The Best Gig In Town

JAZZ ARTISTS
AT THE WHITE HOUSE
1969–1974

To Kevin

Happy Jazz!

EDWARD ALLAN FAINE

 IM PRESS

Takoma Park, MD

PO Box 5346
Takoma Park, MD 20913-5346
301-587-1202
efaine@yahoo.com

ISBN: 978-0-9857952-4-5
LCCN: 2014910276

First printing 2015
Manufactured in the United States of America

Book design by Sandra Jonas

PHOTOGRAPHY CREDITS
Front cover: Frank Sinatra in the East Room
courtesy of the Ollie Atkins Collection (National Archives);
White House, © trekandshoot/Shutterstock

Interior: Harvey Georges (Associated Press), 4; Nixon Presidential
Library, 2, 3, 4, 37, 53, 74, 93, 112, 126, 161, 178, 184, 195; Ollie Atkins
Collection (National Archives), 2, 3, 37, 161; Photofest Inc., 6, 11

To a thousand worthy angels

"The most pleasurable experiences in jazz include count-less fugitive passages, some not much longer than a few seconds—an inspired eight-bar variation in an otherwise leaden recording, a sensational voicing for the brasses in an otherwise routine arrangement. Everyone venerates and as-similates the masters. But the odd personalities that bloom in their shadows, like flowers fracturing an urban pavement, should be valued no less. One example: Frank Newton. . . . Armstrong, Ellington, and Parker are gods. But Newton is one of a thousand worthy angels."

—Gary Giddins, *Visions of Jazz: The First Century*

Contents

Contents

Acknowledgments

As was the case in my previous book *Ellington at the White House, 1969*, I am indebted to the scribes, biographers, and critics, as well as the friendly and efficient staff of the National Archives in College Park, MD, the Library of Congress in Washington, DC, and the Nixon Presidential Library in Yorba Linda, California, who all guided me to the relevant materials in their collections.

I am likewise indebted to the photo providers and processors. Two photos are courtesy of Photofest Inc. in New York City, the rest courtesy of the Ollie Atkins Collection (National Archives) in College Park, Maryland; the Nixon Presidential Library in Yorba Linda, California; and Harvey Georges, Associated Press. The conversion of film photos to digital images courtesy of Visual Image Presentations of Silver Spring, MD, and photo processing by Dave Smith of U-Photo, Beltsville, MD.

I am also indebted to Sandra Jonas of Your Book Partners for her (Sandra) Bullock-like efforts to secure permissions for the quotes used in the book, for her deft editorial eye and writerly pen, and for her typesetting acumen.

Lastly, a thousand thanks to Ms. Jonas for her suggestion to name the book *The Best Gig in Town*—absolutely the most perfect title imaginable.

Setting the Stage

Richard Nixon began his presidency in 1969 with ideas he had been accumulating for fifteen years, since first becoming vice president under Eisenhower. He knew exactly what kind of entertainment policy he wanted and implemented it just a month after taking office. His presidential directive on the matter signaled not only the significance he placed on social affairs at the mansion but also his intention to oversee their planning.

Obsessively attending to every detail of the state dinners, Nixon dictated the dress code, location of the reception line, the menu, wines, seating arrangements, and musical selections. As important as these functions were to him, he disliked having to attend them and made sure to limit their number and duration. But if he did have to socialize, he wanted to maximize the political benefit of every event—his modus operandi throughout his presidency.

So when it came to selecting entertainers, he laid down the following rules:

We need as a basic research document the names of all artists and orchestra leaders, etc., who supported us in the campaign. They should come before others who did not, assuming of course, that their quality is high enough. Under no circumstances can we have in the White House, no matter how good a supporter, an artistic group that is sub-par because this would reflect on both the group and the White House.[1]

Guests who attended the mansion soirees were strategically chosen as well. Like the entertainers, supporters were to have first priority. Chief of Staff H. R. Haldeman made certain of that:

> The president is concerned that we've been conned into invit-ing too many people who basically don't support us to White House events. Obviously every time we do this we're simply re-warding those people who are against us and encouraging their viewpoint . . . Control on the [guest list] has got to be held here [in the West Wing] rather than at the [East Wing] Social Secre-tary's Office because they of course have no basis for evaluating individuals by this [support/non-support] criterion.[2]

The entertainers—and their political loyalties—were especially scrutinized under the Nixon microscope. The entertainers, after all, by virtue of their celebrity, had the potential to influence large segments of the population in support of the president's policies.

Although a devotee of classical music, Nixon appreciated jazz and sup-ported the important role jazz musicians had in spreading American freedom and democracy overseas via the State Department's Jazz Am-bassador program. He was aware of the impact of the daily jazz broad-casts by the Voice of America (VOA) and the occasional United States Information Agency (USIA) documentary film or newsreel screened at commercial theaters, United States Information Service (USIS) posts, and mobile film units around the globe—efforts all begun during the Eisenhower administration when Nixon was vice president. African American jazz musicians were highly effective in countering Soviet propaganda over the treatment of minority blacks in America.

Beginning with Duke Ellington's seventieth-birthday tribute on

April 29, 1969, Nixon hosted thirteen jazz-related performances at the White House throughout his five and a half years in office. This book pays homage to that handful of mid-twentieth-century iconic entertainers and their signature songs: singers Pearl Bailey, Peggy Lee, and Frank Sinatra; pianists Henry Mancini, Bobby Short, and Billy Taylor; New Orleans musicians clarinetist Pete Fountain and trumpeter Al Hirt; and the instrumental groups the Modern Jazz Quartet and the World's Greatest Jazz Band.

But it is the setting, the most famous building in the world, and its lord and master, the most Shakespearean of American presidents, the multifaceted Richard M. Nixon, that make the events so compelling. This book confirms what jazz performers—all performers—have known for some time: the White House is indeed the best gig in town.

To wit:

Singer Marilyn McCoo: "Whenever the President of the United States asks you to come into the nation's most famous residence to perform, you go. It's like a command performance. We were entertainers, which meant we checked our politics at the front door of the White House."

Singer Peggy Lee: "When a citizen of the United States is asked by their President to appear at the White House, I think it's an honor and I feel it's a gracious act for him to make. It was a lovely experience."

Pianist Bobby Short: "When I was in the fourth grade in Danville, Illinois, my teacher went on a sightseeing trip on the East Coast. And when she got back, she told the class about the trip and said, 'Bobby, some day you should play on that beautiful piano at the White House.' And my childhood dream was to play it. That dream has come true tonight."

Singer Pearl Bailey: "When you go there once, you get so excited, you call it the White House. 'You know where I was, honey? I was at the White House.' But when you come out here as often as I do, honey, you call it the *House*."

Clarinetist Pete Fountain: "You know, I still wonder how it happened. It's like a dream to play five state dinners. Most people would love to get one. But five? I just keep shaking my head."

Pianist Billy Taylor: "[Nixon] saw the arts as something that should be encouraged and nurtured and in which the government should be the junior partner. He was extremely supportive of jazz and made me feel most comfortable—and I'm a registered Democrat!"

The Best Gig In Town

Duke Ellington

Ellington—I dig him. He is my generation.
—*Richard Nixon*

April 29, 1969 | Ellington All-Stars Birthday Tribute

O N THE EVENING OF APRIL 29, 1969, President Nixon awarded the Medal of Freedom to Duke Ellington—the first time in U.S. history anyone in jazz had been so honored. To pay tribute to the maestro, a stunning array of jazz greats assembled in the East Room of the White House (another first) and performed twenty-seven Ellington songs in a ninety-minute concert. This stellar evening will undoubtedly be remembered as one of the most glittering in the history of the White House.

Edward Allan Faine has carefully researched and fully documented the event in his book *Ellington at the White House, 1969.* Faine traces the decades-long journey that both Ellington and jazz had to travel to have their music heard in the White House, as well as the machinations leading up to Nixon's approval of the tribute and of Willis Conover as the concert's producer.[1]

Faine then brings Duke's big night alive, presenting vivid details of the banquet, the medal ceremony, and the all-star concert. Such jazz giants as Dave Brubeck, Earl "Fatha" Hines, J. J. Johnson, Gerry Mul-

3

Mary Mayo voicing the familiar "Mood Indigo" backed by trombonist J. J. Johnson.

ligan, and Clark Terry performed Ellington's songs—from "Take the 'A' Train" to "Don't Get Around Much Anymore" to "It Don't Mean a Thing." The audience responded with booming applause throughout the evening.[2]

At the boisterous jam session that followed the concert, guests danced to the music of marine, all-star, and guest musicians, including jazz notables Dizzy Gillespie, Marian McPartland, and Willy "the Lion" Smith. The party lasted until sometime after 2 a.m.

The excitement of Duke's birthday bash no doubt influenced Nixon to schedule subsequent jazz soirees. At some point, after listening to the featured musicians that night, he told Leonard Garment, "If this is jazz, we should have more of it at the White House."[3]

This singular White House jazz event reverberated throughout the jazz arts community like none other before. It was about recognition, about respect, and about honor. It reverberates still.

Ellington's tribute also had an enormous impact on the African American community and on the millions worldwide who viewed a USIA documentary of the event (a White House first) and listened to

4

Duke danced with multiple partners at the jam session. Shown here with Carmen de Lavallade (*top left*); the president's secretary, Rose Mary Woods (*top right*); and a woman identified as Mrs. Joe Williams (*bottom*), with Dr. Arthur Logan nearby.

Duke and Willie "the Lion" Smith sharing a piano bench at the jam session following the all-star concert.

radio broadcasts over Voice of America on Willis Conover's daily jazz program.[4]

Jazz critic Leonard Feather, one of the after-dinner guests, later wrote this about the evening:

> It would have been easy to write off the whole affair cynically as a political ploy. True, it redounded to the president's benefit . . . nevertheless, what took place that night transcended questions of either politics or race. . . .
>
> Respectability was the name of the game, and respectability is what Ellington, more than any other man living or dead, had brought to jazz in his music, his bearing, and his impact on society.[5]

Henry Mancini

It's melodic, it's pretty, and it's tender. It's everything
that you think the kids aren't nowadays.
—*Henry Mancini*

June 30, 1969 | Apollo 10 Astronaut Dinner

FIVE MONTHS INTO HIS ADMINISTRATION, Richard Nixon had only
just begun to fulfill his ardent craving for piano music. At the Ellington seventieth-birthday bash in April, he was treated to jazz piano greats Dave Brubeck, Duke Ellington, Earl Hines, Hank Jones,
and Billy Taylor (and, as he surreptitiously listened to the after-hour
jam from his upper-floor quarters, pianists Leonard Feather, Marian
McPartland, Willy "the Lion" Smith, and George Wein).

Then in May, he invited the popular pianist Peter Nero and his
trio, who were followed early the next month by the classical duo Jack
Lowe and Arthur Whitemore. To close out June, Nixon brought in assumed supporter and popular tunesmith Henry Mancini to entertain
the Apollo 10 astronauts (Eugene A. Cernan, Tom P. Stafford, and
John W. Young), who had circled, but not landed on, the moon the
previous month. Booked because of his hit song "Moon River"? Nah,
too obvious.

Composer, arranger, and sometime-performing pianist Henry Mancini attracted laurels like a magnet. He had received nominations for

seventy-two Grammy Awards and eighteen Academy Awards, winning twenty of the former and four of the latter. He scored many memorable films, including his somewhat auspicious first, *The Creature from the Black Lagoon* in 1952, *Breakfast at Tiffany's* ("Moon River") in 1961, *Hatari* ("Baby Elephant Walk") in 1962, and *Charade* in 1963, and *The Pink Panther*, the first of the series in 1965, which featured the soundtrack sax of Plas Johnson. Mancini referred to Panther's insanely catchy and instantly recognizable jingle as "tippy-toe jewel thief" music.[1]

Mancini had also scored two jazz films—*The Glenn Miller Story* (1953) starring Jimmy Stewart and *The Benny Goodman Story* (1955) starring Steve Allen—both credible as far as Hollywood biopics go.

Singer/actress Lola Albright in an episode of the *Peter Gunn* TV show.

And he contributed the jazz-noir soundtrack to Orson Welles's *Touch of Evil*. But some might argue that Mancini's most notable achievement was his composing and scoring for the pioneering *Peter Gunn* TV program.

For three seasons, 1958–1961, Americans had something hip to watch on television for a change. Peter Gunn, a jazz-loving private eye, played by Craig Stevens, chased down crooks and hung out at a jazz club called Mother's. The background jazz score by Mancini—a first for network TV and never repeated—regularly featured such West Coast jazz musicians as Victor Feldman (piano, vocal), Shelly Manne (drums), Dick Nash (trombone), Ted Nash (tenor sax), and Ronnie Lang (reeds). Significant swathes of the music were heard too—no token dips and dollops. Director Blake Edwards gave Mancini plenty of scenes without dialog to fill.

The show was not without its detractors, however:

One Chicago pianist said, "I think it may kill jazz. All these crime programs with jazz in the background are setting up in people's minds an association between jazz and crime and slick, cheap women" . . . Critics were speaking in condescending tones: "Jazz must be made more than transient background sounds to endure."[2]

Mancini argued that the show was not jazz per se, but jazz-oriented. "We packaged jazz in an interesting way, that's all." Nonetheless, the successful series spawned similar TV shows: the Count Basie Orchestra supplied the *M Squad* theme (1957), written by the Count and Frank Foster (tenor sax), and the Duke Ellington Orchestra could be heard during the opening credits of *Asphalt Jungle* (1961). These shows, along with *Peter Gunn* and the occasional jazz TV special, made possible the unheard of: a weekly jazz music network series, *Jazz Scene U.S.A.*, hosted by Oscar Brown Jr., which hit the airwaves in late 1962. Gunn jacked up the public interest for jazz, helping to sustain the big-band revival for Duke, the Count, and such other bandleaders as Woody Herman, Maynard Ferguson, Oliver Nelson, and Gerald Wilson through the 1960s (in the age of rock and roll, Elvis, and the Beatles, believe it or not). Henry eventually got his own TV show: *The Mancini Generation*, a syndicated variety number with hip guests and plenty of jazz that aired in 1972–73.

The detective series eventually inspired the movie *Gunn*, with songs and themes from the TV series. The soundtrack musicians included Ted Nash and Bud Shank (alto and tenor sax), Plas Johnson (tenor sax), Pete Candoli (trumpet), Dick Nash (trombone), Vince DeRosa (French horn), Bob Bain (guitar), Jimmy Rowles (piano), Ray Brown (bass), Larry Bunker (vibraphone), and Shelly Manne (drums). The composer also appeared briefly as a piano player in a bar sequence.

Every autumn under Friday-night lights all over the United States, marching bands quickstep onto the field, face the crowded stands, and blare out that familiar *Gunn* theme with its constant rumbling bass leitmotif, a distant freight locomotive pounding away:

choom-choom choom-choom choom-choom choom-choom
[and a brass wail on top] waaaaaahh WADA wa wawawa wa wa
   wa WA WADA
choom-choom choom-choom choom-choom choom-choom

As a concert pianist, Mancini was surprisingly competent, given a life's work devoted to composition and orchestration. He had spent two years with the Tex Beneke Swing Orchestra before joining the composing staff at Universal Pictures in Hollywood. Don Piestrup, who wielded a powerful pen as a composer-arranger himself, said of Mancini's sound: "He mixes like a magician. Tightness, relaxation, and rhythm, always in the right proportion. And his French horns are the greatest to be found anywhere in jazz or classical. They're beautifully balanced."[3]

Had he chosen to focus on the keyboard, he could have had a career similar to that of Eddie Heywood ("Canadian Sunset") or Roger Williams ("Autumn Leaves"). He often listened to jazz pianists Art Tatum and Oscar Peterson, although his personal favorites were Erroll Garner and Jimmy Rowles. Still, it was as a composer that he would leave his stamp, as Donald Fagen of the rock group Steely Dan wrote: "Henry Mancini composed the soundtrack for my adolescence . . . all bow before the High Priest of Hollywood Cool."[4]

Henry began his East Room set for the moon-circling astronauts by announcing that he was not going to sing any of the film tunes he had been associated with, but rather just play them.[5] His first number—surprise, surprise—was "Moon River." Mancini crafted the song for Audrey Hepburn to sing in *Breakfast at Tiffany's*. While a radiant and charming screen presence, the pixie-like actress was not a singer. No problem. The wily composer centered his tune on middle C and the surrounding white notes.[6]

Lyricist Johnny Mercer took Henry's melody and fashioned lyrics based on his memories of lying alongside rivulets with childhood friends and dreaming of going out in the world and coming back home to laud their success: "I'm crossing you in style some day." Mercer originally titled the song "Blue River," but after learning that a song by the same title already existed, he changed it to its well-known name. The song's success (it won an Academy Award for Best Original Song in 1961) had a lot to do with the film and its star Audrey Hepburn but benefited from the phrase "my huckleberry friend," which conjures up pure Americana: Huckleberry Finn on a raft drifting down the Mississippi. In actuality, Mercer was referencing his cousin with whom he went "huckleberrying" to gather fruit for homemade ice cream. More than half a century after it was written, the song is the fourth most popular movie theme of all time, after "Over the Rainbow," "As Time Goes By," and "Singin' in the Rain."[7]

Mancini followed "Moon River" with mega-sellers "Dear Heart," "Mr. Lucky," and another Johnny Mercer collaboration, "Days of Wine and Roses," recorded by Andy Williams in 1963 from the film of the same name, starring Jack Lemon and Lee Remick. Director Blake Edwards suggested the title of "Wine" from a phrase in a 1890s poem. Mancini wrote the theme in about half an hour ("It just came out, it rolled out.") and likewise for Mercer ("I can't take credit for that one. God wrote that lyric. All I did was take it down."). And the first to hear it, Mancini's wife, Ginny, said, "My goodness, that undoubtedly is going to win an Academy Award." And it did.[8]

While some consider "Wine" a so-so tune, it has been a favorite of jazz musicians over the years: both the Billy Taylor Trio and the Ray Brown Trio with pianist Gene Harris (Concord) have flat-out swinging versions, and more recently, Maria Schneider and her orchestra (Artist-Share) turned it into a John Coltrane-ish romp.

Next on the program came a medley of three film ballads: "Moment to Moment," recorded by Frank Sinatra from the film of the same name; "In the Arms of Love," recorded by Andy Williams from the film *What Did You Do in the War, Daddy?*; and "The Sweetheart Tree," sung by Robin Ward for Natalie Wood's character, Jackie, in the film *The Great Race*.

Mancini then told the audience, "And all the way this far without a goof! As I said in the beginning, I don't play piano that much. I'm a composer and orchestrator. I play once in a while in concerts. And I came here [to the East Room] this afternoon to try the piano to make sure with the [current] economic mood, I still had eighty-eight keys. It'd be murder to find only sixty keys. I'm happy I'm doing so well. Two up numbers now—two animals—one's pink, the other gray-ish brown, one's a panther, the other's a baby elephant." The familiar bouncy themes followed.

After the "animal" medley, Mancini introduced his then current hit, the best-selling record in America:

About three, four months ago, I was going to do an album, and there was this one piece of music that struck my fancy so I re-corded it. This number was released as a single, but it was desig-nated as the B-side—the suits didn't think too much of it. [The A-side was the Academy Award–nominated "Windmills of Your Mind."] So they started taking it around to the DJs and lo and behold, [after one small station in Orlando, Florida, favored the B-side] everybody started playing it.

Just this past week, it's number one in the country and has passed a million in sales . . . it's a strange kind of record. It's me-lodic, it's pretty, and it's tender. It's everything that you think the kids aren't nowadays. I'm talking about the "Romeo and Juliet" theme, but it shows that—as someone made mention—with [the kids] showing the [war protest] signs, that you can't just judge by what's going on and what's being publicized. What they see in it is a basic beauty, something that communicates love between two people.

Mancini launched into a heartfelt rendering of the "The Theme from Romeo and Juliet," written by composer Nino Rota, who scored the film. The tune was a favorite of Nixon's daughter Julie, who had recently married David Eisenhower.[9]

Before his final number, Mancini admitted to having a good luck charm in the person of Audrey Hepburn. "I've done four films with Audrey . . . up on that screen she is so beautiful, so superior, so touching. People say, 'What inspired "Moon River"?' Audrey. 'What inspired the "Two for the Road" theme?' Audrey again. 'And "Charade"?' The same thing." She was the total inspiration for the next group of songs."

Ms. Hepburn was Nixon's favorite movie actress—he screened nine of her films during his term in office—although he didn't get around

Audrey Hepburn in *Breakfast at Tiffany's*.

to seeing the two scored by Mancini until July 1971 (*Breakfast at Tiffany's*) and December 1972 (*Charade*).[10]

Henry concluded the twenty-eight-minute set with his Audrey Hepburn medley.

A year later, a staffer in the social secretary's office suggested that Mancini be crossed off the list of approved entertainers. "He didn't seem to show much enthusiasm for the President when he was in the previous year." By late that same year, the view on Henry had crystallized: he was declared "definitely anti-Nixon."[11] Was it something he had said during the rehearsal? After the show? Or maybe it was his remarks during the show, when he suggested that the youthful protesters outside the White House gates with their antiwar signs were perhaps being misrepresented, that they, like their parents, were capable of appreciating love and beauty?

It is difficult to reconcile these staff opinions with what actually occurred after the pianist took his final bows in the East Room. The president invited Henry and his wife, Ginny, upstairs for a grand tour of the family quarters, and as Mancini recounted in his memoir,

I asked, "What's your favorite album, Mr. President?"

He pulled one from the shelf [in his private study] and handed it to me. It was Richard Rodgers music for the television series "Victory at Sea." He said, "I sit here by the hour and listen to that album." He had several Lawrence Welk albums, some Montovani, and The Sound of Music, along with some Tchaikovski.

[Taken aback that the East Room piano] I had to play was terrible . . . I couldn't let its condition pass unremarked. "Mr. President, for this piano to be in the White House is unseemly. Surely, the White House deserves a better instrument. After all, artists such as Arthur Rubenstein and Vladimir Horowitz play it."[12]

Nixon's response to Henry's comment is lost to history. Still, the exchange couldn't have tarnished his standing with the White House because Nixon invited the Mancinis to a state dinner for Italian Premier Emilio Colombo on February 18, 1971.

Future presidents took a liking to the Peter Gunn composer as well. Henry was invited to a reception by President Carter, and to perform (along with singer Johnny Mathis) for President Reagan. He found the piano in very good shape this time around.

"Moon River" and the "Peter Gunn Soundtrack" were entered into the Grammy Hall of Fame in 1999, and "The Pink Panther Soundtrack" followed five years later. On the eightieth anniversary of his birth (and a decade after his death), the U.S. Postal Service issued a Henry Mancini commemorative stamp. No pun intended, but that's tough to lick!

Modern Jazz Quartet

*The shah had to come all the way from Iran
for the MJQ to bring some jazz to the White House.
—Milt Jackson (vibist)*

October 21, 1969 | Iranian Reza Shah Pahlavi Dinner

S HAH PAHLAVI, A MOST FAVORED Gulf State partner of the United
States, was a relatively frequent visitor to official Washington—nine
times from 1949 to 1969. Educated in Switzerland, he had secular and
modern tastes in art and music. Indeed, President Kennedy had honored the Iranian leader with the Jerome Robbins Ballet; after Nixon,
President Ford would follow with dancer and singer Ann-Margaret; and
then President Carter would showcase jazz luminaries Dizzy Gillespie,
Earl Hines, and Sarah Vaughan. As President Nixon would oddly put
it the night of the event honoring Pahlavi, the shah has "shown some
tolerance and understanding of American jazz."[1]

Even so, the Modern Jazz Quartet was not an easy sell to President
Nixon. This was a state dinner after all—appearances mattered. What
would JFK have done? Something high class for sure—a symphony
orchestra, a world-renown classical instrumentalist? Nixon had embraced the genre for his official state dinners from the outset (easy for
him because he liked the music): cellist Zara Nelson and pianist Grant
Johansen for the prime minister of Australia; Jack Lowe and Arthur

Whittemore piano duo for the president of Columbia; pianist Eugene List for the president of Ethiopia; violinist Kyung-Wa Chung for the chancellor of Germany; the Romeros' classical guitarists for the president of South Korea; and pianist Leonard Bernstein and violinist Isaac Stern for the prime minister of Israel.

From all indications, the fabled duo of VOA broadcaster and White House advisor Willis Conover and Nixon arts aide Leonard Garment—responsible for assembling the jazz all-stars to celebrate Duke Ellington's seventieth birthday earlier in the year—worked diligently behind the scenes to book the Modern Jazz Quartet, "or as we '*in*' people call them, the MJQ," Nixon told the East Room crowd the night of the event.

In February, Conover had planted the MJQ seed with Social Secretary Lucy Winchester in his bid to become part-time White House impresario. In fact, in a follow-up letter to Lucy, the MJQ was the first group he suggested for the Ellington tribute. Moreover, Conover knew that the MJQ's music "was the kind the Shah goes for," which animated his and his colleagues' efforts to book the group.[2]

MJQ vibraphonist Milt Jackson remembered,

We got the choice [to play the White House] through Willis Conover, you know. He's a big man around here [DC] and I think there was a choice between us and Dionne Warwick with Burt Bacharach accompanying her or something like that so Willis Conover, you know being as cool as he is about jazz and stuff, thought it would be better for the choice of establishing the goodwill thing to have us. Because the Shah [of Iran] is a little better conversant with what's happening as opposed to Mr. Nixon. Let's put it that way.

You know, that whole situation is sadly ironic because, you know, the Shah comes a very long way from where jazz originated, from the roots of jazz, and Mr. Nixon was born right here in the middle of it, and I think the telling point of it is that the Shah had to come all the way from Iran for the MJQ to bring some jazz to the White House.[3]

The White House press release issued on October 18 in time for the Sunday newspapers had this to say:

> The Quartet, consisting of John Lewis, pianist, composer and musical director; Milt Jackson, vibraharpist, composer; Percy Heath, bassist; and Connie Kay, drummer, has been called the "first pure concert ensemble in jazz." Recent performances have included those with the Cincinnati and Minneapolis Symphony Orchestras, as well as the Toronto Symphony and the Symphony Orchestras of Genoa and Tokyo. It has been compared, in its field, with the world renowned Budapest String Quartet.
>
> Before the jazz group was organized in 1952, the four musicians performed individually for a number of the great jazz leaders of the 1940s, including Charlie Parker, Dizzy Gillespie, Miles Davis, Lester Young, Thelonious Monk, J. J. Johnson, Stan Getz, Ella Fitzgerald and Woody Herman.[4]

How could Nixon turn down a group who played with all those symphony orchestras? And in the same league as the Budapest String Quartet, no less. Whew! Eat your heart out, Jack Kennedy.

The Modern Jazz Quartet, perhaps named appropriately when the group began in 1952, was more backward looking than forward. It was a pack of counter-revolutionaries, throwback renegades who relied on the achievements of the past: collective improvisation, emphasis on composition, counterpoint, European borrowings, swing, and the setting of riffs behind the soloists.

And all of this was by design. John Lewis, the unofficial leader of the quartet and its chief composer and arranger, said his "vision for the group was to change the music from just a jam session, or rhythm section and soloist idea, to something more." He also said, "The MJQ has to have variety. We can't bore audiences to death with one idea." So Lewis set out to fashion a collective music that reconciled the composer's belief in predetermination with the improviser's yen for free will, while embracing the secrets of formal composition: tension and release, dynamic shading, and dramatic pause.[5]

Moreover, Lewis instinctively knew that a quartet made up of three percussive instruments and a bass violin (which, in jazz, functions more as a percussive than a stringed instrument) had to vary its repertoire to avoid a repetitive sameness, although the group was accused of it anyway. Hence, the addition of fugues, rondos, concertos, laments, little suites, and carols to the staples of the genre: blues, thirty-two-bar standards, and the occasional odd-time signature piece.

To round out his aural concept, Lewis expanded the role of the drummer, turning superb timekeeper Connie Kay into a miniature symphonic percussion section. In addition to his standard drum kit, Kay used finger cymbals, triangle, chimes, bells, tambourine and tympani, his hands, and the metal loops on his wire brushes in place of sticks. But it was the exquisitely pitched ride cymbals that set Kay apart. Jazz critic Rob Mariani rhapsodized:

> In all music, I don't think there's ever been anything quite like Connie Kay's ride cymbals. You could detect the ping of his ride cymbal out of a thousand—dry and metallic with just a hint of sizzle. Like the drop of vermouth in a dry martini. He must have used very special drumsticks, too, because they added a slightly hollow, "woody" timbre. His cymbals' sound was full, he could play chorus after chorus and barely touch his snare drum, making it all work immaculately with just his high-hat and ride cymbal.[6]

Composer Lewis took advantage of this percussive cornucopia, incorporating the various tinks, pings, and splashes into his many compositions.

Bassist Percy Heath, the MJQ's "all-American" center, held steady compass on the meter and evolved into a singular voice among recognizable voices. Pianist George Shearing, who on club dates would often sit next to the jukebox between sets listening to MJQ records, was overheard on more than one occasion to exclaim, "Percy, Percy, Percy. If you would only join my group, I would swing my ass off."[7]

Fellow pianist and avant-gardist Cecil Taylor had this to say about Lewis: "Talk about an interesting pianist . . . John Lewis. The MJQ was magisterial . . . To me, the MJQ was always about Milt Jackson. He was always beautiful. But if you listen to the delicate things John Lewis is playing behind him?!"[8]

Gary Giddins, another keen observer of the music, further elaborated:

[John Lewis was] an unfettered genius for the melodic phrase, poignant and robust, forthright and shameless . . . More than anyone else, he has combined jazz and classical techniques into an insoluble whole; and yet they often bring him to a terrain one is more likely to associate with Ray Charles.[9]

Yes, John Lewis was a melodist, through and through, in the composing realm certainly as well as in his piano comping and soloing. He commonly set little single-noted rhythmic figures (riffs, if you like) underneath vibist Milt Jackson's fleeting, multi-noted solos, repeating them with variations and, come time for his solo, would twirl the figure into a melodic line with its own expanded or contracted variations. From time to time—surprise—a few chords would punctuate the line being spun. The Count Basie Orchestra of the '30s and '40s had a profound influence on Lewis's style—namely, the leader's spare piano playing, of course, but also the constant riff setting by the individual musicians with and counter to the ensemble and the rhythm section.

Of the band's other principal soloist, Milt Jackson, Lewis said: "There's no other vibraharpist in the world like Milt. He's the most brilliant." In his thorough examination of the vibist's musicality in his 2002 doctoral thesis, Patrick Edward Roulet observed that

Milt Jackson's improvistory style on vibraphone is a result of his early upbringing in the church and his experience singing gospel music combined with the style of jazz he heard played by [bebop innovators] Charlie Parker and Dizzy Gillespie . . . . Jackson's tone on the instrument, a result of his Deagan *Imperial* vibraharp, his custom-made [large ball, soft yarn wound] mallets, and his approach to tone quality distinguish him from other jazz vibraphonists [predecessors Red Norvo and Lionel Hampton and contemporaries Gary Burton and Bobby Hutcherson]. By slowing down the speed of the instrument's vibrator [oscillator to 3.3 rps, vice 10 rps for Hampton], Jackson was able to emulate the sound of his voice . . . . Another aspect of [his] playing style that gives his sound a horn-like or vocal quality is his effective use of the instruments damper pedal . . . . Jackson frames each solo by outlining the structure by utilizing several strategies. He starts and ends his solo with clear opening and closing phrases, and connects each 12-measure chorus using techniques such as octave shifts, motovic patterns, and melodic formulas.[10]

Many others have noted that the vibe master's improvisations exhibit great dynamic variety, sudden outbursts of short notes often joining languid, sustaining phrases. He also had an affinity for the twelve-bar blues and recorded many excellent blues solos. But it was the interplay between the two main soloists, buoyed by the two rhythmmates, that made the group so marvelous. Gary Giddins again:

The MJQ is almost too good. Fixed snapping rhythms embellished with bells and chimes support contrapuntal melodies and compelling improvisation. Clipped, jabbing piano and vivid blues compliment saturated sonorities augmented by bowed bass and accelerated vibraphone vibrato. A seductive book . . . transfigures popular songs into originals and visa versa. The downside is one's natural propensity to take it for granted, especially given how the ensemble's formality can overwhelm the very improvisations it frames, not least the controlled but always palpable tension between Milt Jackson's effusively carnal vibes and John Lewis's elusively rational piano.[11]

The musicians could be heard individually, too, as jazz bassist Ray Drummond recalled:

> I remember hearing one of their concerts at Stanford University in the late 1960s and being truly impressed by the classy musical presentation. . . . The dynamics of their performance were astonishing; I could hear every note from each of the instruments, including the bass fiddle, and they did it with only two talk microphones.[12]

All this discussion of form and process aside, when they wanted to, the MJQ could put a hurt inside you, suspend your disbelief, and shrink your empathetic distance to zero, because they could swing their asses off, pure and simple.

The group would bring their graceful lyricism and jaunty swing to the White House, but they would not replay their old standby hits like "Django," "Bluesology," "Bags' Groove," "Skating in Central Park," "One Never Knows," or "The Cylinder" from their masterwork albums *Fontessa*, *Pyramid*, *Odds Against Tomorrow*, and *European Concert*, to name only a few. Instead, the quartet chose to feature new music from their new record label, Apple—that's right, the Beatles record label.

In 1968 the Beatles hired Ron Kass, an experienced American record company executive to kick-start their entry into the record production business. The MJQ's manager at the time, Monte Kay (no relation to Connie), had been friends with Kass for some time; Kay knew him when he headed the independent World Pacific jazz label. One thing led to another and the MJQ dropped their long-term association with Atlantic Records and joined the new venture. Kass landed a prestige jazz group (the only one he would sign), and Kay landed the opportunity to bring the group to a wider audience in association with the Beatles.[13]

For the MJQ, it was a label switch only; they didn't intend to alter their approach as jazz star Miles Davis and others were doing by electrifying the music and adopting rock rhythms. The content of the MJQ's book would remain the same—just the cover would change.

Their first effort, recorded December 12, 1967, in New York City arrived ready-made at Apple HQ in London. Released by Apple Records in 1968, *Under the Jasmin Tree* featured a lengthy three-part suite: "Three Little Feelings," poised, structured fare with swinging elements but in no way groundbreaking; "Exposure," excellent, programmatic, not unlike "Feelings;" and the two surprises "The Blue Necklace" and "The Jasmin Tree," both based on the Afro-Moorish rhythms of Morocco.[14] Had the jazz critics' worst nightmare come true? Had John Lewis sold out to Beatlemania? Composed anthems for the "Lucy in the Sky with Diamonds" crowd? Just look at the album jacket's provocative psychedelic cover! Had he lost his Euro compass, gone native, joined the Afrocentric "new thing" movement?

None of the above.

Totally unrelated to the label switch, Lewis had accepted a request by the United States Information Agency (USIA) to compose a score for a short documentary film on water conservation in Morocco: *De l'eau et de l'espoir* (About Water and Hope). The MJQ played the music on the soundtrack, which included the Apple tracks "Necklace" and "Jasmin."

The USIA produced numerous short films on water and agricultural projects in Africa and other parts of the world in the 1960s. It was all part of the Cold War competition with the Soviets, who no doubt retaliated with similar films; jazz, for certain, would not have been heard on one of theirs.

Composer John Lewis and his bandmates were no neophytes when it came to film. The MJQ had provided Lewis-scored background music for two documentaries in the mid-1950s and famously for four feature films: *Sait-on jamais,* or *No Sun in Venice* (1957); *Odds Against Tomorrow* (1959), starring Harry Belafonte and Robert Ryan; *Exposure* (1959); and *A Milanese Story* (1959). Lewis even turned down offers to score two notable films: *The Pawnbroker* and *Sounder*. A busy man that John Lewis.[15]

If the question had been asked, "So and so wants jazz on this Moroccan documentary. Who should we get?" Four or five names would have immediately come to mind, Duke Ellington, Henry Mancini, and John Lewis among them. Obviously the latter was chosen, but not in their wildest dreams did the USIA filmmakers expect that the music on their little documentary would appear on an album produced by the Beatles. To top it off, the very same music was played by the MJQ at a disused linoleum factory in London in March 1969 at an event billed as Supershow: The Last Great Jam of the '60s, where the quartet joined rockers Eric Clapton, Jack Bruce, and Stephen Stills. And to top that off, six months later, that same music was performed at the White House for President Nixon and Shah Pahlavi of Iran.

In late March 1969, the MJQ laid down tracks for a second and final album for the Beatles Apple label (it would not be released until October 1969, however) at the new state-of-the-art Trident Studios in London, where the Beatles and other rockers on the roster recorded. John Lewis would use the studio's hand-made Bechstein grand, the same one used by Paul McCartney on "Hey Jude."

The head of A&R at the time, twenty-four-year-old Peter Asher, supervised the sessions. Neither his age (less than half that of John Lewis) nor his background (former pin-up pop star of Peter and Gordon fame) nor his rock 'n' roll studio proclivities (which sought a forward presence for the bass and drums) hampered the outcome: "a perceptively different MJQ album." *Space* contains three tracks that would also be played at the Nixon state dinner: the two Lewis compositions "Visitor from Venus" and "Visitor from Mars," and the adagio from Spanish composer Joaquin Rodrigo's *Concierto de Arunjuez.*

Ah ha, Lewis at it again, catering to the Beatles "Make Love Not War" crowd. Another provocative psychedelic cover! And take a gander at the inside gatefold sleeve proclaiming "love! love! love!" and "war! war! war!" What did it all mean? The MJQ's composer/leader just had to be compromising his principals, right?

Wrong!

Lewis's inspiration for the two outer-space tracks lay elsewhere: "I had been listening to Gustav Holst's *The Planets*, and it was around the same time that Stanley Kubrick made *2001: A Space Odyssey*. That, together with the astronomical and astrological aspects of Venus and Mars, was my inspiration." [16]

The album's final track is the adagio from *Concierto de Aranjuez*. Joaquin Rodrigo composed prolifically for orchestra, chamber ensembles, the stage, and solo instruments, but his fame rests on his work for guitar, premiering in Madrid in 1940 with the *Concierto de Aranjuez*, certainly one of the most popular twentieth-century concertos for any instrument. Virtually every guitarist had recorded it. And its bittersweet adagio is often called upon to evoke the spirit of Spain by documentary filmmakers. [17]

Recognized as one of the world's most beautiful melodies, the Apple version is actually the quartet's third interpretation of the work—they had previously recorded it with a full orchestra and again with Brazilian guitarist Laurindo Almeida (1964).

The first jazz player to honor the *Concierto* was Miles Davis on the Gil Evans collaboration *Sketches of Spain* (Columbia, 1960), and like the MJQ, Miles played the melody straight. In 1975, guitarist Jim Hall recorded another attractive version on *Concierto* (CTI) that featured trumpeter Chet Baker, saxophonist Paul Desmond, and pianist Roland Hannah. Unlike Davis and the MJQ, Hall played a jazzier version of the classical piece.

With their recently recorded new music in hand, including rave reviews for two of its numbers ("Visitor from Venus" and "The Jasmin Tree") received at the out-of-town Supershow tryout in London, the band members were as ready as they would ever be for the Big White Way on Pennsylvania Avenue. As was often the case in those days, the set would be presented as a concert—no introduction by the bandleader, no talk between numbers, only stately bows at the end. The printed playbill would take care of the rest.

Prominent jazz magazine *DownBeat* reporter Charles Suber described what happened the night of the event:

At about 10:30, [along with other reporters not invited to the dinner, we began] the ascent to the second floor via the front marble staircase . . . The President and First Lady flanked the Shah of Iran in the receiving line, a presidential aide tactfully murmuring each guest's name to the President . . . Then directly into the East Room, where about 250 comfortable chairs were arranged in a horseshoe pattern . . . When we were all in place, the President and party took their seats and Mr. Nixon made his introduction of the MJQ with ease and affability. Whether the words were original or not, the impression was gracious . . . The chandelier lights went out and two banks of colored spots hit the MJQ on a small raised platform stage . . . Percy Heath looked more distinguished than anyone in the house . . . Milt Jackson looked somber and somewhat funereal [natural for him] . . . Most of the smiles came from John Lewis and Connie Kay, but they were reserved and introspective . . . The group played flawlessly, but you couldn't say they swung . . . With the first applause it became apparent that this was the chamber music of our American court . . . Leonard Garment and Willis Conover had chosen wisely—it wasn't the blues outside the gate and beyond but it was jazz, and it was not any condescension to have it here and now.[18]

The group opened with "The Blue Necklace," described this way by *Washington Post* jazz critic Hollie I. West:

A restrained rhythmic number that featured abundant and precise interplay between Jackson and Heath and drummer Connie Kay. Pianist Lewis used Indian castanets during the performance. Most notable about the number were the many subtle shadings employed by the group, whether it be in Jackson's circuitous melodies or Heath's short thrust.[19]

West's comments were spot on. This highly structured and percussive vehicle, each instrument in every conceivable combination with the other, had the drummer and bassist front and center. A very active Kay alternatively, and at times simultaneously, rang his triangle, shook his jingle bells, tappety-tapped his snare's skin and rim, while Heath plucked a high-note, clave-like rhythm on his bass. All to no avail, apparently—the audience was lukewarm, giving the number perfunctory applause. The shortness of the piece (less than five minutes) may have had something to do with that. Expectations had yet to be reconciled with reality.[20]

Still in expository territory, the group launched into "Visitor from Venus," another composition-driven piece with no dominant member. Heath and Kay were more in the background than on "Necklace" but still on equal footing with Lewis and Jackson, who stood out more than they did on the first number. Although "Venus" had forward motion, it came close to being too atmospheric. The tune began with the shimmering tones of Milt Jackson's vibes, or as critic Gary Giddens later put it, "a tingling opening crescendo (the kind of thing synthesizers would take care of a few years later)," followed by Percy Heath's rumbling bass and the jingle-bell percussion of Connie Kay.[21]

Next, a steady tick, tick, tick from Kay; a boom, boom, boom from Heath; and a dong, dong, dong from Jackson. Finally, from Lewis, a piano statement, a bit on the precious side, somewhat like the unwinding song of a Swiss music box. As Kay splashed around on his cymbals, Jackson soloed nicely, more so than on the first song, chording more than usual (the "Visitor" is from outer space, you know).

Fans of the musicians in the audience (and there were a number invited) probably expected them to break out at some point with a swinging, bop-driven chorus, but it didn't happen. They stuck to Lewis's script and finished as they began—and again received polite applause.

Overall, a tentative start by the group; musicianship was quite high but this was music for aficionados. That would change with "Visitor from Mars," much closer to earth than its planetary counterpart:

It began with an enchanting and ethereal blues-like theme with

Jackson taking the lead. The quartet's playing was jaunty, even in the portions where Lewis played extremely delicate melody. President Nixon was noticed tapping his finger, although his facial expression was stolid.[22]

The quartet repeated the enchanting theme seven times. At once irresistible and memorable, the bouncy figure was no doubt recalled by many the next day—perhaps whistling it or trying to pick it out on the upstairs piano?

Ba doo doo doo do to-daaaaah
Ba doo doo doo do to-doooooh
Ba doo doo doo do to-deeeeeh
Deeedily deeedily deeedily deeedily dee

Lewis surrounded his theme with foreboding sounds: from here-come-the-boogeyman piano tremolos for himself to Jackson's up-the-basement-staircase vibraharp chords to Kay's cymballing thunder crashes and crisp military rolls to Heath's sustained bass drone. But the up-tempo, improvised segments by himself and Jackson had to be the choicest moments. Nixon was seen tapping his finger again during these infectious interludes. Jackson, his mallets finally unsheaved, unfurled several peerless solos, and Lewis scrolled out snappy ones of his own—as is his wont—quick single-note runs with very little harmonic underpinning, chords implied more than explicitly stated. Appreciative applause bordering on enthusiastic followed this number. The MJQ had finally won them over.

How many in the audience, after hearing the last two pieces and scanning their programs for the titles, assumed the quartet was making a political statement with their music, articulating the polar political anxieties of the times? Ostensibly, this was the group's intent. They were presenting their most recent compositions, but they must have been aware of the conclusions that would be drawn. By obvious inference, the quartet had to be okay with that, perhaps hoping that the current occupant of the White House would fix his gaze on the one planet in the night sky that outshone all others and keep it there.

Next on the program came the adagio from the *Concierto de Aranjuez*. The quartet played the version they had recorded on their album *Space*, performing it rather "straight," not "jazzed up," as some would say. Lewis said of the version, "We don't deviate in any real sense. We make the piece seem that it's ours. Our dynamics and out rhythmic conceptions are all there in the performance of that music. We wanted it to feel like what it is: an impression of Spain."[23]

The MJQ composer assigned himself the lead usually played by acoustic guitar, at least initially, because it was soon mirrored by Jackson's vibraharp, anchored by the deep, bowed bass of Heath—who shone as a soloist later in the piece—while Kay's percussion was ghostly in restraint. Perhaps the most effective moments occurred midway during the quietest part, after the melody had been indelibly planted in the audience's mind, when Lewis played unaccompanied followed by Jackson, also by himself, except for a three-note echo by bassist Heath. Hollie I. West noted,

> Jackson was superb in the deeply expressive way he handled the lead part. Each note was played as if it contained a sea of emotion. The performance brought the biggest applause of the concert and the President burst into a broad smile at the end of the piece.[24]

Lewis was simply following Rodrigo's advice: "It should sound like the hidden breeze that stirs the tree tops."[25] In a later interview, Milt Jackson seconded the consensus but added a cautionary point of view:

> But when we played . . . *Concierto de Aranjuez* [at the White House] you know, this always creates a reaction, I don't care where we play.
>   First of all, even the black folks ooh and aah when they find out that this kind of music is played by jazz musicians—because

they never really dreamed that it could be played that way. And with the people in the White House, you know, with that stiff group they got, they were really shook up because they never came to expect that kind of culture from the black man, you see. They maybe had a little association with jazz from down there on what's-the-name-street—somewhere see, but they stereotype everything we (blacks) do, and consequently the association leads to just one particular area of music. This is one reason we have such an extensive variety in our repertoire, because that's the only way we really get around that kind of thing. They would automatically put us in a particular phase of music, and it would be—and this is where it would be; and you can't *do* that with music.[26]

The group closed the concert with the perky "Jasmin Tree," a Lewis original he later said "was used for . . . a short documentary about the people who live in the desert part of Morocco. Our music has the kind of feel that suggests the music of the people who live in that area." While the jasmine tree itself originated in the Middle East, and is cultivated in only a few countries (principally Morocco), Lewis's tree grew up somewhere else, somewhere in the deep American South in the vicinity of a Black Baptist church.

Irrespective of the tune's origin, the feel was gospel: Percy held the bottom with a steady boom-boom-boom, while drummer Kay (with only two hands and two feet) held a steady clack-clack-clack, sock cymbal clucking away underneath and the triangle keeping the pulse on top instead of the ride cymbal, and then the coup de grace—a tambourine gospel shake that sounded like the quick one-two hand claps of a church choir.

In the midst of this throbbing stew, Lewis on piano and Jackson on vibes twined their way through a folklike ditty, stating the melody, comping, soloing, first one and then the other, back and forth—what was improvised and what was composed would be hard to know on first hearing. Lewis's solo, always simple, always euphonious, always distinctive, single noted, a chord here and there. If Lewis is Basie, then Jackson is Tatum.

About three-quarters of the way through, the gospelish rhythm came to a halt and a new but related melody was introduced (possibly the folk song on which Lewis based his ditty), played in unison by piano, vibes, bass, and (second time through) drums. Following the interlude, it was back to the Moorish church, and the song concluded as it began. *DownBeat* gave the *Under the Jasmin Tree* album a five-star rating (its highest) and said, "Make no mistake about it—the group is capable of generating a great deal of swing, as on "The Jasmin Tree." Amen![27]

The thirty-five-minute concert concluded with respectful and sustained applause from the East Room crowd. At a minimum—one would imagine—they had to be impressed with the quartet's versatility and—to Milt Jackson's point—might have come away with a better appreciation of "culture from the black man."

DownBeat scribe Charles Suber described the scene afterward:

The President and Shah posed briefly for pictures with the MJQ and then we all were free to mingle and party . . . Out came more champagne, and the social aides escorted congressman's wives to the dance floor while I made my way over to Vice President Agnew . . . I asked him if I could have his views on jazz . . . He very pleasantly replied he was a "big band man" ("I used to collect Artie Shaw and Larry Clinton records"), and went on to say that he doesn't hear enough jazz to make any further comments . . . [Earlier a First Lady staffer told Suber she thought she liked jazz and would have to read *DownBeat* magazine sometime]. Yes, [Agnew said], he most certainly liked the MJQ, "particularly the last number ('Jasmin Tree') with the triangle and tambourine in counterpoint" . . . Several of the front line in the Navy dance band said hello—they were ex-stage band musicians [and would certainly know *DownBeat* magazine, even if no one else did].[28]

Washington Star society columnist Betty Beale, who had attended considerably more shindigs at 1600 Pennsylvania Avenue than our intrepid *DownBeat* correspondent, observed that the foursome was about as smooth and as longhair as jazz could get. Still, she noted, it was hard for some people to keep their little feet still.

Alice Roosevelt Longworth, daughter of former president Theodore Roosevelt, and close friend of the Nixons', went up to the four musicians afterward to say how much she liked their concert and then told them she was married right where they were playing. Smiles all around.

After the photo session, John Lewis gifted the president with two record albums, *European Concert* and *Blues at Carnegie Hall*; taken together, these two highly regarded LPs presented a different facet of the MJQ diamond—the more bluesy, swinging side—than was on display earlier in the evening.[29] Nixon's reaction during the concert—the finger tapping and the appreciative smiles—would suggest he might have slapped the platters on his phonograph the next day, but alas, history has no record of such.

Rarely has the White House in its long, long history offered the very latest currents in music of any kind. But on that starry night in October 1969, it came close to doing so. The MJQ may have been in existence for seventeen years (fourteen with the same personnel), but the music they played was fresh and new and exotic. While not in any way associated with the "new thing"—avant-garde and fusion movements of the time—what they played was not *that* far removed from the sonic experiments taking place at the far reaches of jazz. Unquestionably, the music bestowed upon the shah was the most "experimental" of all the jazz presented during the Nixon administration. So it was a good night for the boys in the band and a good night for jazz.

Two months later, at its annual December New York concert in Alice Tully Hall at Lincoln Center, the group replayed the White House concert minus the Rodrigo *Concierto,* along with old favorites and new music from another film score, *Kemek.* While critic John S. Wilson of the *New York Times* generally praised what he heard, the *DownBeat* critic Tami Fiofori did not. Here is a sample of Fiorfori's comments, a typical example of the negative criticism of the time toward the group and a good reason why artists should never read their reviews:

> Their music at Lincoln Center was not particularly modern in terms of the sixties. Neither was it indicative of what the music of the future might be like . . . and whether the music they play is jazz or has any true relation to jazz is open to debate . . . That they were including new works at this concert was different . . . and the impressive titles only succeeded in disappointing those who expected to hear something really new and moving . . . Their excursions into Space Music, "Visitor from Mars" and "Visitor from Venus," borders on mundane romanticism . . . As a voyager, I would rather go into Space with accomplished pilots like [avant-garde bandleader] Sun Ra; flying Eastwards and not necessarily the "American" way as one of the Earth airlines advertises.[30]

In spite of Fiorfori's views, in April 1970 the group was "flying Eastwards the American way," courtesy of the State Department, on a sponsored tour to the Middle East (Lebanon) and East Asia (Bangladesh, Indonesia, and the Philippines).[31] While their playlist is unknown, it would be safe to assume that people of these countries heard selections from their most recent albums, *Under the Jasmin Tree* and *Space*.

Not imagined at the time of their White House appearance was the group's breakup in 1974. Milt Jackson's unhappiness with the repertoire and the lack of financial compensation (compared to rock stars), along with the rigors of constant touring, had taken their toll. Fortunately for jazz, they reunited in 1981 and continued to play a mix of old and new music all over the world, including another stopover at the White House under President Clinton. The end came in 1999 when Milt Jackson passed away. Connie had died in 1994, but Mickey Roker had taken his place at the drums.

The MJQ would become the longest-lived small group in jazz history, chalking up "believe it or not" numbers: forty-seven years as a group, thirty-nine with the same personnel, if one does not count their seven-year sabbatical.

Importantly, all the nonsense heard during the '60s and '70s about the group corseting jazz and smothering bop would fade with time. The quartet went on to amass a stack of masterpiece albums that surpassed all but a few jazz groups in the history of the music. Two of its members are included in the DownBeat Hall of Fame and by general consensus in the more rarified jazz pantheon of which Armstrong, Ellington, and Parker are charter members, Milt Jackson as the greatest virtuoso on vibes in jazz history and John Lewis as a first-rank jazz composer and underrated pianist.

Lewis did on a small scale what Ellington did on a large one—he cloaked the freewheeling improviser into the regality of his compositions. How appropriate, then, that both would appear at the White House only six months apart.

Oh yes, about the "Modern" in MJQ, maybe the critics had it right . . . should have been "Marvelous."

Al Hirt

Even the Secret Service was keeping time.
—*Isabelle Shelton*, Washington Evening Star

December 3, 1969 | Governors Dinner

THE NATION'S GOVERNORS AND THEIR families came to DC for a daylong conference on narcotics, followed by a fancy dinner and musicale at the White House. While the governors caucused during the day, their wives and teenage offspring attended an afternoon briefing in the East Room on dangerous substances. They learned about various harmful drugs and the ingenious methods used to smuggle them into the country. None of the teenagers—to no one's surprise—admitted to having experimented with drugs themselves. One governor's son said there was "a lot of glue sniffing" in his school and he knew two kids who grew marijuana in their bedroom, but he didn't know what they did with it. Another governor's teenage twins remarked that some of the boys at their private school said they used drugs.[1]

Sensitive to charges that the Nixons fancied only traditional chamber music for their after-dinner entertainment, and given that it was a governors dinner, the White House decided to shake, rattle, and roll its conservative image. The administration called upon trumpeter Al Hirt and his New Orleans band as well as the popular 5th Dimension

34

rock ensemble to cap the evening's festivities. Both groups were worthy of cultivation, despite their Democratic leanings: Hirt appeared at the inaugural celebrations for John F. Kennedy in 1961, and the 5th Dimension, who sang at the 1968 Democratic Convention, had been signed to perform at Hubert Humphrey's inaugural had he won the election.[2]

AL HIRT

At the time, Al Hirt was one of the best-known trumpeters in the United States. His stellar resume boasted a string of best-selling RCA record albums that began in 1960; several pop hits, including "Cotton Candy" and his signature tune "Java," which rose to number three on the *Billboard* charts in 1963, earning him a Grammy; numerous TV and film appearances; a sold-out Carnegie Hall concert in 1965; and a pregame appearance at the first Super Bowl in 1967.[3]

Al looked and acted the part of a New Orleans hot trumpet man: rotund, bearded, and full of joie de vivre. To many, after Louis Armstrong and Pete Fountain, he was the public face of New Orleans jazz. Yet he never considered himself a jazz player, famously telling the *New York Times*, "I'm not a jazz trumpet, and never was a jazz trumpet. When I played in the big bands . . . I played first trumpet. I led the trumpet section. I never played jazz or improvised."[4]

Only three months prior to his White House gig, Jumbo, as Al was called, again underlined his disclaimer as a jazz player in a *DownBeat* cover article:

> I never knew why I was looked upon as a jazz player, because I never really considered myself one . . . The most I'd ever done in jazz really was to be a lead trumpet player in a section . . . I never played any jazz solos. I don't say that I can't—I can probably do a little of it, but I never considered it anything earthshaking. It was always something in the vein of somebody else's bag; you know, like I always played something that was influenced by somebody else. I never was a good improviser and never blazed any trails of my own. So I never considered myself a jazzman.[5]

No matter how hard he tried, Al Hirt was never able to convince people he was not a jazz musician.

Al would own up to his technical proclivities on the instrument, however. After all, he was a classically trained, well-apprenticed 1940s swing bandsman who had been awarded *Playboy* magazine's top trumpet prize in 1962 and every year thereafter—for the following fourteen years. True, his name seldom came up in polls or articles in the prominent jazz magazines (in a positive sense). Still, he surrounded himself with solid musicians in the Dixieland tradition, often soloing, although many excursions would have been "routinized," as the jazz guys of the 1920s were fond of saying. He characterized his playing as "a little bit of this and a little bit of that," meaning the traditional Dixieland standards along with country and pop numbers. Modesty aside, Hirt, along with notables such as Pete Fountain, the Dukes of Dixieland and the then newly formed Preservation Hall aggregation, kept the traditional jazz flame burning through the mid-decades of the twentieth century.[6]

Trumpeter Hirt brought a quintet of Louisiana musicians with him for the evening at the White House. On saxophone was Mike Osheski, a relative newcomer, who would not pursue a career in jazz; and on clarinet, Joseph T. "Pee Wee" Spitelera, who had played off and on with Al since the early 1960s and appeared on several of the brass showman's best albums. Pee Wee was highly regarded, frequently mentioned in discussions of legendary New Orleans clarinetists, but never a household name—the consummate sideman with few album titles of his own.[7]

Drummer Paul Ferrera came to Hirt with solid credentials, having played with Santa Pecora, Louis Prima, and the Dukes of Dixieland. All-around keyboard man Wayne DeVillier (pronounced "de-vill-ye-ay") was there that night to sub for the lack of bass violin, add to the volume, and lay down a slow funky groove for Jumbo's horn to romanticize over.[8]

On piano was a little-known freelancer from New Orleans who occasionally played at Al Hirt's Bourbon Street nightclub: Ellis Marsalis. Today, Marsalis is (1) the grand patriarch of the world's most famous jazz family—his four jazz-playing sons are reedman Branford, trumpeter Wynton, trombonist Delfeo, and drummer Jason; (2) a premier New Orleans jazz educator (albeit retired) with an emphasis on jazz studies; and (3) a fine modern jazz pianist conversant in all styles with recordings for the Sony CBS and his own ELM labels. But on that December night, those in the audience who glanced at their programs took little notice of the Marsalis name. Wynton was only nine at the time, three years away from beginning his serious studies on his first trumpet, which would be given to him by—Al Hirt.[9]

When the Al Hirt sextet mounted the East Room stage and performed that evening, a precedent was set. No previous bona fide commercial Dixieland band had played the embryonic music first heard on the streets of New Orleans some six decades before—or at least a contemporary extension thereof—in the president's house (as George Washington called it). Bells did not peal, banners did not unfurl, clarion calls were not heard, and the headlines the next day fell silent on the historical significance. Everyone simply assumed that authentic New Orleans–style bands had played the East Room before. But they hadn't.

Al and his combo opened their set with a rousing version of the New Orleans classic "Down by the Riverside."[10] The East Room crowd response was similarly upbeat, boisterous even. Hirt acknowledged the applause and said, "That was 'Down by the Riverside.' [Laughter.] In case you didn't recognize the melody. [More laughter.] Can you hear us okay? [Even more laughter.] Nobody sleeps when we play! Here's a ballad from last year that you may remember [The Burt Bacharach/Hal David hit] 'This Guy's in Love with You' [made popular by singer Dionne Warwick, but with 'Girl' replacing 'Guy' in the title]."

This time it was the trumpet master alone, backed by drums and keyboards (Marsalis's piano *and* DeVillier's organ), rendering the hummable Bacharach/David collaboration in a respectful, romantic way.

How many minds in that august East Room wandered away to another place, a darkened roadhouse somewhere, sawdust on the floor, a never-ending slow dance, enveloped in the caramel stench of cigarette smoke, beer, and whiskey? How many gave thought to Al's nightspot,

Chez Hirt, on historic Bourbon Street in the French Quarter? The spell was abruptly broken as the combo launched into "Java," Al's chart-busting, Grammy-winning hit written by fellow New Orleans musician Allen Toussaint in 1958. The Crescent City sound wrapped the room, Pee Wee's clarinet piping on top and baritone saxophone and organ filling the bottom in traditional tailgate trombone fashion. "Java" ended on a pop and was greeted with the same enthusiasm as the first number.

Al introduced another change of pace, typical of a Hirt set:

And now I'd like to demonstrate some of the things that you can do with this instrument. Forty years ago when I first started playing it, my father told me some things *I could do with it*! [Laughter.] But my mother always encouraged me, so I'm still at it. And this is an old cornet solo, and it wraps up all the things like the fancy flights and fast tonguing, double tonguing, triple tonguing, and it's all in this one little solo called the "Carnival of Venice."

[Al scattered some impromptu trumpet remarks before starting the familiar melody.] Here are some variations on that melody . . . Here's another feature, some double tonguing. . . And now some triple tonguing. [Obligatory applause, much like accordionists receive for playing "Lady of Spain" at NASCAR speed.] And now here's the last variation and the finale. And we try to get little special effects. I'm going to make you think you hear two trumpets playing. I do this by accentuating the melody notes—the C notes—by playing them a little louder, and the notes that come in between softer. You may get two trumpets playing. You may. [Laughter.]

A drum crescendo swelled amid mounting applause as this circus-like special reached its climax. Al no doubt included this bit of musical acrobatics in his rather short set to emphasize his technical mastery of the trumpet and remind everyone he was, as he liked to put it, a "first trumpet player," a "trumpet showman," and not a jazz player.

Al Hirt and his band in the East Room; (*l to r*): Ellis Marsalis (*p*), Mike Osheski (*s*), Paul Ferrara (*d*), Pee Wee Spitelera (*cl*), Pat Nixon, Richard Nixon, Al Hirt (*tp*), Tricia Nixon, and Wayne Devillier (*kb*).

Hirt began a musical arabesque that halted abruptly in a loud trumpet kiss, the signal for the band to roar off with the standard closer "When the Saints Go Marching In." Originally a gospel hymn (1886), this song has transmogrified itself through so many arrangements, variations of lyrics, and even title changes that it is now more a secular folk song than anything else.[11] Many musicians dread "The Monster" because it so often requested. The jazz musicians at Preservation Hall in New Orleans, for example, got so tired of playing it that the sign announcing the fee schedule ran "$2 for standard requests, $5 for unusual requests, and $10 for 'The Saints.'"

The East Room audience took to clapping during the ensemble playing. Each instrument soloed before the band commenced a long, concluding tease that began with the usual New Orleans three-horn, interlocking weave, which faded into a whispering trumpet line over a steady Marsalis piano vamp, the organ picking an altogether new bass-line melody, followed by another full ensemble blast, then the front line instruments, sequentially alternating note by note, playing "The Saints" melody before bring the show to a close with the ever-so-familiar full-volume Dixieland ride out.

The audience stood and roared. They knew that they had just heard something special. This quintessential American tune, one that had closed a million concerts and dances for the previous six decades, had finally received its first most glorious presentation at the nation's grand mansion.

And the 5th Dimension had to follow that act. To their credit, they held their own.

5TH DIMENSION

The 5th Dimension was a most unlikely entertainment choice for the Nixon White House, not for their Democratic Party leanings as much as their appearance after a daylong conference on drugs! The most popular song in America that summer was their rendition of "Age of Aquarius/ Let the Sunshine In," the two tunes that bookended the enormously popular (and controversial) Broadway hit *Hair*, billed as an "American tribal love/rock musical."

> The musical was actually three shows in one: a celebration of free love and the hippie lifestyle; a satirical attack on the Establishment; and the story of one hippie's decision about whether to avoid the draft and flee to Canada. *Hair* sang the praise of everything from marijuana to masturbation and pretty much thumbed its nose at traditional values . . . At the end of Act I under dramatic lighting, a dozen members of the cast—male and female—stood totally naked in front of the audience. This was the infamous nude scene that shocked folks in America— people naked on stage! In the "let's try anything" atmosphere of the late Sixties, however, the nudity and the musical's rebellious themes fit with the times.[12]

Not that the White House was totally sanguine about the matter, as 5th Dimension lead singer Marilyn McCoo recalled:

A funny thing—or strange thing—happened prior to our appearance. A White House aide sent us a questionnaire, which included a question asking if any of our lyrics referred to drugs or taking drugs. When we asked for a clarification, the White House aide told us that they were interested in a particular song of ours called "Up, Up and Away." Since cocaine was sold in "balloons" or packages, he said, was there a hidden meaning behind "Up, Up and Away"? We replied that it was just a happy song about the joys of riding in a hot air balloon.[13]

It's a good thing they didn't ask whether any of the songs were connected to free love, pot smoking, draft evasion, and nudity. Moreover, and this is difficult to square in any rational way, earlier in the year, Nixon told his aide Haldeman that he wanted to take stronger action on obscenity, and that he had decided he would go to a play in New York where they took off their clothes (*Hair*), and get up and walk out, to dramatize his feelings.[14]

The above aside, it is still hard to imagine the 5th Dimension being invited to 1600 Pennsylvania Avenue in any other year but Nixon's first in office. Confidence in the president had already begun to wane after the "secret" bombing of Cambodia was revealed earlier in the year, as was amply demonstrated by November's "Moratorium," the massive Vietnam protest march in DC. But the national polarizing angst to come had not yet settled across the land—that would arrive after the ground incursion into Cambodia, the Kent State student shootings, the Pentagon Papers flap, the Vietnam air war escalation, and the Watergate morass much later. It was safe for the 5th Dimension to be at the White House in 1969, especially for an administration in need of a hipper image.

The 5th Dimension opened their segment with a three-song medley, "The Declaration" (actual words of the founding document preamble set to music), "A Change Is Going to Come," and "People Got to Be Free." According to singer (and Ms. McCoo's husband) Billy Davis Jr., the opening selections (and not the closing song from *Hair*) caused the group some nervous moments:

Performing that three-part song was our little protest, a political statement if you will. If President Nixon was listening closely, he would have heard us sing that when the government becomes destructive of unalienable rights, the people have the right to institute a new government. We weren't exactly John, Paul, George, and Ringo [the Beatles] singing, "You say you want a revolution," but we were definitely pushing the boundaries.

The weirdest thing happened when we finished "The Declaration." The East Room fell totally silent! There was a long, awkward moment as the U.S. governors and their wives waited to gauge President Nixon's reaction.

I froze in my tracks for several seconds, waiting . . . waiting . . . until President Nixon stood up and clapped his hands. Within seconds, the East Room filled to the rafters with applause. I made eye contact with Marilyn and winked as we bowed, but let me tell you, that was the most nervous moment I've ever had on stage.[15]

The finale of course had to be "Age of Aquarius," and the audience needed no cue by the president to react. The song and the show received high marks from the press. Isabelle Shelton of the *Washington Evening Star*:

There has been nothing like last night's whomping, stomping and ear-splitting—and highly entertaining—program for two generations since a birthday party for Duke Ellington last spring that has musicians across the country still talking.

President Nixon and most of the VIP parents last night were clapping hands and tapping feet right along with their children as trumpeter Al Hirt and his New Orleans band and the 5th Dimension took turns on the podium seeing who could shake the most rafters.

Even the Secret Service was keeping time.

And Vice President Spiro T. Agnew, the last man with whom

most of today's youth would expect to find common ground, was clapping and swaying as the 5th Dimension belted out "The Age of Aquarius" and "Let the Sunshine In," both from the nude anti-establishment hit show, *Hair*.

Democratic Governor Richard Hughes of New Jersey and Republican-elect Linwood Holton of Virginia further livened up the proceedings on stage, dancing with the sequin mini-skirted girl singers in the 5th Dimension. Hilton said he loved "the whole program, all day. It was a great day, a great family day. It's the kind of thing that closes the gap between the two generations."[16]

The president tried to get daughter Tricia to join the governors onstage, in vain, however. So he simply clapped to the beat. Marie Smith of the *Washington Post*:

At the conclusion of the musical extravaganza, President Nixon joined the performers on the stage and said, "Only one other night has there been the excitement of such music in this room, and that was the great jazz of Duke Ellington. This is in the same category. That was a great night and this is a great one." Then turning to the musicians, he said, "I hope you'll all live as long as the Duke and be as good as he is."

Vice President Agnew said he is both a rock and jazz buff, and he thought the program was "great." He added, "We were shaking along with them."

The governors, who bounced in their seats, swaying to the music and applauded President Nixon's declaration that the 5th Dimension "are better than their records."[17]

While the musical quintet wowed the president and the East Room crowd, their appearance did not sit well with everybody, as Marilyn McCoo explained:

We encountered some unexpected controversy *afterward* when

we were criticized in some quarters for "selling out" or losing our "soulful edge" by singing in the Nixon White House, but we never saw it that way. Whenever the President of the United States asks you to come into the nation's most famous residence to perform, you go. It's like a command performance. We were entertainers, which meant we checked our politics at the front door of the White House. If truth be told, we didn't vote for Nixon (we came from families of lifelong Democrats) but that was beside the point.[18]

But they didn't check their politics at the front door, did they? They spoke to power on the issue of civil rights in their opening medley and didn't shy away from singing their "anti-establishment" megahit "Age of Aquarius/Let the Sun Shine In," which won Record of the Year and two Grammys in 1969.

Six weeks after the White House gig, Al Hirt played the national anthem at Super Bowl IV, the second of his five Super Bowl appearances.

Eight months later, Al again played for the president, this time on *his* home turf. Nixon flew to New Orleans for a one-day conference to argue for an orderly end to school segregation.[19] Al and the band, with famed clarinetist Pete Fountain included, greeted Mr. Nixon at his hotel in the heart of the French Quarter. And of course they played "The Saints."

In the spring of 1973, the 5th Dimension toured Turkey and Eastern Europe for the State Department. They broke up in 1975, but the original five reunited in 1990 for another seven-year run.

Peggy Lee

I don't know what it was,
but as long as it's gone, it's all right.
—*Peggy Lee*

February 24, 1970 | French President Pompidou Dinner

Peggy Lee was the quintessential girl in the middle: a pop-jazz singer. She may not have been Ella Fitzgerald, Sarah Vaughan, Billie Holiday, or Betty Carter, but make no mistake, this songstress with the steamy pastel voice *was* a jazz singer. Jazz musicians who worked with her believed passionately in her musical sensibilities.

Peggy came to wide public attention in 1943 on the strength of her first hit, "Why Don't You Do Right?," recorded with the Benny Goodman band. "Do Right," along with other recorded songs from that period, confirmed—to the cognoscenti, at least—her facility for translating jazz and blues for the masses and pegged her, rightly or wrongly, as the "white Billie Holiday."

She next swung toward the mainstream, with a string of pop hits, such as "It's a Good Day," "Mañana," "Golden Earrings," and "Don't Smoke in Bed," some cowritten with her first husband, Dave Barbour. By 1950, she had become the nation's "number one vocalist" with record sales exceeding four million. Peggy was huge!

While her jazz credibility faded, she had garnered a Capitol Records contract and network radio appearances, including her own radio show, and taken her first tentative steps into the world of glitzy nightclubs that would provide the major platform for her talent for the rest of her life.[1]

"You come with me and you can record whatever you want," A&R man Milt Gabler famously said when she switched to Decca Records in 1952. And that she did. First came a single, a galloping treatment of the Rodgers & Hart waltz "Lover," that soon took its place among Peggy's growing list of signature songs. Then the album *Black Coffee*: an eight-song set on the new ten-inch LP format with her nightclub jazz-mates Pete Condoli (trumpet), Jimmy Rowles (piano), Max Wayne (bass), and Ed Shaughnessy (drums). Many consider *Coffee* one of the best female jazz vocal albums ever; it was certainly one of the first concept albums and one of Lee's best. Peggy got her jazz credibility back! She finished second to Ella Fitzgerald for female singer of 1953.[2]

After *Coffee*, Peggy treaded pop waters for a couple of years. Then came a film (*Pete Kelly's Blues*), numerous TV and nightclub appearances, and a return to Capitol Records in 1957 with her inaugural album (*The Man I Love*), charted, arranged, and conducted by Frank Sinatra, which begat her midcareer benchmark, "The Folks Who Live on the Hill."[3]

And the following summer, another surprise hit.

Although Peggy did not write "Fever" (it was penned by Davenport and Cooley and first sung by Little Willie John), she was responsible for the arrangement and some substitute lyrics (the Romeo and Juliette and Pocahontas and Captain Smith verses). It was Peggy who told Howard Roberts to set his guitar aside and just snap his fingers, while bassist Joe Mondragon and drummer Shelley Manne laid down the percolating rhythm. Not only did Peggy have a chart-topper but she had a song that would be eternally hers.[4]

The girl forever in the middle again showed her jazz chops on the superb *Mink Jazz* album partially arranged by jazz legend Benny Carter and released on Capitol Records in 1963. That same year marked the Beatles and the British Invasion, as well as the end of the resurgent interest in jazz that had begun in the mid to late 1950s and the beginning of career difficulties for many jazz and pop-jazz musicians, who found refuge in recording or broadcast studios at home or abroad.[5]

Peggy remained relevant in the 1960s, however, through her occasional TV and nightclub appearances and her bulging portfolio of personal hits, American songbook selections, and songs she herself had written or cowritten, which by 1970 numbered 145. Perhaps not well appreciated at the time, she had become America's first popular female singer-songwriter, spawning acolytes from Joni Mitchell to Norah Jones to Taylor Swift. Increasingly, Peggy began to incorporate contemporary sounds (rock and roll) into her repertoire. A final surprise hit in late 1969 ("Is That All There Is?") would reinvigorate her career and keep her on the scene into the 1990s.[6]

One would have thought that by 1970, a transcendent celebrity like Miss Peggy Lee—on the national scene for nearly three decades—would have already received an invitation to perform at the White House. Not the case, though it finally came . . . by default. Peggy, as it turned out, was the only top-drawer entertainer willing to perform at a state dinner for French President Pompidou.

The White House had been in a quandary early that February. A high-profile artist was needed to entertain Georges Pompidou and his wife in the East Room on the twenty-fourth. But a problem had arisen:

Pompidou had just agreed to sell a hundred and ten Mirage fighter jets to a young man named Maummar al-Quaddafi in Libya. Pompidou had, on the other hand, refused to sell fifty Mirages to Israel [he would tender five gunboats later, however]. Pompidou's eight-day state visit to the United States would inspire vocal demonstrations in several large cities, including San Francisco and New York. As the day of Pompidou's dinner approached, State's list of potential entertainers grew ever shorter. Jewish singers [and instrumentalists as well as their sympaticos] wanted no part of the performance.[7]

In late January, White House impresario Connie Stewart had sent a note to Social Secretary Nancy Winchester: "[Arturo] Rubenstein requested for Pompidou, [Vladimer] Horowitz coming?" It should come as no surprise that these two preeminent classical pianists found themselves otherwise engaged on the night of the state dinner.[8]

One short week before the event, the office of Lee's publicist, Peter Levinson, received a phone call. Could she sing for the Nixons and the Pompidous? Her current single, "Is That All There Is?," was also a hit in France. Peggy agreed, although several protest groups pressured her not to perform.

Nixon went all out to impress President Pompidou and his visiting party—it was the French after all who had invented both ceremony and fashion. The welcoming ceremony and state dinner were meticulously planned.

As was often the case after a state dinner, President Nixon introduced the entertainment in the East Room. That evening, in deference to his guest of honor, Nixon's remarks were simultaneously translated into French by Major General Vernon Walters to accommodate President Pompidou's lack of facility with the English language and perhaps to also appeal to his residual Gaullist chauvinism. Nixon stuck closely to his prepared remarks:

> Our artist tonight, Miss Peggy Lee, comes from the heartland of America . . . From the farm in North Dakota she went to Hollywood, and then to New York, and then finally to the pinnacle of success in the musical world. An indication of her success is that she's sold more than ten million records, and they're still selling. She has many other capabilities. She's an artist, she writes poetry, she's a sculptor, and she's a diplomat . . . because one of her very best selling records is entitled *Big Spender*, [and] she's not singing that tonight. [Laughter.][9]

Miss Lee, dressed conservatively with one long string of pearls and a long-sleeved black dress, drifted onto the East Room stage and immediately launched an up-tempo version of "Almost Like Being in Love," which she had sung numerous times before. Her swinging backup band consisted of members of the Marine Orchestra and her traveling jazz combo: stalwarts Lou Levy on piano, Mundell Lowe on guitar, and five-year associate Grady Tate on drums. Peggy followed her opening cooker with renditions of two pop-chart items: "Something," the George Harrison *Abbey Road* ballad and "Spinning Wheel" by the rock group Blood, Sweat & Tears.

For several years, Peggy had been in an "if you can't beat them join them" mode, embracing the rock sound like never before. Her first outing occurred on her *A Natural Woman* album, which, in addition to "Spinning Wheel," featured her version of Otis Redding's "Dock of the Bay," Aretha's "Woman" (of course), Sly Stone's "Everyday People," and tunes by Percy Mayfield and Randy Newman. As to be expected, the closer the tune to the blues, the more successful the outcome. Some in the East Room that night had probably heard her take on "Spinning Wheel"—she had sung it on the *The Ed Sullivan Show* the previous April, and the single had been regularly spun on the radio since its release months before.

"Something," on the other hand, was fresh off the *Is That All There Is?* album that had arrived on the charts only the previous month. And, like *A Natural Woman*, the more recent LP included compositions by new artists like Randy Newman, Neil Diamond, and the Lieber and Stoller songwriting juggernaut. Peggy would sing "Something" to the rest of the nation later in the week on *The Ed Sullivan Show* and five weeks after that at the Hotel Shoreham in Washington, DC.

After the president's introduction, there was no way Peggy would sing "Big Spender," but she did offer a warm reading of a tune from the 1966 *Big Spender* album: Michel Legrand's "Watch What Happens" (from the film *The Umbrellas of Cherbourg*). A languid flute solo introduced the tune before Peggy lazily sketched the lyrics in that whispery cotton-candy way of hers that fans of three decades knew only so well. Her jazz combo then kicked off an upbeat "Someday My Prince Will Come" from the Disney film *Snow White and the Seven Dwarfs*; over

the years, this Morey/Churchill tune had been a favorite of jazz musicians, from Dave Brubeck to Miles Davis to Bill Evans.

Following this rather tight five-song set, when Peggy took her first
bows to lukewarm applause and quickly left the stage, the audience
might have assumed that it was part of the act—and it was. But the
muted response irked her and she belted down a stiff drink, according
to her publicist, Peter Levinson. "She gave me this look of exaspera-
tion: '*God.*' The music was too sophisticated for that audience, and she
knew it."

Drummer Tate had a mixed take on the evening. "Peggy didn't
drink as much as people said she drank. There was a thing where she
wanted to be almost incoherent at times, but that was one of her crips,
one of the things she depended on when all else fails . . . She wanted
to be mysterious. And out of it . . . [that night] she ended up very
strange . . . to herself, and to everybody."

Levinson further recalled, "The makeup lady says to me, horrified,
'You can't believe how much cognac she just had.' Now the audience
is kind of shifting around, and she's on the stage, and I see the cognac
had hit her."[10]

Peggy regained center stage and engaged in some offbeat nightclub
banter, the sort of thing she had been doing since the early 1950s; she
loved to talk onstage. That night, Peggy patter was her undoing.

"I want to thank you so very much for making me feel so welcome here," she said, with an overdose of breathy sultriness. "Do
you realize I've tried to be here a number of times? And, uh . . .
it's a very kind of wonderfully warm feeling, and Mr. President
and Mrs. Nixon . . . you have a lovely house." [Laughter.]

Stranger still were her unusual cadences, subtexts, unpredict-
able non sequiturs. "I'm very fond of poetry . . . among other
things," she confided in an old Mae West accent apparently meant
to seem ironic. It brought no laugh from the crowd. And her
next bit came completely out of left field:

"One of my favorite humorous verses is by [the Lithuanian-born Academy Award–nominated screenwriter and humorist-poet] Samuel Hoffenstein from his book *Pencil in the Air* [Kessinger Publications] and it's very short. And it goes like this:

"Everywhere I go
I go too
And spoil *ever*-thang."

This self-deprecating downer representation of the insecure little girl inside her drew sparse, confused laughter. But Peggy seemed undeterred.

"You know, that poem keeps me in line now and then," she continued. "There's another one written by Princess Grace [of Monaco] when she was fourteen years old, and I think she wrote rather profoundly." Now Lee lapsed into a little-girl voice:

"I hate to see the sun go down
And squeeze itself into the ground
'Cuz some warm night it might get stuck
And in the mornin' not get up.

"Isn't that divine? Do you like her poem? I love it. I really wish she'd kept on writing, but I know she's happier now [giggle]. You know, more serious poetry isn't that well accepted. In fact, to quote one writer, 'To publish a book of verse is like dropping a rose petal down the Grand Canyon and waiting for the echo. . . . And I know. I wrote a book of verse and I dropped it into the Grand Canyon.'"[11]

Peggy went on, "But then I couldn't say that all poetry is not accepted because lyrics are poetry and they are accepted. Although, so many today are sentimental, sad, down. And I, for the most part, prefer the song of the optimist, because without the optimist, the pessimist would never know how happy he wasn't, *right*? And then I couldn't say that all lyrics are poetry because so many things they are writing today are little stories, little vignettes."[12]

Her rap on poetry was neither coquettish nor dilettantish; she genuinely loved the spoken word, as one would expect of a lyricist of her caliber. She read poetry regularly on her radio show way back in 1952, reciting William Butler Yeats before singing "These Foolish Things," for example.[13]

Her patter, especially the remark about the optimist and pessimist, was no doubt her way of introducing her current surprise hit song. A most unusual pop number, written by chart-masters Leiber and Stoller, "Is That All There Is?" intersperses morbid spoken verse with a catchy hook, a song that could easily be a turnoff on first hearing—as it was in fact for Peggy—but one that gathers meaning upon repeated hearing.

After all, a song that describes the narrator's memory of her house burning down (it happened to Peggy twice as a child), a trip to a so-so circus, and lost love (she knew only too well) but advises us to "keep on dancing . . . and have a ball" is the stuff of an Oprah Winfrey show. So it has a "keep smiling in the face of adversity" side, though on first hearing, it may not be too clear.

It was reasonable to assume that most in the audience had heard this buzz song of the year, especially because of its mysterious quality and the controversy it generated. The single version of "Is That All There Is?" had been out for an entire year. Throughout 1969, Peggy sang it at her nightclub engagements and on national TV; an album of the same name had filled record store bins for the previous three months; and the trade press was humming with speculation that Peggy would win a Grammy for the song (which she did, two weeks after the Nixon event).[14]

Yet the song was a bummer to the East Room glitterati; it received only polite applause. Maybe Peggy's spoken opening phrase had turned them off. In a near whisper, she had uttered, "I remember when I was a little girl, our house caught on fire—and it did, Mr. Nixon."

After the lukewarm response," Peggy said, "Well, I don't want to sing good night right now, if you don't mind. Do you?"

Only a few in the audience answered no.

"You've all been to Disneyland I presume. No? Well, you must go. I'm going to be Tinkerbell someday. [Long pause.] I don't think any of you have been to Disneyland. Don't you know what Tinkerbell does? She hits that peanut-butter jar and files over the Matterhorn. I think she's about seventy-five. So that's my next job. [Peggy was fifty at the time.] No, she does something magic, because she turns the lights on. I do something different. I turn them off."

After some stage business (a lowering of some of the lights in the East Room), Miss Lee offered her signature tune "Fever," accompanied by the familiar finger-popping bass- and drum-only riff. This was not the sultry, sexy version most would be familiar with, but a playful cabaret version. Drummer Tate "put on the pots" all the way through to an extended coda, where Peggy interspersed various raps between the song's final two lines: "Fe-vah! Fe-vah! I boin. I boin? I burn. I bin. Oh, look out for the Indians . . . Fever. What a lovely way to learn . . . You know what you learn? You learn not to kiss chickens. You know why? Ask me why."

Someone in the audience asked why.

"Because they have such funny lips [she awkwardly mimicked a noisy chicken kiss]. There is no other reason. I had a pet chicken, Mr. President, thank you for mentioning my home state North Dakota. But you didn't know this about me. I had a pet chicken and I thought it was an Irish Setter but it was a Rhode Island Red. I fed that chicken gravel, promised it wheat, did everything. It went the way of all chickens. Don't blame me I was only four years old.

"'What a lovely way to burn.' I was a terrible cook. Out damn spot. No I doth jest. Thou knowest I doth jest. I certainly doth, dothest I. 'What a lovely way to burn.' I'm smoking more and enjoying it less. Yes sir! 'Yes sir that's my baby'" [several times into a fade].

Her fascination with chickens began in her North Dakota youth, where she regularly fed and plucked them. Her 1950s pianist Joe Harnell recalled:

She would entertain us by doing an impression of what chickens would do when it rained on the farm; they would stand in the rain and drown. The water would fall into their nostrils. She'd stand up straight, with this funny expression on her face, and fall forward onto the floor.[15]

Thank goodness Nixon's guests were spared this barnyard tale.

Peggy and her full combo suddenly erupted into a bouncy "Why Don't You Do Right?," her first hit with the Benny Goodman band. She followed this with another 1940s hit: the 2.5 million-seller "Mañana," a tune she cowrote with husband Dave Barbour. It's hard to imagine anyone singing this politically incorrect song in the nation's capital today (the lyrics insinuate that Latinos are lackadaisical). Peggy warbled the tune at times in a mock Latin voice that featured call-and-response "mañanas" with the band; some in the audience joined in as well.

Following the applause, she addressed the guest of honor: "I wanted so much to sing a song for his Excellency President and Madame Pompidou. I learned one song in French; maybe I'll sing four bars. I sent my daughter to school to learn French. You know how mothers are. Would you mind if I sang a little of it, Mister President, I'm going to try. Oh, lord, this is hard!"

Peggy whispered, chanteuse-style, several bars of "La Vie en Rose," a song she used to sing back at the Copa in 1951.[16] "I must learn to speak French," she lamented. "My daughter learned. We went to France. She called room service. She said her words very well. And they assumed that she spoke very well, and they spoke very rapidly, and she hung up. And she's never spoken another word!"

As if she had totally confused the French president, she leapt into a bit about a new, very short song she had written, and sang, "I don't know what it was, but as long as it's gone, it's all right!"[17] Peggy had used "The Short Song" before, having composed it specifically to rescue a show that wasn't going well.

This time, the song came too late.

Still, she continued, "You like it! I want to record it, but it's so short. I wonder if you would sing it with me." She rehearsed the lines with the

By all appearances, the Pompidous and Nixons enjoyed Peggy Lee's performance; (*l to r*): President Pompidou, Mrs. Pompidou, President Nixon, Peggy Lee, and Mrs. Nixon.

audience—following the bouncing-ball style—and jump-started them into a surprisingly credible sing-along.

In closing her first show at the White House, Peggy said, "I've waited so long to sing here that I really . . . I thank you so much for asking me. And I thank you so much for making me feel so welcome." She then segued into her final song, the touching and poignant "Here's to You," which had an appropriately nostalgic "Auld Lang Syne" feel.

She had written this gentle waltz (with Dick Hazzard) for Cary Grant to sing to his daughter thirty years before and had been using it for some time as her closer. The lyrics were predominantly farewells in a number of languages—*a votre sante, vaya con dios, shalom, salut, pace, l'chaim*—ending with the spoken words "angels on your pillows." While she would sing this song for years to come, she would soon adopt a new closer: "I'll Be Seeing You."[18]

By all appearances, the Pompidous and Nixons liked the performance. The French president was the first one onstage to congratulate the vocalist at the end of the program (he kissed her hand), followed by President and Mrs. Nixon (the latter kissed Miss Lee on the cheek) and Mrs. Pompidou. Peggy told the *Chicago Daily News* that all four of them were "very gracious."[19] The heads of state and their wives might have been the only ones to enjoy the show.

Under the banner "Sing-Along with Peggy," the *Washington Post* claimed that "the program of pop music didn't make a hit with some of the serious music lovers at the dinner," spotlighting only the sing-along organized by Peggy.[20]

Betty Beale of the *Washington Star* was less kind:

It was late when the entertainment was over. Usually performances are limited to 20 minutes, but singer Peggy Lee's program lasted quite a bit longer. Although Miss Lee is tops as a recording artist and there were people there who love her records, they thought the nightclub act, which was pitched for the average nightclub mentality, did not belong in the East Room of the President's House, certainly not before such a sophisticated audience. Her act once again proved, as was proven in the Johnson administration more than once, that any singer who won't sing without a microphone shouldn't be allowed to sing in that comparatively small room, especially when backed up by a full orchestra. . . . Last night the sound was sometimes deafening.[21]

Two years later Ms. Beale would rant again:

Peggy Lee, who sang for President and Mrs. Pompidou of France two years ago, was also a disaster on that stage. Indeed, it could be that any singer who won't perform without clutching a mike should not be there.[22]

Beale, who covered White House social events on a regular basis for the *Washington Star*, often lobbied for "highbrow" (opera singers and classical pianists) and railed against "lowbrow" entertainment (anything other), so her comments can be put into context. But there were others who shared her view. The *Chicago Daily News* headlined with "Peggy's Feverish Act Leaves White House Cold." According to reporter Vera Glaser,

Singer Peggy Lee's sexy routine "misfired" at the diplomatically sensitive White House dinner for French President Georges Pompidou, a source close to President Nixon said Friday.

The misfire is officially viewed as such an international boo-boo that U.S. protocol chief Emil (Bus) Mosbacher is expected to take it up with the White House when he finishes escorting the French visitors around the country.

The buxom blonde Miss Lee would have wowed 'em in Las Vegas, but her style went over like a lead balloon with the high-brow White House audience . . . .

It was a disaster," a French journalist said. "America has much better to offer." He described his country as "too polite to express their feelings" and suggested the act "made a worse impression on the Americans than the French."

One of the ranking women in attendance that evening was furious. "Did you see what she [Peggy Lee] did to President Nixon?" she told Glaser. "She went up and put her hands on him. He made a fast step back, but she was faster. She planted a kiss. You know how Quakers are about public mushmouth-ing." A source from the State Department explained that such close contact with the president was forbidden. A person "must extend his hand first for a handshake."[23]

Inside the White House, appointment secretary Dwight Chapin prepared a critique of the dinner for Nixon aide H. R. Haldeman. Regarding the performance, Chapin had this to say:

I am sure the President is going to mention something to the effect that [Major] General Walters had to lean over and keep interpreting comments made during the performance by Miss Lee to President Pompidou. This must have been distracting for the President and those around him. Unfortunately, I am afraid that the only answer is to have a type of entertainment that does not need interpretation on those occasions when a foreign-speaking Head of State is present.

Hmm. How did the general interpret the chicken kiss? A French chicken kiss? Chapin is correct, though—an instrumentalist would have been a better choice for a non-English-speaking head of state. French mime Marcel Marceau would have been even better! Still, from all appearances, Pompidou enjoyed the show.

More from Chapin:

The entertainment last night went from 10:50 until 11:32. I am not sure what the current ruling is on length of entertainment and what control we have of the star once he or she starts performing. One thing is for sure—Miss Lee would have been much better off if she had held her performance to 20 minutes. It should be short and sweet and the audience should be left wanting more.[24]

Broadway-producer-in-waiting Chapin (as well as Betty Beale) should have known that most White House musicales exceeded thirty minutes and many ran to an hour. A forty-two-minute program was short by Peggy Lee standards. Five weeks later at the Hotel Shoreham in downtown DC, her show featured a fifteen-song set (with between-number raps, to be sure) that lasted more than an hour, and the audience gave her a standing ovation and begged for more at the end. Ah, but that was to be expected from an audience with an "average night-club mentality."

Kidding aside, had Peggy dropped several raps—and maybe even moved the "Short Song" up in the program to warm up the audience sooner—and had the White House started the program before 10:50 (bedtime for most Washingtonians is 10:30), the program would have had a much better reception. The point is that the songs and the singing weren't the problem.

If a sizable portion of the audience were seeing and hearing Miss Lee for the first time, a cool response might have been expected. After all, Peggy was an acquired taste. One of the first fan letters she ever received was prescient: "Some singers . . . hit you over the head the first time you hear them. You're the kind it takes a while to catch up with."[25]

A month after the "disaster," *Washington Post* jazz critic Hollie West interviewed Miss Lee:

Her last appearance in Washington . . . caused a ripple of reaction about what some characterized a "sexy" routine. Miss Lee called these reports of the performance inaccurate: "If one person writes an inaccurate report, one shouldn't spend the rest of his life commenting on it," she says. "When a citizen of the United States is asked by their President to appear at the White House, I think it's an honor and I feel it's a gracious act for him to make. It was a lovely experience. My program was checked in advance."[26]

Miss Peggy Lee had the last laugh, however. President Ronald Reagan invited her back to the White House in 1988, this time to attend a dinner party for thirty guests, after which she performed. At her table, she dined with Secretary of State George Schulz, Oscar de la Renta, and dancer Rudolph Nureyev. The guest of honor was French President Francois Mitterand.[27]

Two of Peggy's songs—"Fever" and "Is That All There Is?"—both sung at the White House in 1970, were entered into the Grammy Hall Fame in 1998 and 1999, respectively.

World's Greatest Jazz Band

I like jazz. It was an excellent band.
—*Richard Nixon*

March 19, 1970 | Evening at the White House

AN ENTERTAINER'S PATH TO THE White House can be straightforward, as in a presidential directive: "Let's have Fred Waring and the Pennsylvanians sing for the *Reader's Digest*'s fiftieth anniversary dinner." Or it can be circuitous, the result of a series of happy accidents. The World's Greatest Jazz Band traveled the latter course.

In January 1970, President Nixon decided to hold a series of performances called Evenings at the White House. Somewhat more informal than white-tie dinners, these programs would bring in a wide range of entertainers. Starting around 8 p.m., they would last about an hour, followed by (maybe) a receiving line, (maybe) a reception, and (maybe) dancing.[1]

A great idea, really. Why wait for a state dinner or an annual governor's conference or a moon landing to hold an event? Set something up on a regular basis, invite supporters and potential converts, gain pander credits with constituencies, and obtain publicity for the president.

The first Evening went to longtime Republican supporter and TV comedian Red Skelton in January, followed in February by the cast of the Broadway musical *1776*. An okay start, but who to bring in for March? Why, of course, famed British actor Nicol Williamson. Didn't he receive a Tony Award nomination for Best Actor for *Inadmissible Evidence* in 1966? And portray Hamlet in London and on Broadway in 1969? And didn't he also appear in the film versions of *Inadmissible Evidence* (1968) and *Hamlet* (1969)?[2] Yes—but why a Brit? And why Nicol?

Shortly after taking office the previous March, President Nixon visited Prime Minister Wilson of Great Britain at Chequers, the official country residence of Britain's prime ministers. The two leaders sat by themselves on a sofa after dinner and were seen talking with some animation.

"Everyone wondered what [we] were talking about. Now I can tell you," President Nixon said to the audience gathered in the East Room for Nicol Williamson's big night at the White House. "The Prime Minister was telling me about a great new star that had come on the scene. He said that the new star was probably the best new Hamlet. He said, 'You should see him in London.' I said, 'I can't stay another day.' So because I couldn't stay in London, that star is here tonight—the man the Prime Minister says is the greatest Hamlet."[3]

His conversation with Wilson had stuck in Nixon's mind—and on his tongue. Later in 1969, items began to appear in the American press about the president's interest in Williamson's work. The clippings reached the desk of Abe Schneider, the CEO of Columbia Pictures, the company responsible for distributing the movie version of Williamson's *Hamlet*. The CEO immediately checked if President Nixon would like to see the film, but was told no; he then asked if the president would be open to an hour or so of *Hamlet* in person. In late January 1970, the White House informed the delighted CEO that it would be happy to devote an Evening to the British thespian.[4]

By February 20, 1970, Nicol had agreed to appear at the March 19 event and promised to send details of his performance—there was no mention of a jazz band at that point, however. The next day, Chief of Staff Haldeman sent a memo to Nixon's secretary, Rosemary Woods, also intended for the president's eyes, and a copy to First Lady aide

Connie Stewart, outlining the president's rather interesting thoughts on the Williamson Evening and on the series of programs in general:

> For the March 19 Evening at the White House that will feature Nicol Williamson, the President wants to be sure that we concentrate on people who will appreciate the great importance of this performance. We should get some of the key drama critics from all over the country. We should not have people who would not realize what an outstanding performance this really is (I don't know exactly how you figure out how to meet that standard). As a general rule, he feels that Evenings at the White House should be regarded in a similar category to State Dinners rather than like Church Services [held in the East Room on Sundays]. That is, we should not include anybody below the top levels of government and it should be top level from outside also. We should not erode down to the Administrative Assistant or secretary level and should within government, concentrate on those at Level 5 and above and their comparable counterparts from outside.[5]

As a consummate actor, a surprisingly capable singer, and an amateur piano and trumpet player, Williamson instinctively knew that an hour-long recitation of Shakespeare could not hold an East Room audience—even one purged of administrative assistants and secretaries. So, unbeknownst to the White House, Williamson decided to deliver a one-man theatrical performance. He also decided to sing, and for that, he would need a backup band. Given his somewhat esoteric taste in music, which included traditional jazz standards of the 1920s and 1930s, he called upon the newly formed nine-man group called the World's Greatest Jazz Band (WGJB).[6]

Williamson had known several members of the band for years (jazz clubs being the only kind of nightlife he regularly enjoyed). The year before, while doing *Hamlet* in Boston, he sat in with them after the theatre each night, sometimes playing the trumpet, sometimes singing. And what made this swing-Dixieland band unique among all others? Three of its members had participated in a recording session thirty-one years before when they waxed four Shakespeare sonnets set to music by Englishman Arthur Young and sung by Marion Mann. Nicol knew this, of course; in fact, he would sing three of those sonnets with the band at his White House Evening.[7]

The World's Greatest Jazz Band? Not really. But hey, what a lineup! Billy Butterfield and Yank Lawson (trumpets), Lou McGarity and Kai Winding (trombones), Bud Freeman (tenor saxophone), Bob Wilbur (clarinet and soprano saxophone), Ralph Sutton (piano), Bob Haggart (bass), and Gus Johnson (drums). Saxophonist Freeman, a man of inestimable wit, recounted in his memoir,

> Surprisingly enough, there wasn't as much controversy over the name "The World's Greatest Jazz Band" as I thought there would be. Every time that I told people the name of the band, they would invariably ask who was in the band. Just recently a jazz critic I had not seen in a long time asked me what I was doing. I told him that I was playing with the World's Greatest Jazz Band."
>
> "Oh yeah! Which one?" he asked.[8]

The band with the awkward name nonetheless had a sterling pedigree: three of its members—Haggart, Lawson, and Butterfield—were sidemen with the Bob Crosby Bob Cats. During the height of the Swing Era in the late 1930s, the Bob Cats ranked high in fan polls, topped only by the Benny Goodman, Glen Miller, and the Artie Shaw orchestras. But they were an anomaly, not really a swing band—more an extension of the 1920s hot groups, more Dixieland than swing. To be sure, they played and recorded ballad and novelty tunes to fill their coffers, but the jazz numbers were what they and their diehard fans lived for.[9]

Individually, the guys ranked high in the fan polls too, with bassist Haggart usually leading his category. If the Bob Cats had a soul, it was "Hag," as he was called. His tenure was the longest. He contributed numerous arrangements and co-composed and arranged some of their greatest hits, like the novelty tune "Big Noise from Winnetka," the romantic evergreen "What's New?," and the Dixieland standard "South Rampart Street Parade."[10]

John "Yank" Lawson, whose gruff, biting, and sometimes hectoring trumpet solos, open or muted, did not receive the acclaim of a Bunny Berigan or a Harry James, was nonetheless regarded as their equal by musicians and critics. Billy Butterfield, who later mastered flugelhorn, had a pure, shining tone with airborne lyricism—a romanticist, most would say. The two meshed like sweet-and-sour pork: "Billy and I just seem to understand each other's playing. It isn't a conscious thing. Both of us seem to realize what should happen and we fall into it together."[11]

When the Swing Era shuttered in the mid-1940s, Bob Cat alumni (and others) moved into the recording and broadcast studios to sustain their careers. Still, they moonlighted regularly to pursue their passions. In the early 1950s, Lawson and Haggart formed a band (with trombonist Lou McGarity on board) and recorded a series of small-band tributes to jazz pioneers King Oliver, Jelly Roll Morton, Bix Beiderbecke, and Louis Armstrong.[12]

Yank and Hag then participated in the Louis Armstrong *Musical Autobiography* sessions, helping Louis recreate many of his earlier triumphs. Yank played the trumpet parts of the great King Oliver and went on to play a double trumpet session with Louis at the 1962 Newport Jazz Festival.

After several tours with the reunion Bob Cats through the late 1950s and into the 1960s, as well as contributions to wealthy businessman Dick Gibson's annual jazz parties in Colorado, Yank and Hag left their steady gig at the NBC studios (*The Johnny Carson Show*). With financial backing from Gibson, they formed the World's Greatest Jazz Band. Neither of the co-leaders was enamored with the name their benefactor had bestowed on the group, but both bowed to his superior marketing skills (that is, his very deep pockets and self-delegated role as unpaid manager).[13]

Former Bob Cat member Billy Butterfield was the first to join the WGJB. Trombonist and big-band alumnus Lou McGarity, who had been playing with the duo on their various projects since the early 1950s, probably didn't even have to be asked. No doubt that was the case with pianist Ralph Sutton, considered by many as the best living exponent of the New York stride school of Willy "the Lion" Smith, James P. Johnson, and Fats Waller. Sutton had played with the boys at several Bob Cat reunions and at the Gibson jazz parties.[14]

On tenor saxophone: a ringer, the legendary Bud Freeman of the Austin High School Gang from Chicago (members included Jimmy and Dick McPartland), who had recorded with Hag, Yank, and McGarity in the mid-1940s and jammed with them occasionally thereafter at clubs and concerts. Freeman was the first significant white jazz tenor player. Compared with jazz saxophone innovators Coleman Hawkins, Ben Webster, and Lester Young, he had a lighter sound than Hawkins and Webster—although certainly not pallid—and a rawer sound than Young (to which he is often likened) but with a tougher articulation.

Through his six-decade career, however, Freeman sounded like no one but himself, a sentiment echoed by his fellow tenor masters:

Coleman Hawkins, 1941: "Lester Young is great on phrasing. For origin of ideas I would rank him first . . . Bud Freeman has a lot in common with Les Young; he phrases well and puts a lot of thought into his playing."

Ben Webster, 1973: "The guys who matter, the real ones, are the guys who never mooched off somebody else's stuff, who did something completely their own and never gave a shit about showin' everybody how much or how fast they could get over it. Lester was like that. Benny Carter, too. And so was Bud Freeman; everybody keeps forgetting about him. But, man, you hear him play two notes, and you *know*, no mistake, who's in town."

Lester Young, 1952: "Because nobody played like him. That's what knocked me out."[15]

Next enlisted was clarinetist and soprano saxophone player Bob Wilber, a traditionalist, who at the time had recently emerged from the long shadow cast by his old teacher, New Orleans master Sidney Bechet. After years of wandering in the wilderness, taking one step after another backward and suffering a resultant loss of identity and confidence, Wilber discovered a curved soprano saxophone in a music store, an original voice on the instrument, and a sense of who he was musically. He became better known and appreciated after he formed the Soprano Summit group with Kenny Davern.[16]

The second trombone chair for the White House Evening (Carl Fontana was the usual second trombone at the time) was filled by another ringer: bop trombonist Kai Winding, who, together with bop pioneer J. J. Johnson, co-led the popular trombone duo Jay & Kai; they enjoyed a decade-long run into the early 1960s. It was most fitting for Kai to make it to the White House—J. J. had attended the Duke Ellington seventieth-birthday celebration the year before.

Rounding out the nine-piece WGJB was Gus Johnson Jr., a drummer who played with some of the most famous jazz artists of the post WWII era: Earl Hines, Cootie Williams, Count Basie, Lena Horne, Ella Fitzgerald, Buck Clayton, and Woody Herman. He moved to Denver in 1968 to be the WGJB drummer and stayed with them for the ten-year duration of the band. Trombonist Urbie Green, who played at Duke Ellington's birthday party the year before, called Gus "Father Time," referring, of course, to his peerless timekeeping, not his age.

Thus formed, the powerful six-horn frontline WGJB began its quest to keep the Dixieland-to-mainstream spirit alive during a relatively dim time for such music. Marketing-maven Gibson got to work.[17]

The group made its official bow at the Riverboat Room in Manhattan in November 1968, but not until it opened the following year at the Downbeat on a Friday night did things get moving. The first sign came after the first Monday off. On Tuesday evening, as the musicians mounted the bandstand, a packed house gave them an ovation before they even played one note. Respect. From that point on, they were a howling success.[18]

In less then two months, the new wonder band found itself among legendary big-name bands—Basie, Les Brown, Ellington, Hampton, Lombardo, Severinson—performing at President Nixon's inaugural festivities on January 21, 1969. Gibson then booked the band on the nightclub circuit, on TV shows, and at the Newport Jazz Festival in July 1969. That same year in November, New York's Roosevelt Hotel instituted a full-time jazz policy with "guess who" in charge of booking the music. Gibson promptly announced that the WGJB would play the room for four months each year.[19] The White House gig, however, had less to do with Gibson's marketing acumen than with good old-fashioned serendipity.

At the time, London-based drama critic Kenneth Tynan, a friend of Nicol Williamson as well as an advisor to Britain's National Theatre Company, was courting Nicol for a role in one of the company's upcoming theatrical productions. When Tynan learned of the White House project, Nicol readily accepted his offer to go along for the ride as aide-de-camp. For this we are indebted, for in 1975, Mr. Tynan chronicled the whole mad escapade in his book *The Sound of Two Hands Clapping.*[20]

As is well known from hundreds of "let's put on a show" movies, theatrical enterprises are plagued with inadequate planning, personality clashes, technical mishaps, and debilitating doubts, so it seems a miracle they ever reach opening night. This endeavor would be no exception.

Williamson learned in London on February 11 that President Nixon wanted a "Shakespearean recital" five weeks hence on March 19 and that Columbia Pictures would pay all expenses. By February 15, Nicol had conjured up a more ambitious program than anyone in Washington ever imagined: "I don't want to read bits of Shakespeare, or even bits of other books, or even just read. I want to give them something breathtaking, something not many people can do."

He planned to sing as well as act, and the WGJB would accompany him. He would inform the White House of his decision in good time, but in the interim he had an album of songs to record for Columbia—the final session to conclude on March 8.

A notice of Nicole's upcoming event appeared in the *New York Times* on February 24, a sign he viewed ominously: "It's all final now. That's when you start to panic."[21]

Wednesday, March 11. A scare. Upon learning that his nemesis drama critic Walter Kerr of the *New York Times* had been invited to attend the performance, Nicol instructed his New York agent to get the White House to disinvite Kerr, which they refused to do. "It's off. The whole thing is off. Forget it."

A panicked Tynan called Kerr and requested that he graciously withdraw, which wasn't necessary, because he couldn't make it anyway. Nicol finally contacted Tynan: "Listen to this. The White House has just called [my New York agent] back. They finally got mad and said to him, 'Who's running this show—Mr. Williamson or Mr. Nixon?' [My agent] responded coolly: 'Mr. Williamson is running the *show*. The President is running the *country*.'"

Tynan told Williamson the news about Kerr, and the *show* was back on.[22]

After a boozy flight across the pond on March 11 and a smooth check-in at the St. Regis Hotel in New York City, Nicol unveiled his grand plan for Tynan and his New York agent, which, by then, had taken on pretentious airs: *Nicol Williamson in Five Hundred Years of Entertainment in Poetry, Drama, and Song.* For the opening of the program, he told them, Hamlet, the speech to the players, and possibly "To be or not to be." Then more Shakespeare, Macbeth seeing the dagger, Malvolio finding the letter, Hotspur confronting Henry IV, and the Shakespeare jazz vocal pieces "Sigh No More, Ladies," "Blow, Blow, Thou Winter Wind," and "When Icicles Hang by the Wall."

From the modern repertoire: Willy Loman's protest against the callousness of superannuation ("A man is not a piece of fruit") from

68

Arthur Miller's *Death of a Salesman*; Bill Maitland's attack on the un-caring coolness of the young from John Osborn's *Inadmissable Evidence*; an extract from T. S. Elliot's *Little Giddins*; an erotic poem by E. E. Cummings; and the final pages of Samuel Beckett's novel *How It Is*. In addition, Nicol would sing "Baby, Won't You Please Come Home?," "Darktown Strutters Ball," and another Shakespeare tune about Macbeth, "Dunsiname Blues." To give the star a pause for breath, the WGJB would play "South Rampart Street Parade" and Kid Ory's "Savoy Blues."[23]

A forty-five-minute act had been expected, but this would run longer. Could Nicol prepare and learn all his material in a week? Especially with no director to keep him disciplined? Against logic, two more pieces were added: the comic set piece *Treasurer's Report* by Robert Benchley and the subversive Yeats's "The Second Coming."

The trio taxied to the Grill, the basement jazz room of the Roosevelt Hotel where the WGJB was playing (booked there courtesy of manager Gibson). Champagne all around. Nicol took the stand and sang "Baby, Won't You Please Come Home," a first casual rehearsal for a song on the program. Nicol was in bed by 4 a.m., but by noon the next day, he and his friends were in Washington, DC, to inspect the nation's performance hall. By nightfall, they were back in New York City. The wee hours found Nicol "in rehearsal" at Jimmy Ryan's jazz club singing "Sister Kate."[24]

Friday, March 13. Less than a week to go—the significance of the date did not escape our intrepid thespian. Down to business, he spent the day memorizing the nonmusical parts. Tynan was convinced Nicol couldn't possibly learn all the material; he would have to read some. The program would top seventy minutes. After late-afternoon vodka sours, our star settled on the show's ending: Prospero's last line from *Midsummer's Night Dream*. He rehearsed the line while standing: "Our little life—is rounded—with a sleep." He mimed unscrewing a bottle cap and swallowing handful after handful of pills. Rolling his eyes, he clutched at his throat and collapsed on the carpet.

Saturday, March 14. The star lost most of the day, having stayed at Jimmy Ryan's club the previous night until 4:30 a.m. He attended a rehearsal by the band at the Roosevelt Grill. Intimidated by their preparedness, he disappeared into the night.

Sunday, March 15. An egg-sized bump surrounded by contusions had formed on Nicol's forehead. "I got back to the hotel at 5 a.m., pissed out of my mind. While I was taking off my trousers in the bathroom, I fell and knocked myself out. The moral is: If you are pissed out of your mind, keep your trousers on."

Later that day, after even more champagne and no time spent on rehearsal, Nicol told his agent, "I don't think I can ever act again."[25]

Monday–Tuesday, March 16–17. As Tynan described those lost days, the one constant factor was a steady drain on Manhattan's supplies of wines imported from the communes of Bourgogne. A partial rehearsal was managed somehow, with our headliner painfully aware that he was terribly unready for Thursday. Nearly all were surprised by his presentation of the modernists: John Osborne, Arthur Miller, and Samuel Beckett. After Beckett's staccato tirade of negation from *How It Is*, taken by Nicol at tracer-bullet speed, tenor man Bud Freeman walked over and shook his hand: "You're one hell of a tenor sax player. I thought I knew you pretty well, Nicol, but man—as the jazz people say—that was *something else.*"[26]

Two days from showtime and it was discovered that "director" Nicol had no technical staff and no one to light the act or cue the musicians. Following midnight calls to the White House, a young stage manager was booked and the agent's secretary was roped into giving the music cues.

Wednesday, March 18. The first full rehearsal was held for an invited audience at the Roosevelt Grill. Fluffs were made and lines missed. Nicol was less than sanguine: "Tomorrow night will be something disquieting, disturbing, weird."

And it was off to Washington, DC, for our star and his steady companion, Tynan. Both were in bed by 3 a.m.

Thursday, March 19. To the White House by limo for the final rehearsal. At the gate, an ill-advised exchange:

Guard: Are you the entertainment?
Nicol: Yes. To be exact, I *am* the entertainment. In just one moment, a dove will escape from my hip pocket and I shall pull the flags of all nations out of my mouth.[27]

The limo is waved on; why not—the "Entertainment" had been living a charmed life up to that point. Rightly performed at half pressure, the rehearsal proceeded without a glitch—sixty-four minutes long. Hag, for one, had to be somewhat relaxed; he had played the White House before in a combo led by Skitch Henderson, which included trumpeter Clark Terry and guitarist Toots Theilmans. Together, they had provided the music for Lady Bird Johnson's birthday party on December 22, 1968.[28]

Afterward, a press conference for society columnists arranged by the social secretary's office:

Columnist #1: What was that first song Mr. Williamson sang?
Agent: "Sigh No More."
Columnist #1: What show is it from?
Agent: *Much Ado About Nothing.*
Columnist #1: Is that a musical?[29]

The big night arrived. The royal court and guests gathered in the East Room and settled into their assigned places. Many of them believed they were about to witness a milestone—the first legitimate actor to give a solo performance at the White House—but it was misplaced. Renowned actor Frederick March had read Sinclair Lewis and Hemingway to President Kennedy and his guests a decade prior. Nonetheless, anticipation was nervously high. The overly dressed aristocrats squirmed in their seats. The aroma of freshly powdered wigs tickled noses. Fans fluttered. Snuffboxes snapped open, clicked shut.

The king and queen finally entered to prolonged applause and seated themselves front and center. The king rose to tell the assembled how he had heard about Nicol Williamson from Prime Minister Heath more than a year before. And fortunately for the king, he knew nothing of what that casual conversation had set in motion; he would only know what was to follow.

Suddenly, a heralding blast by the WGJB—the evening's performance was about to begin. First up, a short mock-Elizabethan overture by the band. Thus summoned, fellow player Nicol Williamson, wearing informal brown slacks and a blue cashmere shirt with a paisley scarf tied casually at his neck, sauntered forth to issue a Shakespearean soliloquy. In a voice characterized by a North Country nasal twang (*Washington Post* drama critic Richard L. Coe) or alternatively, a quick twang, the sort of sound a man might make if he spoke rapidly while carelessly pinching the bridge of his nose (*New York Times* drama critic Walter Kerr), Williamson essayed Hamlet's speech to the players: "Speak the speech I pray you, as I pronounced it to you . . . trippingly on the tongue."[30]

A proper bow, polite applause, and another WGJB fanfare followed. Mr. Williamson then limned a Samuel Beckett poem, followed by another rather silly fanfare with two howling clinkers that caused Bob Haggart to go bug-eyed with shock.[31] If the mock-Elizabethen overture and the musical bridges sounded lame, it was because a dumbstruck Hag had been told to compose and arrange them only two days before. They were purposeful, though, giving the Entertainment time to catch his breath and rearrange his thoughts. At this point, some in the audience—one could only imagine—adjusted their high expectations for the evening downward. Patience would be rewarded, however.

A return to the bard: Williamson, as Hotspur, confronted the King as in *Henry IV, Part 1*: "England forever and always." Another fanfare,

New Orleans style in this instance, and the literary focus shifted to twentieth-century America. The distinguished British actor then extolled a short bit from the script of John Osborne's play *Inadmissible Evidence*, his onstage performance of which had earned him numerous awards.

An experienced thespian, Williamson lightened the mood considerably with a sly reading of a short, humorous, and ribald E. E. Cummings poem "May I feel said he." As the crowd titters faded, the WGJB—unleashed at last—roared off in a rousing ensemble version of "Sigh No More, Ladies, Sigh No More" (*Much Ado About Nothing*, act 2, scene 3), lyrics by William Shakespeare, melody by Arthur Young, and verse sung by Nicol. Wholly at home as a singer, Williamson sang true to the vaguely familiar chorus:

Then sigh not so, but let them go
And be you blithe and bonny,
Converting all your sounds of woe
Into Hey, nonny nonny

Many in the audience would have been mildly surprised by Nicol's pungent but rather pleasant tenor singing and would have thought it reminiscent of another performer. Someone from the 1940s? Dick Haymes? Bob Eberle? Maybe someone from the 1950s? Perry Como? Andy Williams? As Kenneth Tynan put it: "The trouble with Nicol's singing voice may well be that it makes you think of everyone but Nicol."[32]

The song "Sigh No More" was arranged by bassist Bob Haggart— no surprise there. That had been his role with the band from the outset, but in this case, all he had to do was dust off the score he made for the Bob Cats thirty-one years prior. Fellow Bob Cats Butterfield and Lawson had little trouble—one can assume—relearning their old parts.

On the whole, the literary aspects of the evening complemented the musical selections and vice versa, as above: a sexy E. E. Cummings smile piece followed by the bard's blithe and bonny air, which might

have been one of the first songs ever written for the women's lib movement. (You really don't need men—just let them go and sing "Hey,
nonny nonny" instead).

Another case in point: Williamson next recited Hamlet's most fa-
mous speech with the line "To be or not to be," and then he and the
WGJB followed with "Dunsinane Blues," a retelling of the story of
Macbeth by fellow Brit Johnny Dankworth, who had written it for
his jazz-singer wife Cleo Laine. Nicol knew Dankworth and his tune;
Nicol had appeared in a musical (if only for one night) set to music by
Dankworth: T. S. Elliot's *Sweeney Agonistes*.

Each verse of the bouncy "Dunsinane Blues" is punctuated with
"Macbeth, Macbeth," which Nicol appropriately emphasized. Hmm?
No song out there to sing about Hamlet? Not really needed, not with
a "Dunsinane" verse like this:

Now's the time for you to be—
A wary 'un:
I wasn't really born, it was a—
Caesarean[33]

Our star player retreated offstage for a deserved rest, and for the
first time in the program, the WGJB took flight on Kid Ory's "Savoy
Blues." The band featured numerous solos—Ralph Sutton's striding
piano, Bob Wilbur's woody chalumeau register clarinet, Kai Winding's
bop trombone (adequately fulfilling its assigned tailgate role), and Yank
Lawson's cornet—before culminating in a rocking full ensemble out-
chorus. Trombonist Winding would no doubt have had an affinity for
this tune, having been written at the turn of the century by Kid Ory,
the first significant jazz trombonist; not that horn-men Butterfield and
Lawson would feel much differently. After all, it was Kid Ory who, having one of the best jazz bands in New Orleans in the early 1900s, first
hired their trumpet idols Joe "King" Oliver and Louis Armstrong.[34]

Williamson returned to the stage and (instead of the scene of Malvolio finding the letter from *Macbeth*, which had been scrapped only the

day before) began: "Now is the winter of our discontent." Shakespeare turned in his grave, as did King Richard III, as likely did some in the audience when the WGJB followed this performance with "Winter" (*Love's Labor Lost*, act 5, scene 2), vocal again by Williamson, the song's chorus unfamiliar to most but with an unforgettable last line:

Then nightly sings the staring owl,
Tu-whit;
Tu-who, a merry note,
While greasy Joan doth keel the pot.[35]

How many in the audience could process "greasy Joan" and what does "keel the pot" mean anyway? Tynan (in the audience) noted that the songs—especially "Dunsinane Blues" and "Winter"—had warmed the audience up. The president smiled and the rounds of applause were fuller and more frequent, helping to overcome the program's tense start.[36]

Nicol began another recitation (out of sequence—it should have come later—but he recovered), "The Second Coming" by poet W. B. Yeats, this one no doubt vaguely familiar to many in the audience:

Things fall a part; the center cannot hold;
Mere anarchy is loosed upon the world

In London the boys had deliberately chosen this admonitory piece to relate to what they called local reality (the fact that Nixon sat at the center of a very fragile Vietnam war policy).[37] Did anyone catch the irony? The WGJB followed the classic Yeats verse with a change of pace, the Charles Williams and Clarence Warfield New Orleans classic, the sweet, late-at-night "Baby, Won't You Please Come Home," played and sung as a slow ballad. Our British warbler sang the familiar words in a hushed tone, backed only by the rhythm section; outstanding solos followed by trumpeter Yank Lawson and Billy Butterfield on flugelhorn. (For fans of this tune, trumpeter Miles Davis has a gorgeous bal-

Nicol Williamson and the World's Greatest Jazz Band. *Left to right*: Nicol (*far left*), Ralph Sutton (*p, behind Nicol*), Bob Wilbur (*cl*), Bud Freeman (*ts*), Bob Haggart (*b*), Yank Lawson (*tp*), Gus Johnson (*d*), Billy Butterfield (*tp*), Lou McGarity (*tb*),and Kai Winding (*tb*).

lad version taken at an even slower tempo on his *Seven Steps to Heaven* Columbia album.)

To demonstrate his acting chops on pure Americana, Nicol enacted the powerful scene from *Death of Salesman* by Arthur Miller in which an irate Willy Loman tells his boss how and why he became a salesman. Since nearly everything in *Salesman* is dark, angry, or sad, the stage was again reset, this time for American humor, and who better for Nicol to recite than Robert Benchley and his delightful *Treasurer's Report*. One cannot always gauge audience reaction to material of this sort, but for certain, they had to be impressed. Williamson was acting it out from memory, not reading it, as he did with all the pieces he presented.

The fifth silly WGJB fanfare of the evening prodded Nicol into an amazing virtuoso, high-speed rant on Samuel Beckett: "When the panting stops, yes, yes, screams in the mud, yes, yes." How many other actors could have pulled that off? How many of today's actors or rappers? Recall how enthralled sax-man Bud Freeman was at his rehearsal version. Tynan captured this moment:

The way Nicol punctuated [Beckett] into lucidity is a technical *tour de force.* I have never heard his voice more hypnotic: as it rises from a wintry monotone to a high urgent, terrified whinny, you would think he was a medium, possessed and shaken by an unquiet demon. Nixon's face was rigid and expressionless, but he stared straight into Nicol's eyes. I don't think he has ever heard anything quite like this before.[38]

While the audience was catching its breath, a marching-band drumroll launched the WGJB into its most famous Dixieland number, "South Rampart Street Parade." Several strains of this tune would be familiar to nearly every American. But probably unknown to most: this classic evocation of a New Orleans parade was cowritten by Haggart and Bob Cat drummer Ray Bauduc and first recorded back in 1937. Hag's superb (but difficult) arrangement was immediately available as a printed orchestration, and it still reverberates to this day in saloons, ballrooms, and concert halls all over the world.[39]

Williamson closed the show with Bardish snippets from this and that—"Oh what a rogue and peasant slave am I"—before the proverbial curtain dropped on Prospero's famous last line from *Midsummer's Night Dream*:

We are such stuff as dreams are made of
And our little life is rounded with a sleep

The WGJB sounded the end with another unnecessary and silly fanfare.

The well-chosen audience of assorted high-ranking officials, diplomats, presidents of major corporations, and drama critics from across the land apparently all loved the show. Their insistent applause called the players back for a final bow. President and Mrs. Nixon requested an encore, which Williamson and the band honored with "Blow, Blow, Thou Winter Wind," words by Shakespeare (*As You Like It*), melody by Arthur Young, and arrangement by Hag. They had cut "Wind" from the program because they felt the show was running too long. As it turned out, it was the perfect closer:

Heigh-ho! sing, heigh-ho! unto the green holly;
Most friendship is feigning, most loving mere folly;
Then, heigh-ho, the holly!
This life is most jolly.[40]

The dailies were as effusive as the audience over the performance. "Hamlet Set to Jazz at White House" headlined the *Washington Evening Star*. Even the after-show received decent coverage:

Williamson made a quick change into dinner jacket and black tie (wide lapels, velvet, elegant) then stood with the Nixons to meet and chat with guests.

"Why was I invited here?" asked TV host Dick Cavett, with wonderment, watching the receiving line, [although he enjoyed the show immensely]. He and his wife came from New York for the occasion. (Obviously pleased by the invitation, he said several times on his talk show 24 hours earlier: "I'm going to the White House tomorrow night.") [Cavett, the most cerebral and literate of the extant night-show hosts, was invited because it was hoped that he would, as the president wanted, appreciate the great importance of the performance and convey such to his like-minded audience and that he would of course continue to invite administration officials to appear on his show. In 1970 alone, he invited nine, eight officials after the White House invitation].

The receiving line dispersed about 11 p.m., and the Nixons took their leave. Meanwhile, Williamson was recalling that he and his fellow performers had gone through some deep doubts about their unusual show. "It didn't seem to click until our last rehearsal today," he said. [If they only knew, eh, Nicol?][41]

Tenor saxophonist Freeman recounted the following about the show and its preparation:

Nicol had very little time to prepare for the tremendous amount of material he had to remember. I played at all the rehearsals, they were tedious and difficult, and I didn't have to remember anything . . . He gave the White House and its guests the show of the year. Isn't it interesting that a Scottish actor could get the [WGJB] into the White House.[42]

More from "Hamlet Set to Jazz at White House":

The jazzmen took over the state dining room, where tables were set up, and the White House soon was vibrating to what may turn out to be music's "new thing"—that jazz beat . . . They did "Darktown Strutters Ball" with all that marvelous talent. People called: "More . . . More." [It's unlikely that "Darktown" would be played at a "politically correct" White House today, even though its composer, Shelton Brooks, is an African American]. Williamson, obliging with "I Can't Give You Anything But Love, Baby," along with the band, told them: "We want an evening that swings . . . but let's hope we don't wake up the people upstairs!"

At one point, Nick Williamson, as his jazz buddies call him, was playing a trumpet in the direction of the other end of the big room, where Lou McGarity was answering him on the trombone. And Yank Lawson took the floor to begin, amid much laughter: "To be or not to be . . ." in pseudo-Williamson style. The [WGJB's] manager, Dick Gibson, said the band will be back in Washington May 12 at the Shoreham Hotel. [The marketing wizard at it again, placing an ad for an upcoming WGJB event in the newspaper . . . for free].[43]

As of early morning, they had all adjourned to Georgetown's Blues Alley, a prominent DC jazz club where trumpeter Charlie Shavers was playing. The WGJB sat in, as did Nicol, and it was well past 3 a.m. before the night ended.[44]

Under the headline "'Prime' Hamlet," *Washington Post* reporter Marie Smith captured President Nixon's own critique of the performance:

"I'll tell any prime minister or king who comes around this place he (Williamson) is the best Hamlet I've seen," said Mr. Nixon. He added, "I'm going to see the (Hamlet) movie in Florida."

The President added that he liked all the Shakespearean pieces. He said, "The ones you always like are the familiar ones. The ones I would not know are the *Death of a Salesman* and *Inadmissible Evidence*. The ones I know are the historical ones."[45]

By 1970, *Salesman* had become an American classic. Nixon told the *Washington Star* reporter, however, that he was particularly moved by the actor's interpretation of the key speech in Arthur Miller's *Death of a Salesman*. He told Tynan: "It's so wonderful the way he changes so quickly. One thing ends, something completely different begins. And to think your Prime Minister started it all." Nixon even told Williamson he could take the program twice over. "You must come and do it again."[46]

Asked how he liked the music, the President said, "I like jazz. It was an excellent band." Mrs. Nixon termed the program "sophisticated" and "great." Williamson summed up his feelings at the end of the evening. "I feel it's been an honor for me. I was surprised everyone liked it so much."[47]

Yet, not everyone liked it. East Wing aide Connie Stewart didn't, and by implication, others in the executive mansion didn't as well. Ten months later, she responded to internal White House criticism of another Evening by referring back to this one: "Sometimes we bomb at the White House. The Nicol Williamson Evening was another example of an original program written for the White House that was only moderately successful, and mostly because of the presence of the [WGJB]."[48]

Well, at least, the band came out unscathed. But what about the drama critics—what did they think of it? Ted Kalem of *Time* magazine, besides not objecting to his wife dancing with Williamson at the after-show party, later wrote most favorably of Williamson:

Some actors occupy the stage; a few rule it. Some actors hold an audience; a few possess it. Some actors light up a scene; a few ignite the play. These combustible few blaze with the x factor of acting—intensity, intelligence, and authority. There is royalty apart from role, and when an Olivier, Gielgud, Nicol Williamson, or Irene Papas treads the stage, their fellow actors are as rapt as the audience.[49]

Critic Richard L. Coe of the *Washington Post*, apparently tickled by the incongruity of it all—Shakespeare and jazz for goodness sake—filed a faux *Variety* notice that, despite its use of showbiz lingo, was crammed with details not usually found in coverage of White House events:

> Class bookers should check British thesp Nicol Williamson [gives credits in shorthand] in new combo with the World's Greatest Jazz Band of Yank Lawson and Bob Haggart . . . Known for mod treatment of classics as well as savvy way with smart stuff (T. S. Elliot and Samuel Beckett), thesp cooked up novel touch. This adds band [list of instruments and musicians]. Between Williamson's highlights, group blares fine beats, with specials by Shakespeare, Arthur Young, John Ducksworth [*sic*], Clarence Williams, Charles Warfield and Shelton Brooks [lyricists and composers of tunes played].[50]

After their raucous night at the mansion, the WGJB was off to play clubs and concerts around the world. The band performed at Newport again in 1972 and in the years 1974–1976. They made a stopover at the Nixon Presidential Appreciation Day (campaign) rally in Miami on March 9, 1972 (Lionel Hampton was also on the bill), which secured their "committed" spot on the White House celebrity list. Their grandest gig was yet to come, however.

President Ford invited them to play the White House again. This time, they appeared, not in the East Room, but in an erected tent on the South Lawn, along with jazz vocalist Ella Fitzgerald and others for America's bicentennial celebration on July 20, 1976, in a Salute to American Music concert.[51] The WGJB disbanded in 1978, but Lawson-Haggart marched on through the 1990s.

President Nixon kept his promise. On April 3, 1970, he screened *Hamlet,* not at Key Biscayne, Florida, but at Camp David. History does not record what Nixon thought of Williamson's portrayal. We do know, however, that Nixon viewed *Patton* the night after *Hamlet* and again on April 25, only five days before he announced the U.S. ground invasion of Cambodia on national television.[52]

Nicol Williamson went on to sing the role of Henry VIII in the Broadway musical *Rex* in 1974 and star in films, notably *Robin and Marian* (1976) and *Excalibur* (1981). More importantly, his Hamlet portrayal is generally considered to be second only to that of fellow Brit John Gielgud.[53]

Bobby Short Trio

That dream has come true tonight.
—Bobby Short

April 4, 1970 | Duke and Duchess of Windsor Dinner

FOR ANY NUMBER OF POSSIBLE reasons, the Nixons invited the duke and duchess of Windsor and a hundred of their closest jet-set friends to the White House for a private dinner party. Perhaps the president and First Lady wanted to repay a past kindness or to honor the nobility of a close political ally or to stage a fashionable soiree not seen in the White House since the time of Jacqueline Kennedy—or all three. Back in 1964, the Windsors had invited the Nixons to tea at New York's Waldorf Astoria Hotel so younger daughter Julie—an avid history buff during high school—could meet the duke. Two years later, the Windsors gave a formal dinner party for the Nixon family in Paris. In his toast to the famous couple at the 1970 White House shindig, Nixon remarked, "Julie wanted to reciprocate for the tea and dinner, but our New York apartment wasn't big enough and that is why I ran for President."[1]

In thanking his host in his toast, the duke spoke of other trips he had made to Washington. One occurred some fifty years prior, when, as the young prince of Wales, he visited a very ill President Woodrow Wilson. Another occurred on June 1, 1942, when the Roosevelts held a luncheon in his honor. That visit came while the duke was governor and commander in chief of the Bahamas. (In 1936, he renounced the British throne to marry the twice-divorced American Wallis Warfield Simpson, who would become the duchess of Windsor, in what was described then as "the romance of the century"—hence, Julie's teenage interest in the duke.) Later, during the Eisenhower administration, the duke stopped by to discuss golf with Ike. In concluding his reciprocal toast, the almost-king japed, "I feel more kindly about the White House than did many of my countrymen when they were here in 1812."[2]

Once the Windsors had been invited to dinner, it was important to invite American royalty as well. In addition to administration officials and military brass, the guest list included several ambassadors and corporate CEOs with their fashionably dressed wives, several of the duke's golfing chums, professionals Arnold Palmer and Billy Casper, and "U.S. Princess" Alice Longworth Roosevelt (famed daughter of Theodore), John Coolidge (son of Calvin), film dance star Fred Astaire, and Charles Lindbergh and his writer wife, Anne Morrow.

John Coolidge was in the audience, not because he was a Short fan per se or a jet-setter in good standing, but because it was his lucky night, having been selected from the register of living descendants of former presidents compiled by the First Lady's staff. Later in the year, Nixon (through his aide Haldeman) cited these invitations, along with those to luminaries like Lindbergh, as acts of civility, hallmarks of his administration that should be publicized.[3]

As for the entertainment for the evening, it was only proper to invite the royal couple's favorite "society" pianist, Bobby Short, whom they had seen and heard numerous times going back to the 1950s. Their first meeting took place at the Beverly Club in New York City, as Bobby recalled in his memoir, *Life and Times of a Saloon Singer*:

They wanted to meet me when the show was over. The Duke, a keen amateur drummer, was the first to extend his hand. "Mr. Short, we love the drums that roll before you came on and when you take a bow." Indeed, the Duke was one fine drummer; in fact, the other Duke—Ellington that is—recalled, "He sat in with us on drums in London and surprised everybody, including my drummer Sonny Greer."[4]

On March 27, in her *Washington Post* article, headlined "Windsor Entertainment Booked," social correspondent Marie Smith provided more details:

> Short is coming from the Café Carlyle in New York where he performs six nights a week, eight months a year, and will be accompanied by Richard Sheridan on drums and Beverly Peer on bass.
>
> Joining Short on the program from the West Coast will be The Young Saints, a group of 27 young singers and musicians whose repertoire includes everything from the classics and spirituals to jazz and contemporary sounds . . . [the group has] provided background on recordings for many top artists, including Pat Boone, Peggy Lee, Bobby Darin, Debbie Reynolds and Frankie Laine, and [has] appeared in Las Vegas with Danny Kaye and on several TV shows.[5]

The Young Saints had been on the social secretary's radar screen as a possible entertainment option for some time. Interestingly, their manager, Ted Short, was Bobby's nephew, who—according to Bobby—had also recommended him to the White House along with the Windsors. In fact, Ted had initially asked Bobby if he would sing on the same program with the Saints. Bobby replied, "At a dinner for the Duke and Duchess of Windsor. At the White House! Yes, of course.'" And the action began.[6]

It is not uncommon for an intermediary to invite an entertainer to perform at the nation's mansion. That way, both sides are saved embarrassment in case of a "no" answer. In any event, it's hard to imagine anyone else other than the dapper crooner performing for the man who gave up his crown for the woman he loved.

In a rather unusual and candid interview with the singer on March 31, four days before the event, *Washington Post* reporter Smith revealed that the White House was letting Bobby select his own songs. One of them—according to Bobby—the black militants used to find objectionable: blues singer Bessie Smith's classic "Gimme a Pigfoot," a song about Harlem rent parties with references to reefers and gin first recorded in 1933 under the aegis of legendary talent-scout John Hammond. "But the militants no longer find it objectionable. They think it is very urgent now," Bobby told Smith, and he added, "It used to be that any song that mentioned race was considered racially offensive, but now some of those lyrics are camp."[7]

Mr. Short ran down the rest of the program for reporter Smith: the Duke's favorite, "Bye Bye Blackbird," and three songs by Cole Porter— "I've a Shooting Box in Scotland," "I'm Throwing a Ball Tonight," and "Black and White Baby of Mine"—as well as "Whoever You Are, I Love You" from *Promises, Promises* (the Neil Simon play with music and lyrics by Burt Bacharach and Hal David), and English songwriter Ivor Novello's "And Her Mother Came Too."

The interview also revealed some interesting facets of Bobby's personal life:

Those who used to object to his songs involving race can't accuse him of not having done his share in behalf of civil rights. He was in the vanguard of the civil rights march in Washington in the summer of 1963, and joined in the sympathy march in Harlem on the day of the big march in Selma, Alabama, to get the vote for blacks. Although a Democrat politically, Short worked in [Republican] New York Mayor John Lindsay's two campaigns and he said, "I worked hard." He said he has never met President and Mrs. Nixon. Short admitted he is "very excited" about his forthcoming appearance at the White House. "I played in Washington as a child at the old Howard Theatre and I've been back only for television shows, not to perform," he said. A decade ago Short told a friend he wouldn't appear in Washington because it was "a Jim Crow town." But, he said yesterday, things have changed since then. "In those days you could hardly try on clothes in a department store if you were black and you had trouble getting a room in a hotel."[8]

Because of his performance venues, the songs he sang, the audiences he drew, and, yes, even the faultless and inventive way he dressed, Bobby acquired a reputation as a "cabaret" singer, a "supper club" singer, or a "saloon" singer (Bobby always preferred the latter). For these very same reasons, he acquired another reputation, one that had to hurt, one that had circulated on the cabaret circuit in the form of a joke: An impresario opens a room and wants to hire an entertainer. "Get me a white Bobby Short," he says. "What do you mean?" comes the answer. "Bobby Short is the white Bobby Short!"[9]

Regarding his impeccable, male-model appearance, jazz guitarist Bucky Pizzarelli had this to say: "Mr. Short is why the tuxedo was invented. When boys go to rent tuxes for the prom, they should be shown a picture of Bobby in a tux, to see its promise. It would be like showing a movie of Babe Ruth to a singles hitter or a Monet to someone purchasing acrylics."[10]

But Mr. Short was a jazz singer and a jazz piano player. He may not have cracked many Top 30 jazz lists, but he was a skater on the jazz ice, not just a spectator in the stands. Noted Atlantic Records producer Nesuhi Ertegun has characterized his talents thus:

Bobby is a superlative pianist, in the best tradition of [stride pianists] Fats Waller, James P. Johnson and Willie "the Lion" Smith. His choice of songs and his singing style are so unique that many overlook his enormous gifts as a pianist . . . Bobby gets inside a song more deeply than anyone in popular music, with the exception of Mabel Mercer [and let's not forget Frank Sinatra.] Like Mabel, he and the song go through a long period of getting to know each other before Bobby decides on atmosphere, on tempo, on rhythmic embellishments, etc. He is faithful to the composer, but at the same time he most definitely adds the weight and wisdom and musicality of his own personality.[11]

Bobby's devotion to the lyrics and his exacting diction put him in that ambrosial class with his idols Mercer and Sinatra, despite a coarse tinge to his voice (laryngitis was a lifelong malady) and a sometimes uneven delivery, whether he was slightly rushing ahead or lagging behind his own accompaniment and that of his rhythm mates. The boundless energy he brought to every performance more than made up for any minor flaws. Everything worked in his favor. His voice was immediately recognizable, the sine qua non of every jazz performer.

Others hear him as more pop than jazz. Take *DownBeat* reviewer Joe Klee, for example:

> The music of the Gershwin brothers has been a favorite with the kind of warm, personal singers who enjoy treading that thin line separating the pop singer from the jazz vocalist. Some, such as Ella Fitzgerald, have come from the jazz field. Some, such as Barbra Streisand, have come from Broadway. Some, such as Bobby Short, have come from that home ground of affluent America known as Park Avenue. Mr. Short has a healthy respect for jazz and was influenced by much of it, Ellington in particular. He sings with the kind of musicality and respect for lyrics that has characterized the best popular singers from Crosby and Wiley to Streisand and Ray Charles.[12]

In short—and no pun intended—Bobby Short is to the singing voice as Pee Wee Russell is to the clarinet. As saxophonist Bud Freeman said in Jean Bach's documentary film *A Great Day in Harlem,* "A hundred years from now we'll hear more of Pee Wee Russell's playing than of Benny Goodman's, who was a great artist." Equally, it could be said—quite arrogantly—that in the future we'll hear more of Bobby Short's singing than of Frank Sinatra's.

Short was all about unearthing or dusting off downright obscure or merely neglected songs in the American canon, as he elaborates further in his *Saloon Singer* memoir:

Musical trivia and tracing show tunes became a hobby of mine long ago. A useful pastime considering how many people revel in the out-of-the-way, obscure, and just plain forgotten or discarded Broadway show tunes. Many of my friends love to play the game of singing a few lines and asking their group what show the song is from . . . it isn't all that uncommon for someone to send me a piece of music in the mail from a show that never saw the light of day after an out-of-town opening.[13]

Fashion editors are not always invited to White House dinners but they were out in force for this one. As *Newsday* fashion editor Nina Hyde reported,

Saturday night the women wore beautiful, low-key dresses and simple hairstyles to show off their glorious jewels. There were several versions of the organdy printed dress with ruffled hem, with a peasant or country look, often worn with a matching triangle edged in ruffles. Mrs. Richard Pistell's see-through printed organdy by Saint Laurent was ankle length and she wore it with a long chunky jade and gold necklace by David Webb. Christina Ford [Henry Ford's wife, who also attended the dinner for French President Pompidou when Peggy Lee sang] asked Greek designer Kimitri Kritsas to make something right for the White House and he delivered to her in Washington an orange and white printed organdy V plunge dress with ruffled hem and stole. "Henry told me to wear jewels, she said, fingering her diamond and jade necklace from Van Cleef and Arpels. "He said people would think he was cheap if I didn't wear some jewelry." Mrs. Britton Browne wore Larry Aldrich's version of the peasant dress in patchwork printed silk and a huge pin centered at the neckline. Anne Morrow Lindberg's version of the dress was a deep red print that she wore with a coral necklace.

Mrs. Loel Guiness—the Duke and Duchess often stay with her and her husband [the Duke's golfing buddy] in Florida— chose a pale mauve cape-effect chiffon dress by Dior to show off a necklace of pear-shaped diamonds. Mrs. John Sherman Cooper's simple fitted yellow silk crepe was the perfect foil for her diamond and sapphire wide dog collar. Mrs. Edwin Hilson's turquoise chiffon dress showed off well her diamond bib necklace.

There were two pairs of exactly matching dresses [heaven forbid!]. Mrs. Arthur Gardner and Mary Brooks were wearing the same floral printed dress by Sarmi, and the wife of Congressman Busch and Mrs. Reginald Short, Bobby Short's sister-in-law, had on identical white silk and worsted gowns.[14]

As for the wives of the two heads of state,

The Duchess of Windsor . . . wore a Givenchy white silk crepe with long sleeves and a jeweled coin belt. She wore ruby earrings encircled with two rows of diamonds.

Mrs. Nixon's Sarmi gown was yellow silk with a bodice of daisy lace accented by tiny chalk beads. The narrow shawl collar and cuffs were of the same yellow silk as the full skirt, and a white satin ribbon marked the slightly raised waistline.[15]

Dressed in their Hamptons fashions, the upper crust assembled in the Red Room and dined on a meal fit for only themselves. Meanwhile, Bobby and the Young Saints cooled their nervous heels:

Today I cannot remember how cool or how nervous we were as we stood waiting downstairs while the guests were at dinner . . .

the kids from California—all thirty of them—all looked as if they hadn't had a decent meal in days. We had been asked to sing, but the White House was not offering us supper . . . At last the Nixons and their guests emerged after coffee in the Red Room, and the duchess spotted me in the hall. "Oh, David, there's Mr. Short," she cried out, breaking loose from the group. [The duke's friends called him David—his full name: Edward Albert Christian George Andrew Patrick David.] Suddenly I was being greeted by the Duke of Windsor and the Nixons; an unexpected way to meet the president of your country. The Young Saints disappeared into the East Room, which had been set up with gold ballroom chairs facing a stage. Mr. Nixon introduced me with ease and charm, mentioning I was from Danville, Illinois.[16]

At that point, Bobby took his place at the Steinway, and backed by longtime associates Beverly Peer on bass and Richard Sheridan on drums, he began his twenty-minute, eight-song set with the perfect opener, Cole Porter's rollicking "I'm Throwing a Ball Tonight."[17] Those in the room unfamiliar with Mr. Short probably wondered why they had heard so little of this energetic, raspy-voiced wonder. By evening's end, they had no doubt made a mental note to have their maid stop by the record shop and pick up an album or two.

The party continued with Porter's "That Black and White Baby of Mine," which Bobby brightened by whistling several tuneful choruses and finger tapping the piano top. He then set a peg for the uninitiated to hang their new hats on: a bossa nova treatment of Burt Bacharach and Hal David's recent Grammy-winning "Raindrops Keep Falling on My Head." The award-winning duo wrote the song for a specific movie (*Butch Cassidy and the Sundance Kid*), for a specific character (Cassidy, played by Paul Newman), and, indeed, for a specific scene (a brief bucolic idyll in the midst of a Western chase). Nice song, but what was it doing in that movie, really?

Short followed "Raindrops" by another one from the Bacharach/

David team: "Whoever You Are I Love You," a lovingly rendered ballad, nearly impossible to improve upon, except by dimming the East Room lights.

Bobby next plucked another winner from his bag of esoteric but delightful songs: "I Have a Shooting Box in Scotland." If the jet-setters of this period had an anthem, this surely would have been it. Bobby sang the chorus twice, and since the tune lacks a bridge, drummer Sheridan simulated a soft-shoe tap dance using his brushes on the snare drum. Bobby called out, "I apologize, Fred," directed to guest Fred Astaire in the audience. The trio repeated the "Shooting Box" lyrics and immediately moved into "Her Mother Came Too." No small talk between numbers was the rule for this set, as it was most nights at the Café Carlyle. It was Short's modus operandi: "Time is short in a saloon, so I make no complicated references, and I never natter on about the original production [of the song]." The meet-and-greet chatter, to the extent that there was any, was prior to the show and between sets—Bobby didn't want to become too familiar.[18]

"Mother," by the Englishman Novello, as tuneful a song as the others, had piqued Bobby's interest sometime ago, as did the next number, "Cake Walking Babies (from Home)," made famous by the "Empress of the Blues" Bessie Smith. This song, based on a Caribbean-derived dance, began in the key of J for joyous, then gradually dissolved into a slow blues for several measures, before it was suddenly reawakened at racehorse tempo for the sprint to the finish line.

Short closed his set with a two-song medley: the familiar "Bye Bye Blackbird," performed à la Miles Davis—muted flugelhorn pressed close to the mic, slow, quiet, almost whispered—which Bobby melded into the unfamiliar but the equally languorous "I'm Just a Little Blackbird Looking for a Bluebird." Throughout the evening, the Duke of Windsor tapped his cane on the floor and swung in his seat in rhythm with the music, but when he heard Short sing "Bye Bye Blackbird," according to *Post* reporter Smith, "the former king raised his hands in applause."[19]

The first to treat the usually upbeat "Bye Bye Blackbird" in dirgelike fashion is not precisely known, although it was probably Bobby (he recorded his version in 1955, Miles in 1956). In any case, producer Nesuhi Ertegun of Atlantic Records remembered:

> I'll never forget when he did "Blackbird." I think we did only one take. It was so perfect, so *right*, although it was a totally new approach to this "standard." Bobby chose a much slower tempo than usual and he imbued the song with melancholy and despair. When he finished, I was speechless. It was a triumph, one of the greatest moments of music I had ever heard.[20]

While some in the audience might have entertained the idea that Bobby was using his East Room stage as a pulpit—half the songs he presented had a racial cast—his carefully chosen song set likely served another purpose, as he made clear in his *Saloon Singer* memoir:

> I have never mixed preaching and entertaining. Clearly, I was no Leadbelly [Delta blues singer], and songs heavily laden with messages about the rights of man are not for me. But songs come along that allow me to speak my mind without getting on a soapbox. Rodgers and Hammerstein had written such a song for *South Pacific*. The lyrics of "Carefully Taught" made it clear that racial prejudice is instilled in people in a structured and careful way, as any of the other things they learn in life. *South Pacific* was an enormous hit in New York, and I have been singing "Carefully Taught" . . . as a salute to the show. The number never fails to bring cheers from the audience. And I hoped it made them think.[21]

In his selected playlist for the evening, Bobby was not making a point about racial relations so much as about himself. He was more than an interpreter of white songs by white composers for a white clientele; his palette was more colorful than that. And he wanted America to know.

With his toe-tapping set concluded, the singer/pianist then introduced the Young Saints, who proceeded to tear it up with their mixed brand of rock, soul, and gospel. Julie Nixon said she liked "When the Saints Come Marching In" best, while husband David Eisenhower liked "Oh Happy Day." Bobby joined the Young Saints for the rousing two-song finale: Duke Ellington's "Jump for Joy" (also sung in the East Room by bluesman Joe Williams at Ellington's seventieth-birthday bash the year before) and Bessie Smith's "Gimme a Pigfoot" (as the saloon singer had promised). Somehow the East Room crystal glass chandeliers held steadfast through it all.

At the show's end, President Nixon joined the group onstage and thanked them for their performance:

"It's a long way from Watts [the Saints' home base] to the White House, and I want you to know it's a long way from [my birthplace] Whittier to the White House." Mrs. Nixon, who accompanied the President on the stage to thank the performers, told the group that she had grown up in an area near Watts [Artesia, actually].

The Duke and Duchess also went on stage to thank the performers. The pink-cheeked, blue-eyed Duke told Short, "Now I have a bad hip and can't dance." Just as President Nixon began his remarks, the Duke turned his face to the audience and was blinded by the spotlights. "I'm going to get off now, I can't see," he said. The Duchess, ever attentive, whispered, "David, shut up, the president's talking." President Nixon paused and waited for the Duchess to help the Duke to his chair.[22]

Bobby's memoir includes a striking photograph of this moment, similar to the one shown on the following page: the assemblage onstage with Bobby dead center, the duke and the Nixons on the right, family members and the duchess on the left, and the Saints huddled around in back.

After bidding the Windsors goodnight, the Nixons, as usual, retired to their private quarters upstairs, but the party wasn't over. Julie and David Eisenhower and scores of guests remained to talk or dance to

Bobby Short (*center*), joined by the Duke of Windsor and President and Mrs. Nixon (*right*); family members and the Duchess of Windsor (*left*); and the Saints (*background*).

the Marine Combo. Social Secretary Lucy Winchester asked Bobby to play for dancing in the great hall. At 12:30 Bobby sat down at the grand piano with the eagle legs and, with Richard Sheridan on drums and Beverly Peer on bass, played for another thirty or forty-five minutes.

Fred Astaire was even goaded into dancing with society reporter Betty Beale. As the world's greatest and most famous ballroom dancer perfunctorily led Beale around the floor, he told her, "I never liked ballroom dancing. I don't even dance for benefits." Astaire had been invited that night not only because of the many songs he had introduced on the silver screen that Bobby had been keeping alive nightly at the Café Carlyle, but also because the White House had learned that the two were old friends.

As the guests circled around Bobby while he played, he told them,

When I was in the fourth grade in Danville, Illinois, my teacher went on a sightseeing trip on the East Coast. And when she got back she told the class about her trip and said, 'Bobby, some day you should play on that beautiful piano at the White House' . . .

And my childhood dream was to play it. That dream has come true tonight.[23]

The party finally came to a close and Bobby found himself thinking of nothing but food:

The kids from Watts were not the only hungry ones. The White House staff went into action, and a reservation was made at a restaurant not too far away. Cars and a special bus got us to a late supper. All thirty Young Saints with their organist and music director, and my group of family and friends. Luckily, I had tucked a credit card into the inside pocket of my tailcoat.[24]

Luckily, that credit card had a sizable balance, and the investment was well worth it. Bobby was invited back to the White House four more times, as a guest at Jimmy Carter's "Gershwin Night," twice as a performer for Ronald Reagan, and once for Bill Clinton. He was fed every time.

Pearl Bailey Trio

He gave me the chair. He gave me the chair.
—*Pearl Bailey*

April 10, 1970 | German Chancellor Brandt Dinner

HAVING BECOME THE CHANCELLOR OF Germany only four months prior, Wilhelm "Willy" Brandt was in town for a get-acquainted meeting with President Nixon. This visit was perhaps a bit more necessary than usual, because on the night of the German election, Nixon dialed former Chancellor Kiesinger and mistakenly offered congratulations. Also on the agenda was Germany's controversial *Ostpolitik*, or reconciliation with the Communist East.[1]

Brandt's first taste of Washington after-dinner entertainment would be the irrepressible Pearl Bailey, who, along with Lionel Hampton, topped the short list of African American celebrities with long-term Republican affiliations.[2] Going back to the Eisenhower years, her political connections would extend through the Nixon administration into the George H. W. Bush era. Both Presidents Ford and Reagan would appoint her as delegate to the United Nations. She became close friends with the Fords, appearing in campaign commercials and joining them in the White House to watch returns on election night. President Ronald Reagan awarded Pearl the Presidential Medal of Freedom in 1988.

In short, this was one entertainer who did not have to be included on any of the Nixon-supporter lists—although her name appeared on them all—because her loyalties were that well known. For Pearl, this would be the first of two East Room appearances during the Nixon administration and the first in a string of headline-grabbing appearances at the White House, as entertainer or guest.

As usual, the social secretary's office prepared background information on Pearl for the after-dinner program and the press:

[Born in Newport News, Virginia, but] reared in Washington, D.C., where her father was a minister, Pearl Bailey followed in the footsteps of her brother Bill Bailey, the famous tap dancer. As a teenager she won an amateur contest at the Pearl Theater in Philadelphia, and was soon performing in small nightclubs in Washington and vaudeville. When the U.S. entered WWII, Miss Bailey joined the first USO touring troupe, singing for military audiences all over the country.

In 1944, after her second USO tour, bandleader Cab Calloway invited Ms. Bailey to join his bill at the Strand Theater when another was taken ill. She caused a sensation and was soon starring regularly on the New York-Las Vegas-California circuit. She is currently playing opposite Cab Calloway in the Broadway hit musical *Hello, Dolly*, in which she has starred for more than two years, first in New York and now on national tour. For her role in *Hello, Dolly*, Miss Bailey won a Tony Award and Entertainer of the Year Award in 1968 from *Cue* magazine.

Miss Bailey made her stage debut in 1946 in *Saint Louis Woman*. She also starred in numerous films, including *Carmen Jones*, *St. Louis Woman* with Nat King Cole, *Porgy and Bess* with Sidney Poitier and Dorothy Dandridge, and *That Certain Feeling* with Bob Hope.[3]

No matter where one places Pearl in the musical arena—jazz, pop jazz, or popular entertainer—her backup trio was "you know, like jazz, you would say jazz," Pearl told the East Room crowd that night. Her trio included jazz giant Milt Hilton on bass, who played at the seventieth-birthday bash Nixon held for Duke Ellington the year before. Rounding out the trio was Don Abney on the piano and a last-minute substitute for Pearl's jazz-great husband, Louis Bellson, on drums.

Milt Hinton was considered the dean of jazz bass players. Nick-named "the Judge," Milt played with virtually every jazz and popular artist from Louis Armstrong, Art Tatum, Benny Carter, Duke Elling-ton, Benny Goodman, Billie Holiday, Dizzy Gillespie, John Coltrane, and the Marsalis Brothers to Barbra Streisand, Bette Midler, and Paul McCartney.[4] He is reputed to have amassed the most voluminous dis-cography of anyone in the jazz and popular fields ever.

In 2001, Milt entered the long-running DownBeat Jazz Hall of Fame. Only six other bassists have been so honored in the Hall's sixty-two years: Jimmy Blanton, Ray Brown, Ron Carter, Paul Chambers, Jaco Pastorius, and Charles Mingus. His honorary doctorates and awards are too numerous to cite; for his last, bestowed in 2000, he saw his name installed on the ASCAP Wall of Fame.

An avid photographer, Milt collected thousands of images, many of which have appeared in jazz documentaries, notably 1994's *Great Day in Harlem*, and in books: *Bass Line: The Stories and Photographs of Milt Hinton* (University of Temple Press, 1988) and *Overtime: The Jazz Pho-tographs of Milt Hinton* (Pomegranate, 1996).[5]

Don Abney, another of those under-the-radar jazz players, "was an excellent piano accompanist as well as a refined jazz performer, com-fortable in both mainstream and modern styles." Like section-mate Hinton, he played with a jazz Who's Who through five decades. He recorded with Louis Armstrong, worked with vocalists Ella Fitzgerald and Carmen McRae, trombonist Kai Winding, and drummer Louis Bellson in the 1950s.[6] Spending most of his time in California studios in the 1960s, he led his own trio from 1969–71 and worked with singers Rosemary Clooney, Jack Jones, and, of course, the Pearl.

Once the dignitaries and invited guests settled themselves in the East Room after the state dinner, President Nixon, as usual, introduced the program:

> We were trying to make a decision as to what kind of musical program would most appeal to our distinguished guests this evening, and the choice was hard, as it always is. But it was made much easier by the fact that Mr. David Merrick, one of America's most distinguished producers, found it possible to change a performance of *Hello, Dolly* that was scheduled for tonight, in Detroit, to tomorrow, Sunday night. And as a result, we have one of the premier stars of the American—or should I say—the world music scene.
>
> For those of you who will remember the 1956 [Eisenhower] inauguration, Pearl Bailey sang at that occasion. I remember many of those songs, but one in particular—"Bill Bailey"—she is going to sing tonight. While the chancellor has not heard "Hello, Dolly," or Mrs. Brandt has not, I imagine that everyone in this room has heard it, in person, or on television, and there have been many great Dollys—Carol Channing, Ginger Rogers—but I hear that the greatest Dolly Levi is Pearl Bailey, and she is here tonight [raises voice]—Pearl Bailey.[7]

Sustained applause greeted Pearl as she took center stage on the East Room riser wearing a sequined pantsuit and addressed the audience:

Oh my. This is a nice intimate room, yes, yes. Could you widen the lights so they can see more of me, or is this all of me? Wouldn't want to fall—I wouldn't know who to sue if I should fall. Is there a special person, Mr. President, you sue, or do you just generally sue if you fall? I can't even see the president it's so dark in here. Where is the president? Is he in here? Oh, there you are,

Mr. President. Well, that's the way I'm going to work mostly, in that direction. [Laughter.]

Pearl's improvisatory comedic talent—honed to perfection on the nightclub circuit years ago—would be on full display throughout the evening, a talent undiminished by her recent turns behind the footlights and in front of television and movie cameras. Fellow jazz singer-entertainer Bobby Short characterized Pearl thus:

Pearl literally reached out to her audience when she was performing—and won them over in one huge embrace. Her easy banter, her unpretentious style, was endearing. They always worked, except on this night [in London in the early 1950s]—the applause had finally stopped at the end of the show when someone tossed a penny on stage. The coin landed right at her feet. Never at a loss, Pearl just kicked it around for a second with her satin-covered toe, then with a mix of acid and oil said, "My mother always told me that only one kind of animal throws a scent."[8]

Backed by her trio, Ms. Bailey half sang and half spoke her first song, an up-tempo version of the widely popular Burt Bacharach/Hal David tune "What the World Needs Now," usually heard in waltz time. Pearl dropped "Wives and Lovers," the next tune listed on the program, for "Mame," from the Merrick-produced Broadway show of the same name. She told the audience, "I know the words a little better." Pearl sounded tentative on her first two numbers, clearly not her usual full-throated belt-it-out self, but that would soon change.

At the completion of "Mame," Ms. Bailey rocketed into the first of several between-number raps:

You know, I was about fourteen years old—a few years ago, eighteen to twenty years ago. I have a beautiful philosophy I think every woman should use—I don't mind, I will always tell you my age, but I will never tell you the number of years I have lived. [A laugh.] The man enjoyed that . . . I thought the women would enjoy it better.

I had a ballad and I won an amateur contest with it—a beautiful song—and to me all ballads should be sung sitting perched atop a piano—that is the way I always see it in the movies. [Pearl struggled to get up on the piano, prompting the president to get into the act, moving a chair into place for her to use as a stepladder.] You use good wood, Mr. President . . . yes, class all the way. [Nixon gets up, arranges chair] Don't bang it. [Laughter.] Oh, Mr. President! [Scolding] Is the country going to talk about us! [Laughter.]

Where is this darling man who came to visit us? Chancellor, . . . we have so much fun—you must come over more often. Well, I don't want to sound snobbish because I am a very humble woman. Wait till I tell them I had my feet on the president's chair, with my shoes on yet. Yes sir, I tell you . . . I have my dinner menu program, and I'll have the chancellor sign that . . . in English, if you could. I don't want to beg, and, of course, I'm delighted to be here, but Mr. President . . . if you don't need the chair.

The song Pearl had started to introduce, the lovely ballad "Poor Butterfly," written by Raymond Hubbell in 1916, is finally sung, uncharacteristically sweet and mellow.

Then appearing a bit more confident, Pearl tackled an up-tempo rendition of "That's Life," made famous by Frank Sinatra. At song's end, Chancellor Brandt handed Pearl a signed menu program.

Thank you, I don't have my glasses. I'll take it home and read it. Are there any other celebrities here? I've already picked up a couple of things: a chair and a book. The plants you have here [that ring the stage], they're lovely, Mr. President. I love the idea of having them around the stage . . . I have a lovely yard. If they need the sunlight, I'll take them along to put by the chair.

It was time for "Hello, Dolly," the hit song by Jerry Herman from the show of the same name. Everyone knows the Louis Armstrong version, which turned out to be a late career-defining hit for the gravel-voiced jazzman. But few are aware that it was Louis's rendition (recorded and released while the show was still in tryouts) that gave the show its name—originally it was to be called *Dolly (A Damned Exasperating Woman).*[9]

Pearl sang her version softly first time through, little girl lightly, but second time around, she belted it out in her best red-hot-mama, throaty-voiced style; she had been doing this in her almost nightly theatrical performances for the past two years.

I must tell you something—my feet are killing me, I thought they'd stop here—people know that about me all around the country. Oh dear, I thought they would stop here. No respect, be quiet, you'll be out in a minute, and you can go home and rest. I'm talking to my feet.

You know the musicians, it's such a class place, and this is the White House, you know. So I brought these lovely musicians along—they're lovely, but, of course, then you would put them . . . you know, like jazz, you would say jazz—but you have such a higher class room here, I thought you would like a little classical music. And especially for our guest, and I love class, it's just more expensive, but I like class. [Laughter.] I thought this would be the type of music you would be more used to hearing in here [Pearl had that right.] So I asked the people here if they would get me a fiddle player so that you would feel more at home. They said all right.

Pearl greeted the musician that had just joined the group onstage: "What is your name, darling?"

"My name is Master Sergeant Ben Sanger . . . with the Marine Band."

"So you see, Chancellor, our marines play fiddle too—isn't that exciting! Do you know the classics? Then you would know the 'St. Louis Blues.' You start off."

The marine fashioned an appropriate intro and then reverted to accompaniment as Pearl lazily sketched the familiar lines "I hate to see that evening sun go down," filling the spaces with good-natured taunts at fiddler Sanger. The trio entered at the turnaround, and a lively second version resulted, which they gradually attenuated into the background while Pearl substituted scat lyrics for the familiar melody: "Bye, bye, good-bye, thank you, Sergeant, bye, bye."

Pearl was not being flip when she called the "St. Louis Blues" a classic. This popular musical landmark has a tango—yes, a tango!—sweetly nested in its blues; unprecedented, but oh so perfect. While Pearl may not have been the first to sing the W. C. Handy masterpiece in the White House (any one of the many operatic stars or choral groups could have), she was probably the first African American popular entertainer to do so. Neither the White House nor the press made mention of this milestone occurrence. It was sad in a way: "St. Louis Blues" was at the time the second most frequently recorded song in America—after "Silent Night."[10]

(Showing nonpartisan colors, Pearl would later attend President Carter's first White House Jazz Festival held on the South Lawn in the summer of 1978 as an invited guest. And guess who appeared onstage to jam after the program was over? Accompanied by her drummer husband, Louis Bellson, and pianist Billy Taylor, Pearl sang the "St. Louis Blues," sung earlier that evening by none other than the daughter of W. C. Handy.)

After the applause subsided, Pearl said, "In 1956, a wonderful man was at an inauguration, a wonderful man. He [Nixon] was the vice president of our country. Here's the president's favorite song."

The trio introduced "Bill Bailey" but Pearl interrupted them with a request to pianist Abney to pick up the tempo. He complied, and it was off to the races with a tune Pearl had sung so often that if she'd had a nickel for every time . . . yet how many in the audience knew that this

Hughie Cannon song was considered ragtime when it was written in 1902, and not—as many have assumed—named for Pearl's famous tap dancing brother, Bill Bailey? This last number allowed the "lovely jazz musicians" to stretch out and solo before Pearl took her final bow amid extended and enthusiastic applause.

President Nixon returned to the riser and, likely thinking he would get in the last word, told the assembled: "I hope the marines can fight as well as they fiddle."

But that was not the end of the show. No one else—no one—got the last word when Pearl Bailey was in the House. Myra MacPherson described what happened in the *Washington Post* the next day under the headline "Pearl Breaks Them Up":

As she finished the performance flashing a wide grin, Miss Bailey picked up the President's chair and carried it out the side door. With an even wider grin, she came back, picked up a geranium pot and carried it out the side door. At this point, President Nixon jumped up and helped her carry the geranium pot out. Everybody in the room jumped up laughing and applauding, and the act was over.

As she came back to pose for pictures with President and Mrs. Nixon and Chancellor and Mrs. Brandt, she sang another chorus of "Hello, Dolly," substituting the words "Hello, Richard" and "Hello, Willy" while clasping President Nixon's hand and Chancellor Brandt's hand together. Then she kissed Mr. Nixon and he threw up his hands as if he were giving a cheer. He said, "I think we'll all agree Pearl Bailey has given us one of the most memorable evenings in the East Room."

In the end, the President actually gave her his chair to take home with her. It was one of the four special chairs, covered in black, and gilded. Pearl Bailey went upstairs with the Nixons after the performance and came back down beaming. "He gave me the chair. He gave me the chair."

Miss Bailey said the President also made her "Ambassador of Love," which she said she wanted to be. She said the President told her she was the first one he ever gave a chair to. "I was going to take the geraniums, too," she added, "but he gave me the chair and made me an ambassador, I guess I can grow my own geraniums."[11]

David Frost/Billy Taylor

This Christmas at the White House, Santa Claus
came down the chimney and met Wally Hickel going up.
—David Frost

December 18, 1970 | Christmas Evening at the White House

O N MAY 4, 1977, THIRTY-TWO months after Richard Milhous
Nixon resigned the presidency, television host David Frost sat
down with him for his first post-resignation interview. Broadcast to the
nation, the interview was the most widely watched TV news program
of its time, and now, of course, it has been immortalized in the Broadway play and Ron Howard film *Frost/Nixon*. The two had met before,
in a more congenial and much less contentious setting, and while no
one was keeping score, it was Richard Nixon who bested David Frost
the first time around.

In mid-November 1970, planning began for an Evening at the White
House on December 18 to celebrate the one hundredth memorial year
of Charles Dickens's birth (he was born on Friday, February 7). The
entertainment had not yet been chosen, although it was understood
that David Frost would be a likely candidate.[1]

By November 19, the arrangements had taken shape. White House aide Leonard Garment had suggested that David Frost read Dylan Thomas's *A Winter's Tale* or *A Child's Christmas in Wales* (he would read the latter). Staffer Carol Harford floated the idea that British actor/writer Emlyn Williams might do something from the *Pickwick Papers*, such as "Mr. Pickwick's Christmas," or an abridged version of a *Christmas Carol* (Frost would do the latter).

To serve as Emlyn's American counterpart, she thought that the grand dame of American theater, Helen Hayes, would be perfect.[2] As for the music to intersperse before, between, and after readings, Harford recommended Pro Musica, a twelve-person outfit from nearby Columbia Union College in Takoma Park, Maryland, that played old instruments in period costume. The group had previously appeared at a White House worship service on May 4, 1969.

For whatever reasons, Harford's suggestions didn't make the cut, but David Frost and the Army Chorus (a Nixon favorite) did, along with jazz pianist Billy Taylor, Frost's musical conductor from his TV show. Billy was appointed the program's musical director, and his presence on the bill—it can reasonably be assumed—was due entirely to Frost (and perhaps this was what former jazz clarinetist Len Garment had in mind all along). A point to ponder here: If Emlyn Williams, or any other actor, had been selected for the Christmas show, would Billy Taylor have been chosen? Doubtful. And if David Frost had been less than sympathetic toward the Nixon administration, would he have been picked as host? Double doubtful.

Another point to consider: Due to the late start in planning this event, the White House staff probably didn't have that many options. While the Army Chorus can be ordered up at any time, other entertainers are not that readily available in December—even for a White House gig—given only a two- to three-week notice.

Once the cast was set, the program morphed into David Frost's History of Christmas—if you can't have an American actor, then a Brit reading American Christmas literature would do just fine. Notice of the event was released on December 10, which included a biographical sketch of the host (excerpted below):

David Frost, who has been called an "interviewer's interviewer," is the host of the 90-minute syndicated talk-variety television series, *The David Frost Show*, which is shown five times a week on 70 TV stations. He also stars in the London Weekend TV series, *Frost on Friday, Frost on Saturday*, and *Frost on Sunday*, an interview variety show. He is England's top TV personality and one of the most influential figures in the United States . . . [He rocketed to fame on his TV show] for the BBC *That Was the Week That Was.*[3]

With Frost as its star and cocreator, *That Was the Week That Was* was one of the greatest entertainment phenomena in the 1960s. In England, it became the favorite show to watch, and when it crossed the Atlantic in 1964, it brought Frost immediate personal success in the United States. He then had prize-winning shows on two British networks, broadcasts in Canada and Australia, and a wide variety of guest appearances on U.S. television programs. His syndicated series began in July 1969, and he served as moderator for British television's coverage of the historic Apollo 11 moon shot and a year later for the British elections.

The press was informed that Billy Taylor would accompany Mr. Frost—no surprise for those who had been watching *The David Frost Show* for the past year. Billy not only served as musical conductor of the house band, but also occasionally performed with his trio or a larger jazz group. As *DownBeat* magazine noted, the band was unique for a talk show: "While [the other TV shows boasted] large, smooth, well-oiled orchestras mainly made up of studio veterans, the Frost band [under Billy] was smaller [eleven pieces], younger, hipper, and admirably well balanced, musically and racially."[4]

Billy's early lights were pianists Fats Waller and Art Tatum, although both were filtered through the prism of Bud Powell while Billy apprenticed with tenor man Ben Webster's small groups and the Gillespie/Pettiford band on 52nd Street in the 1940s. He graduated from that incubus to play with many of the jazz luminaries of the 1950s and 1960s. Taylor is one of those transcendent figures better known for his tireless work on behalf of his art as a promoter, teacher, lecturer and radio and television personality than for his piano playing. But these extracurricular activities did not obscure his standing as an exceptional musician. In his 2005 book, *The Fifty Greatest Jazz Pianists of All Time*, Gene Rizzo ranked Billy at number seventeen (some might argue for a different rank, but *no one* would argue his inclusion on the list), and Len Lyons in his 1983 book, *The Great Jazz Pianists*, included Billy among the twenty-five then-living pianists.[5]

Billy was one of three featured pianists (along with Dave Brubeck and Earl Hines) at the Duke Ellington seventieth-birthday bash at the White House in April 1969. He would finally command the spotlight, along with his trio, later in the Nixon presidency at a state dinner for President Houphouët-Boigny of the Ivory Coast.

On the morning of the Christmas show, President Nixon spied a group of children touring the White House. After being informed they were the singing Little Angels from Korea, he invited the twenty-seven eight- to fifteen-year-olds on the spur of the moment to come back that night and sing. Talk about being in the right place at the right time!

That evening on the nation's premier stage—the East Room of the White House—the children in their Korean costumes and braids opened the show. After they sang, they rushed to the president and each gave him a hearty kiss, except for two little boys who sedately shook hands, to the absolute delight of the hundred-plus invited guests, cabinet members, and staff seated in front of the riser. After the applause and laughter died down, President Nixon took the stage:

> Well, after that sort of added starter for our program tonight, all of us will have to admit that's a hard act to follow. But we do have as a special guest tonight, one who can follow any act and certainly surpass it. He is one who—without question—is considered to be the top television personality of Britain, and to those who have seen him in the United States, he is considered

to be one of the top—if not the top—television interviewers in our country.

As a matter of fact, he has had more people from the present administration on his program than most other television commentators—not that that is a reflection on the others—or on him, either—but whatever the case may be. Vice President Agnew of course has been a guest of David Frost and [Director of Communications] Herb Klein, [HEW Secretary] Bob Finch, Transportation Secretary Volpe, and I understand some others [yes, like Secretary of Labor George Schulz].

As a matter of fact, last night at the dinner for Prime Minister Heath, I learned from Mrs. Freeman that Mr. Frost, while he was in Washington for this Friday's Evening at the White House, was hoping to get [Attorney General] Mitchell for his program, and I said, "Oh, you mean John?" And she said, 'Oh no, Martha.' [Laughter.]

So you see, there are many things to come. But I simply want to say that we have had many very fine and outstanding programs at these Evenings at the White House—this one is very special and particularly for the Christmas season because David Frost is one who has a reputation far beyond that of simply being a television interviewer who brings out the best—and sometimes the worst—in people.

But in any event, he brings out whoever they are, and he also has a very great ability, an ability which is so very well known in England—and we are learning to learn so well in this country—an ability that he will demonstrate so well tonight in the whole field of presenting what we call a one-man show performance. It is a one-man performance in the sense that he does have some backup. Billy Taylor is here—he was here with Duke Ellington—he will be the musical director for the program for David Frost, and he will also be assisted by our very fine Army Chorus, under the direction of [Captain] Allen Crowell . . . [Please welcome] David Frost.[6]

Nixon's introduction is notable on two counts: (1) it was spoken without notes, as was his style for these occasions (although suggested remarks had been prepared as usual); not all presidents have been this articulate in the role of toastmaster; and (2) his praise for Frost as a media friend of the administration should leave no doubt about why he was chosen for the event.

While Frost was a congenial television host and deserved lavish praise for his groundbreaking news show *That Was the Week That Was*, he was never a host in the mold of a Jack Paar or a Dick Cavett from this period, or of a David Letterman or a Jay Leno of today. Against type, Frost chose to present his History of Christmas as if he were a late-night TV comedian, which he might have successfully done at other ceremonial occasions, but at the White House during the Christmas season, his material was sort of cheesy.

Lacking only a "Heeeerrre's David," Frost burst onto the East Room stage and went right into his opening monologue. He recounted a recent experience in England involving a nervous MC, who was supposed to make the customary introduction "Pray silence for David Frost," but instead said, "Pray for the silence of Mr. David Frost." (The audience laughed.)

Then he turned to anecdotes about child nativity plays: an appropriately costumed Mary and Joseph go to the Bethlehem Inn, knock on the door, and say, "Can we please have a room?" and the little innkeeper says, "I'm terribly sorry, there is no room at the inn . . . would you like to come in for a cocktail?" (Laughter.) At another nativity play, a little girl is overheard saying, "Anybody can be a shepherd, but it's bloody hard being a virgin." (Muffled laughter.) Next, Frost told the audience about two church signs he had spotted in New York only recently: one read "Come to Church on Sunday and Avoid the Christmas Rush," and "If You Are Tired of Sin Come Inside," but someone had scribbled below, "If Not, Call Judson 2111."

Frost continued his opening monologue of tired jokes for another five minutes before unveiling his History of Christmas that began with a boorish parody on the story of creation, substituting Conrad Hilton creating hotels for God creating the world. "Hilton begat a hotel on each day, and on the seventh day, he rested." The *Washington Post* reported the next day that some people glanced at noted evangelist Billy Graham in the audience during this routine. Graham smiled, however.[7]

At long last, the Army Chorus entered, singing the traditional "God Rest Ye Merry Gentlemen." Frost continued the program with a recitation of a first-century Roman poet complaining about his Christmas presents, followed by two seasonal songs by the chorus: "Here We Come A-wassailing" and "Love and Joy."

Finally—finally!—pianist Billy Taylor is heard accompanying the chorus on "A Christmas Day in the Morning." Based on the well-articulated notes and ringing chords, music fans in the audience would have likely guessed that the pianist was an accomplished one. Knowledgeable jazz fans (assuming some were in the audience) would have identified Billy Taylor—his sound was that unique. Marian McPartland, an accomplished jazz pianist in her own right, had this to say in a *DownBeat* magazine article about Billy's recognizable sound: "It's funny, he uses his left hand—the chords—in a certain way, not quite like anybody else does. A certain voicing, I guess maybe I notice that, having listened to Billy so much at the Hickory House [jazz club in New York City].[8]

Time-traveler Frost next essayed a Shakespearean reference to Christmas—a description of King Arthur's Christmas feast—and then moved on to a puritan pamphlet of 1645 titled *The Arraignment, Conviction, and Imprisonment of Christmas* and an 1850 piece on the evils of plum pudding. Somehow in the midst of all this, the Army Chorus ably sang traditional carols.

The highlight of the show followed, certainly for jazz fans and perhaps for others as well: the gospel "Stable down the Road," penned by none other than Billy Taylor, with lyrics by poet/storyteller Laura J. Bobrow. Billy, his jazz bassist, and the Army Chorus, featuring soloist Barry Hemphill, all joined in. Make no mistake, the song might have been non-secular, and soloist Hemphill might have vocalized as in church, but as far as Taylor and his bassist were concerned, this was a swinging jazz number all the way. Taylor took a lengthy solo of Ta-

David Frost shaking hands with President Nixon at his Christmas Evening at the White House, joined by Billy Taylor (*left*) and the Army Chorus (*background*).

tumesque single-note runs that eventually gave way to an equally long segment of church-bell-ringing block chords (more Bud Powell than Art Tatum). No drum kit was needed here—Billy programmed coordinated finger-snapping by the chorus in its stead. The audience response was loud and long.

The concert could have ended with "Stable down the Road," but it was far from over. Mr. Frost read a Christmas love letter published in the English *Spectator* magazine in 1711, followed by a recitation from the end of Charles Dickens's *Christmas Carol*, the famed family repast at Bob Crotchet's home. Here, a most unforgivable sin was committed: Frost stepped on one of the most famous last sentences in all of English literature: "'God bless us, everyone,' said Tiny Tim." As soon as he uttered that line, Frost rushed out an attempted joke: "Miss Vicky was not available for comment," a reference to the squeaky-voiced, ukulele-playing 1960s pop star Tiny Tim and his TV bride Miss Vicky. By so doing, the moment was lost, and the audience was denied their emotional release. The Army Chorus sang "Christmas Bells" and erased the Dickens faux pas from collective memory, at least temporarily.

Mr. Frost turned to White House Christmases past and waxed nostalgic anecdotes about presidents John Adams in 1800, Andrew Jackson in 1829, Rutherford B. Hayes in 1877, and Franklin D. Roosevelt in 1941. Then, in a seeming departure from the general rule to abstain from political commentary, Frost said, "This Christmas at the White House, Santa Claus came down the chimney and met Wally Hickel going up."

Nixon had fired Secretary of the Interior Wally Hickel only twenty-three days earlier (on Thanksgiving Eve) for his public letter the previous May urging the president to give more respect to the views of young people. This letter became public on the heels of the Kent State shooting of war-protesting college students by the Ohio State National Guard. (Nixon had postponed the firing of Hickel until after the Congressional midterm elections.) Frost was not trying to make a broader point here (displeasure with the Kent State shootings or the Vietnam War, for example); it was just another lame attempt at humor. His political blunder was greeted with "a moment of embarrassed titter," said the *Washington Post* the next day.

On with the show! Next read by Frost were *Christmas Bells*, a poem by Longfellow; a *London Times* report of an unauthorized Christmas Eve truce arranged by Allied and German WWI troops and the singing of "Silent Night" across the trenches (captured in the 2006 French film *Joyeux Noel*); three humorous pieces—an Ogden Nash verse, a Robert Benchley essay on Christmases past and present, and Dylan Thomas's *A Child's Christmas in Wales*; and finally, a traditional seasonal song by the Army Chorus.

Billy, back at the piano with his bassist, soloist Bryan Sanders, and the Chorus then rendered a heart-tugging version of "Christmas Song (Chestnuts Roasting on an Open Fire)" by Bob Wells (lyrics) and Mel Tormé, famously seared into the American consciousness by Nat King Cole. Believe it or not, this tune was written in only forty-five minutes on a hot July day in 1946 and was then initially rejected by the publisher: "No one's going to buy a tune that's only good for one day of the year."[9] It became Nat Cole's biggest-selling record ever. (For the definitive jazz instrumental version, listen to saxophonist Pharoah Sanders on *A Prayer before Dawn*, Theresa Records, 1987.)

Rather than close the show on the Cole classic, Frost plowed through another attempt at humor, this time about Santa Claus caught in a holding pattern on Christmas Eve, unable to land his toy-laden sleigh. An end was in sight when Frost read his self-proclaimed favorite yuletide piece, "The House of Christmas" by G. K. Chesterton, and Billy and the Chorus offered in succession: "Noel, Noel," "Joy to the World," and "Good King Wenceslaus." But instead of concluding on these rousing seasonal songs, Frost read in its entirety the famous letter to the editor "Yes, Virginia, there is a Santa Claus" before everyone sang "Come Let Us Adore Him."

That Was the Show That Was! All sixty-nine minutes of it, including Nixon's introduction. One could imagine that many in the audience not only sighed "Thank God it's over," but also wished they had been given a crack at editing the program before it was presented. The music was superb—that wasn't the problem—and there was nothing wrong with the literary selections by themselves either. Frost simply included too many, without thought to dramatic pacing.

Compared to Mr. Frost's effort, Peggy Lee's White House appearance earlier in the year, which had been slammed as too long, was a mere cameo.

━━

Right after the show, White House aide Dick Moore sent a memo to Dwight Chapin with his critique: "The Little Angels were the greatest opening act I've ever seen. David Frost was probably not the best choice—his nightclub stuff was out of place. Stand-up's material [should] be screened in advance." Mr. Moore did not comment on the music.[10]

Dwight Chapin passed this critique on to Impresario Connie Stewart, assistant to First Lady Pat Nixon. Her response to Moore was perhaps somewhat defensive—after all, he was stepping on her East Wing turf. Nonetheless, it was very telling:

We have wrestled long and hard with the problems of entertainers in the White House. The White House is a unique stage for any performer and you can never anticipate exactly how successful any one performance will be nor what unusual circumstances might arise the night of a performance that will make the headlines the next day in the paper.

The problem with a show such as the David Frost Evening at the White House is that the "Evening" was built around an idea (i.e., Christmas) and not a performer. When the program is based on an idea, it means an original script or program must be produced and have its opening night at the White House with no try-out in New Haven. And sometimes we bomb at the White House. The [Shakespearean actor] Nicol Williamson "Evening" was another example of an original program written for the White House which was only moderately successful and mostly because of the presence of the World's Greatest Jazz Band, much the same as the Korean Angels made such an impact the night of the Frost Show. We do best when we select a performer with a known talent and just let him "do his own thing."

I can assure you we do exert as much control as possible over performer's "scripts." Performers are very sensitive about anyone tampering with their material and we must always be on the alert for the cry of censorship, a cry that we have heard several times. We review each program; be it readings or musical selections or whatever, and make our suggestions as to what would be the most appropriate for the White House. However, the performer has the final control when he stands on the stage, and often the performers do things we have advised against, or spring unexpected things.[11]

Luckily, some of the music at this event can be heard on *From David Frost & Billy Taylor: Merry Christmas* (Bell Records, 1970). David Frost narrated as well as reading his favorite yuletide poem, Chesterton's "The House of Christmas." As for the music, Billy had his trio and orchestra (from the Frost TV show) and an adult (and children's) choir, along with guest singers like Gerri Granger. They covered three numbers from the Nixon event: "Joy to the World," Mel Tormé's "Christmas Song," and, importantly, Taylor's "Stable down the Road." This third song, particularly Billy's treatment thereof, needs to be heard—who knows, it could even become a seasonal classic someday. The U.S. Army is doing its part to keep this Taylor gem alive, as can be heard on the Army Band website.[12]

Billy was quite pleased with the Frost/Taylor album, saying it was one of the best albums he'd ever done.[13] Undeniably, it ranks right up there with other jazz and voice jewels like trumpeter Donald Byrd's *A New Perspective* (Blue Note, 1963), pianist Andrew Hill's *Lift Every Voice* (Blue Note, 1969), and, more recently, guitarist Kenny Burrell's effort with the Harlem Boy's Choir, *Love Is the Answer* (Concord, 1998).

As for David Frost, he would come off much better the second time around. In the film *Frost/Nixon*, the casual viewer is left with the impression that, money aside, Frost was selected for the televised interview because Nixon viewed him as a media lightweight.[14] Back in 1970, however, Nixon viewed Frost as a media friend sympathetic to his administration, as Nixon's introductory remarks to Frost's History of Christmas make abundantly clear. No doubt, Frost was considered less a cream puff and more a friendly "fair and balanced" questioner when Nixon agreed to the televised interview. Unfortunately for him, Nixon did not heed other comments he had included in his introduction: "David Frost is one who has a reputation far beyond that of simply being a television interviewer who brings out the best—and sometimes the worst—in people, but in any event, he brings out whoever they are."

Indeed. Against expectations, Frost brought out Nixon, securing an admission of wrongdoing on Watergate matters and a public apology for it. See the movie.

Pete Fountain

I guess just the Republicans like jazz.
—*Pete Fountain*

June 15, 1972 | Mexican President Echeverria Dinner

WITH RESPECT TO ENTERTAINMENT, 1971 and 1972 were down years for the Nixon White House—only twenty-five social events were held. No jazz group appeared at the White House in 1971, and Pete Fountain would be the only one in 1972.

President Nixon was out on the stump most of the time in 1972. That was also the year of his fabled breakthrough trips to China and the Soviet Union. But something else happened early in 1972 that put a damper on social gatherings at the mansion: the Feraci affair.

It began innocently enough. The White House had set aside the evening of January 28 for a dinner and musicale for Lila and DeWitt Wallace, the cofounders of the *Reader's Digest*, to celebrate the popular magazine's fiftieth anniversary.[1] After his prominent guests settled in the East Room for the entertainment, the president took the stage and spoke at length on the importance of the *Digest* to America and to the world. Then he asked Mrs. Nixon and the Wallaces to join him on the riser.

Nixon read the Medal of Freedom citation for DeWitt and slipped the medal around his neck. He repeated the procedure for Lila. DeWitt spoke for both of them, saying, "I am absolutely flabbergasted, and I'm sure Lila is too. We rather suspected some shenanigans might be going on, but . . . I thought at most it would be a carving set or something of that sort."

Little did he know that his suspected shenanigans would soon follow.[2]

The honorees took their seats while the MC in chief introduced an "evening of nostalgia in song" by Ray Conniff and his singers. Before he stepped down off the riser, Nixon said, "If the music is square, [he raised his voice] it's because I like it square."

A chorus of sixteen—eight women and eight men—marched single file across the stage in front of a barrier separating them from their backup six-piece combo. A black-haired female member of the Conniff troupe stood almost center stage behind a mic and held up a cloth sign that read "STOP THE KILLING." She then addressed President Nixon, sitting in the front row just below her:

Stop bombing human beings, animals and vegetation. You go to church on Sunday and pray to Jesus Christ. If Jesus Christ were here tonight, you would not dare to drop another bomb. Bless the [anti-war] Berrigans and bless [Pentagon Papers leaker] Daniel Ellsburg.[3]

Near the close of her speech, Conniff, who had just arrived onstage, reached for the banner, but Miss Feraci yanked it back and folded it up. Speech over. Before any of the 163 guests realized her pitch was anything but part of the act, the singers—including Miss Feraci—swung listlessly into "Ma, He's Making Eyes at Me."[4]

When the music stopped, Conniff stepped forward and said, "Thank you very much and good evening. I want you all to know what a thrill it is to be here in the White House. [Pause.] I assure you, the first part of our program was as big a shock to me, Mr. President, as it was to you."

This remark received lengthy, enthusiastic applause spiked with exuberant shouts, and then from all over the room came the cry, "Throw her out."

"All right," said Conniff, who asked Ms. Feraci to leave. She did. Applause followed her to the exit. Conniff returned to his mic and addressed the president, "All I can say is I must apologize. I guess I'll have to make sure from now on that my singers listen to your speeches. They don't seem to know what is going on."

After brief questioning by the Secret Service and a slight exchange with Press Secretary Herb Klein, the thirty-year-old Canadian session singer from Los Angeles, hired by Conniff only the week before, was released into the capital night air.

Meanwhile, back upstairs at the gala, the singers were chorusing through "God Bless America" to close their upstaged program. Nixon stepped up to the riser to congratulate Conniff, who told him off-mic how sorry he was about Ms. Feraci's action. According to Conniff, Nixon said, "Oh, forget it, those things will happen."

At the after-party, many of the invited guests swapped comments about the evening's scene-stealer. Secretary of State William P. Rogers: "I'm sure she's just a mixed-up youngster." Comedian Bob Hope: "It's a shame, a sad state of affairs when someone can get into this place, and does something like that." Actor Fred MacMurray: "Billy Graham was purple." Graham said, "You expect anything these days." Church leader Norman Vincent Peale joined the amen chorus three days later in a letter to the president: "The incident of the foolish little girl cuts no ice . . . I had a hard time controlling my religion; I wanted to get up and throw her out myself."[5]

Surprisingly, the "affair" drew only "moderate coverage" in the thirteen newspapers the White House regularly tracked and, most important to the White House, "light" coverage given to Herb Klein's suggestion that the "oobie-doobie girl" could be arrested. But for what crime? Insulting the president? Feraci received some publicity traction back home in California for several months, and that was it. She never sang again professionally.[6]

The White House staff had been put on notice, however. One could never be too vigilant when it came to entertainers, especially a choral group of contract singers who had signed up for an unpaid White House gig less than two weeks before the event.[7]

Even with a White House staff on heightened alert, minimal loyalty scrubbing had to be given to Pete Fountain and his band prior to their White House engagement. It wasn't necessary. From a White House perspective, a safer choice could not have been made.

On the surface, the Fountain group had to be okay; after all, Mr. Fountain had starred for two years on the *Lawrence Welk Show* in the late '50s. Welk himself was a well-known GOP supporter. Moreover, the White House didn't have a problem with the other Dixielanders—Al Hirt's band and the World's Greatest Jazz Band—that had played the East Room in 1969 and 1970, respectively.

More significant, as part of Al Hirt's Dixieland band, Pete had greeted President Nixon at his hotel in the heart of the French Quarter on August 14, 1970, when the president flew to New Orleans for a one-day conference on ending school segregation. Upon his arrival at the Royal Orleans Hotel, Mr. Nixon spoke to an assembled crowd from a platform in the middle of St. Louis Street. It was there that Pete received his first invitation to the White House . . . publicly: "Mrs. Nixon and I want to express our great appreciation to all of you for this wonderfully warm welcome. To Al Hirt and Pete Fountain, how about a hand for them? [Applause.] We've had Al at the White House. Pete, you've got to come too."[8]

A week later, Pete got it in writing:

Dear Mr. Fountain:

It is always a pleasure to come to New Orleans, but the lively greeting you gave us at the hotel last Friday helped to make this latest trip the best of all. I was delighted to see you, and as I mentioned, we will have to talk you into coming to the White House in the near future. There is more than one fan in the Nixon family [daughter Julie could be one], and the records you thoughtfully brought for me will be not only mementos of

a wonderful welcome but also, I hope, tokens of another oppor-
tunity to enjoy your company and your music.
With best wishes,
Sincerely, Richard Nixon[9]

Not leaving anything to chance—presidents are known to be fickle—
the crafty clarinetist later sent a record album to the White House, to
which pen pal Richard Nixon replied in May of 1971: "Needless to say,
it will provide all the Nixons with an opportunity to enjoy your music until we again have an occasion to share your talents in person."[10]

Pete made sure that the letters from Nixon were printed in the *New
Orleans States-Item* newspaper; no way was he letting the president off
the hook. Like Duke Ellington before him, and Frank Sinatra after
him, diligence paid off. Pete's invite finally came in early 1972, possibly as early as February when the state visit by the Mexican president
was finalized, but certainly before April 29 when Pat Nixon revealed
at the White House Correspondent's Association Dinner that she and
her husband had invited Fountain to the dinner honoring Mexican
President and Mrs. Echeverria.[11]

If the White House staff had any reservations about the band's political leanings, they were put to rest on the day of the event. Pete and
the band showed up at the rehearsal that afternoon, each one wearing
a "Re-elect the President" button. Smart move, Pete, no matter your
political affiliation! They didn't wear the buttons at the evening's performance, however.

A New Orleans band was a superb choice for President Echeverria. After all, Mexican music was one of the ingredients in the New Orleans
jazz gumbo, the "Spanish Tinge," as jazz immortal Jelly Roll Morton
so aptly put it. The State Department knew that Echeverria was unlikely a European classical music fan, and believed one of his sons was
a jazz drummer (rock and roll, actually). In addition, a band from the
Crescent City was a superb election-year choice for President Nixon

(talk about your Southern strategy!). And why not pick the most well-known living New Orleans musician of the time? Louis Armstrong had passed away the year before.

The talent Pete brought with him was his then current band, which, he boasted, was

> composed of the best musicians in [New Orleans]: Jack Delaney and Jimmy Duggan on trombones, Connie Jones and Mike Serpas on trumpets, Earl Vuiovich on piano, Charlie Lodice on drums, Stick Felix on bass, and my idol on tenor sax—*Eddie Miller* . . . It is the best band I have ever had . . . we have a ball together.
>
> We play mostly traditional songs . . . "When the Saint's Go Marching In," "Wolverine Blues," or "Clarinet Marmalade" . . . We update the show constantly, and it pays off . . . Now we get some of the younger set in the club. The Nashville sound has helped that.[12]

Talk about a band of like-minded souls: lead trumpeter Connie Jones first played with Pete in 1952, with trombonist Jack Delaney in 1946, and with sax man Eddie Miller way before that. Pete "stole" bassist Stick Felix from Al Hirt in 1960 (Jumbo forgave him) and Felix would remain with him into the next century, which prompted Pete to remark in 2003, "Stick—I think we played the Last Supper together." Drummer Charlie Lodice had paid his dues with the Dukes of Dixieland and other New Orleans outfits.

Tenor saxophonist Eddie Miller, who attended the same New Orleans High School (Warren Easton) as Pete (but nineteen years before), had a national jazz reputation—not so much from the *Pete Kelly's Blues* TV series of the 1950s, but mostly from his seven-year stint with the Bob Crosby Bob Cats in the '40s, where he was far and away the most popular member. Miller became the fifth Bob Cat member to get a gig at the Nixon White House. Before him, former Bob Cats Billy Butterfield, Bob Haggart, and Yank Lawson of the World's Greatest

Jazz Band appeared there on March 19, 1970, and Ray Conniff, with his Singers, *really* shook the crystal chandeliers with the help of Carol Feraci in early 1972. Ray had played trombone with the Cats for two years before joining Artie Shaw in 1940.

Miller's much-admired tenor style featured floating rhythmic phrases, regular use of the upper register, and easy, legato constructions. Equally effective on ballads as on up-tempo numbers, his svelte, lowing tenor brought to mind either Bud Freeman or Paul Gonsalves, or both.

Miller's style adapted well to both studio work (nine years with 20th Century Fox) and countless freelance recordings with various swing/Dixie veterans. He toured with the Bob Cat Reunion Band and appeared with the embryonic WGJB before joining his pal Pete in 1967 for a nine-year residence:

> I had known Pete since he was a teenager, way back in the 1940s. [This guy] took me to hear Pete play, and [he was] only about 17 then. We always kept in touch, and when Pete came to the coast to work with Lawrence Welk we spent a lot of time together. He went back to New Orleans, and then asked me to join his band. It was a great time. I like Pete; he is a fine player, and a nice guy. He'll stop and speak with the guy who is sweeping the street, there's nothing big time about his attitude at all.

Unaware of the historical significance of the evening—the first authentic Dixieland group to perform for a foreign head of state in White House history—President Nixon opened the evening's entertainment in a light vein, or as the *New Orleans Times-Picayune* headlined the next day, "Fountain Butt of Nixon Joke": "We had hoped to have President and Mrs. Echeverria's son [a rock and roll drummer] here tonight, but he had an engagement coming up Tuesday in Los Angeles." Mr. Nixon then told the two hundred guests seated in the East Room that he asked comedian Jack Benny (who was a guest) to perform, "but he forgot to bring his violin," so he settled on a third choice, Pete Fountain. "Who really is a first choice," the president said with a grin.[13]

Well known for his self-deprecating humor, Pete took the joke in stride and stomped off the first number in his rather short set. He would adhere, as other performers had not, to the guidelines the White House had set regarding length of show, finishing in less than thirty minutes. Interestingly, and appropriately, Pete selected four turn-of-the-century Crescent City classics for the program—all directly or indirectly associated with the horn that he described as "the hardest of all horns to play and probably the most neglected of all instruments."[14]

He opened with "Clarinet Marmalade," a ragtimey, march-derived piece made famous by the New Orleans–based Original Dixieland Jazz Band (ODJB), the first band to put jazz on record in 1917.[15] It was cowritten by two ODJB members, pianist Henry Ragas and clarinetist Larry Shields. The number not only became Shield's vehicle, showing his liquid, lithe tone to particularly good advantage, but was also recorded by standout 1920s bands like Bix and Tram (Bix Beiderbecke and Frankie Trumbauer) and the Fletcher Henderson Orchestra. By the late 1930s, "Marmalade" had become a member in good standing in the Dixieland canon, a favorite of clarinetists like Irving Fazola (who died at age thirty-six) and Benny Goodman, both of whom, as Pete has often said, were his two primary influences on the instrument.

But no one would mistake Pete for swingman Goodman; he was closer to Faz and such New Orleans clarinet masters as Jimmy Noone, Johnny Dodds, Barney Bigard, Edmond Hall, Albert Nicholas, and Omer Simeon, all of whom Pete has cited as influences (they all played in Louis Armstrong's band at one time or another). Pete's sound is N'Awlins all the way: broad vibrato, woody, loud, and very effective in the low and medium registers. He referred to it as "fat," which he believed was attained by the way he opened his throat when he played. At times, that fat sound conjured up a young Sidney Bechet on soprano saxophone.

Excursions into the piping high register of his instrument aside, Pete could still hold his own with any brass/sax heavy front line, like the group he brought to the White House. Unfortunately, a recording of their East Room performance is not to be found at the Nixon

Library, and only one recording by the group is available—*Alive in New Orleans* (Laserlight, 1998)—on which they play a different set of Southland standards.

"High Society" followed. This tune—another "good old good one," as Louis Armstrong used to say—began in 1901 as a standard brass band march used in nearly all the early New Orleans street parades. It was elevated to culture-transcendent status by New Orleans clarinetist Alphonse Picou, who first adapted the piccolo counter-melody (obbligato) part to clarinet. Musicologist Gunther Schuller says George Baquet was the first; maybe so, but Picou unquestionably popularized it. "High Society" thus became a test piece that all aspiring clarinetists had to "cut" before they could get a job. Other instrumentalists took up the challenge as well. Sidney Bechet had once been astonished to hear a young Louis Armstrong race effortlessly through the famous clarinet solo . . . on trumpet.[16] Modern jazz players, such as Charlie Parker, often quoted parts in their solos. Obviously, Pete would not have stood under the White House spotlight had he not passed the "Society" test. In this number, he skimmed atop the ensemble like Peter Piper picking a peck of pickled peppers, resembling second idol Benny Goodman more than his main man, Faz.

Next, Pete slowed things down with "Just a Closer Walk with Thee," one of the hymns most often played at New Orleans funerals in the earliest days of jazz. "A Closer Walk," an almost-hit single off the bestselling *Pete Fountain's New Orleans* album, became his signature piece, his biography title, and, over the years, his most requested number. When asked if the song was one of his favorites, Pete replied, "One of my favorites? I have to play it every night whether it's my favorite or not!"[17] On this number perhaps more than any other, Pete's voice, his fat sound, is readily discernible: long-held, wide vibrato notes interspersed with perfectly articulated cave-resonant short ones.

The set ended on the leg-shaking, head-bobbing "Muskrat Ramble"—another tune most Americans have heard, and know, but can't always name. The song was composed before 1920 by (arguably) the first jazz trombonist, New Orleans native Edward "Kid" Ory. It was Kid

Ory who—having the best jazz band in New Orleans in 1918—gave teenager Louis Armstrong his first trumpet-playing job. It was Louis Armstrong who—returning the favor—asked Kid Ory (and others) to record a series of sides (now known as the Hot Fives), beginning in November 1925, that would change the shape of jazz and with it the course of twentieth-century music. And it was the Hot Five session of February 26, 1926, that saw the first recording of what is now one of the most popular tunes in the Dixieland canon, "Muskrat Ramble." Some say it was Louis Armstrong who gave the song to Kid Ory (probably apocryphal). More likely, Ory put it together from bits and pieces of the common stock of unpublished and unrecorded music in *fin de siecle* New Orleans. And, by the way, "Cornet Chop Suey," recorded at the same Hot Five session as "Muskrat Ramble," opens with a four-bar a cappella introduction by Armstrong patterned after the clarinet chorus of "High Society" developed by Alphonse Picou.[18]

The full weight of Fountain's little big band—think of it, two trumpets, two trombones, two strong woodwinds, with piano, bass, and drums (a nonet)—just had to be felt as well as heard, especially by

Pete Fountain shaking hands with Nixon, joined by President Escheverria (*right*); Mrs. Escheverria and Mrs. Nixon (*behind Nixon*); and Fountain's nine-piece band.

the presidents and their wives seated in the first row. No one ever accused a Dixieland band of subtlety, especially performing a tune like "Muskrat," and with Pete's band, and its front line of strong blowers, the guests would have no doubt had their backs pressed to their chairs as if the East Room were a jumbo airliner in steep ascent mode.

The *Washington Post* filed a lackluster review of the musical portion of the evening—no mention of the tunes played, just generalities. It could have been written without the benefit of actually having been there:

> But as the chandeliers dimmed, and Fountain began the sharp plaintive wail of Dixieland, a good bit of foot tappery commenced and many distinguished necks craned to follow the solo passages of Fountain's eight man backup. Earl Vuiovich, the jazz pianist, said the White House piano was marvelous and that he would be delighted to make off with it if he could figure out how . . . The White House, for all its proper formality, appeared to have hit on the traditional southern formula for large parties in old houses—wash the chandeliers, play the music loud, pack the people in and hope for the best. It usually works, and it did.[19]

The *Washington Star* awarded "olés!" to the performance and noted that the Mexican contingent reveled in it: "It was a jam session that brought the joy to our [East Room] guests that we get when they bring out their mariachis."[20]

As for the others: One row of guests wanted to write a letter asking the president to please take Pete Fountain . . . and his band with him to all summit meetings so all the world could hear real American jazz.

Not a bad idea, really. The only real support the government was giving to spread the jazz word overseas at the time was the daily VOA broadcasts by Willis Conover, and the band trips sponsored by the State Department. Duke Ellington and his orchestra had toured the Soviet Union the previous October, then split November between Eastern Europe and Latin America before they conquered the Far East in January. Guitarist Charlie Byrd and his trio, and the Thad Jones/Mel Lewis Jazz Orchestra would both spread the music around the globe during 1972.

As for Mr. Fountain, he passed his audition with flying colors. Pete was invited back to play the White House four more times, twice for Ronald Reagan, and twice for George H. W. Bush. Commenting in 2003 on his performances at 1600 Pennsylvania Avenue, Pete said: "You know, I still wonder how it happened. It's like a dream to play five state dinners. Most people would love to get one. But five? I just keep shaking my head." And then he quipped: "I guess just Republicans like jazz." From Pete's perspective, it probably looked that way.[21]

Two nights after Pete and the boys closed their East Room set for President Nixon, some other boys, this group wearing surgical rubber gloves, walked into the Democratic National Committee headquarters in the fashionable Watergate office-apartment complex and began rifling files and planting bugs—at least until they were caught. This "third-rate burglary," as it was called, would set off a chain of events that would chase Richard Nixon out of the White House into a waiting helicopter in August 1974 and end his presidency.

Frank Sinatra

Jesus Christ, I'm back. I'm back, baby, I'm back.
—*Frank Sinatra*

April 17, 1973 | Italian Prime Minister Andreotti Dinner

AFTER RICHARD NIXON WON A second term by a comfortable twenty percentage points, the pace of social events at the White House accelerated. Twenty-one were held in 1973 even as the ship of state began to take on Watergate. Along with the usual smattering of classical favorites (constituting nearly a third of the events), the White House invited a new crop of entertainers handpicked from a slightly different roster. Nixon reached outside and tapped old friend Paul Keyes to be the new White House impresario. Producer and writer of the TV show *Laugh-In*, Keyes had advised Nixon on his campaign television appearances. With his longtime Hollywood ties, Keyes naturally gravitated toward showbiz Republican stalwarts—as was no doubt Nixon's intent.

Although the president appointed Keyes in early 1973, no one saw him at the White House until he showed up at a rehearsal by opera singer Mary Costa on April 10. From that time on, Keyes just took over, and Francis Albert Sinatra was his first beneficiary. But, as we shall see, Keyes received a royal assist from both the president and vice president, who had been courting Ol' Blue Eyes for some time (and vice versa). No other performer, with the possible exception of Duke Ellington, worked as hard as Frank Sinatra did to obtain his star turn under the East Room lights. Sinatra even changed his national politics to get the gig.[1]

FROM BLUE TO RED

Starting in his youth in the 1930s and continuing to the late 1960s, Sinatra was a true blue Democrat. He carried placards for Democratic candidates in hometown parades long before he could read them, accompanied his mother on her Democratic precinct rounds, and sometime later, in 1944, named his firstborn son Franklin after FDR. That year, the bobby-soxers' delight campaigned widely for Roosevelt, speaking and singing to mostly youthful audiences. For that he received his first invitation to the White House, a short tea with Franklin D. himself. He donated at least $5,000 to the campaign and, in a nationally broadcast election-eve rally at Madison Square Garden, dropped a new lyric into the Adair and Dennis song "Everything Happens to Me":

They asked me down to Washington
To have a cup of tea
The Republicans started squawking
They're mad as they can be[2]

Sinatra did not actively campaign for FDR's predecessor Harry Truman in 1948 nor did he support Henry Wallace, who was running as a left-wing third-party candidate. He nonetheless remained committed to civil rights and left-of-center causes. On the former, Sinatra was the first white celebrity to champion the rights of African Americans.

Sinatra strongly supported Adlai Stevenson in his losing bids for the presidency against Dwight D. Eisenhower in 1952 and 1956. In 1952, he sang and spoke for Stevenson at a large election-eve rally at the Hollywood Palladium. In 1956, he not only campaigned widely for Stevenson but also sang the national anthem at the opening session of the Democratic National Convention. Like many other convention-eers, he spotted the rising political star shooting across the firmament and adjusted his sights accordingly. Sinatra's relationship with John F. Kennedy, as it would develop both publicly and privately, became the closest in history between a major party presidential nominee and an entertainer, then or since.

By 1959 a friendship had developed between Frank and Jack. The attraction, though complex (Frank's pal Peter Lawford was married to Jack's sister Pat, for instance) was nonetheless based on clear political motives on both sides. JFK wanted an intermediary between himself and both organized labor and organized crime (yes, Frank was friends with reputed Chicago gangster Sam Giancana); he also wanted a celebrity recruiter and fund-raiser—and who else but Frank. For his part, to be simple about it, Sinatra wanted access to power and respectability (he had everything else).

His recorded voice was soon blaring from Kennedy sound trucks with substitute lyrics for his hit single "High Hopes," chosen as the presidential campaign song:

K-E-Double-N-E-D-Y
Jack's the nation's favorite guy

. . . .

Oops, there goes the opposition – KERPLOP![3]

Sinatra's further public role in the 1960 campaign was focused on fund-raising. He famously marshaled an army of Hollywood stars to entertain at a convention-eve fund-raiser that brought in some $300,000. Then during the fall campaign, he performed at several such events and at a huge election-eve rally in Newark.

As president-elect, Kennedy prevailed on Sinatra to organize a pre-inaugural gala, and did he ever! He flew in jazz singer Ella Fitzgerald from Australia, actor Sidney Poitier from France, and Gene Kelly from Switzerland, as well as buying out the house of the Broadway show *Gypsy* for the night so singer Ethel Merman could appear. He hired Nelson Riddle to arrange and conduct the orchestra. "May have been the most stunning assembly of theatrical talent ever brought together for a single show," said the *New York Times*. Not incidentally, it raised $1.4 million for the Democrats.

But the party was over after friend Jack became President Kennedy. Those once-useful ties to Giancana did Frank in. Under pressure from FBI Chief Edgar Hoover, brother Bobby (then attorney general), and wife Jackie, the "friendship" came to a rather inglorious end in the spring of 1962. Sinatra was informed that, contrary to previous assurances, the president would not be staying at Sinatra's much-refurbished Palm Springs home (where he had built a helipad for the chief executive's helicopter). Instead, for "security reasons," Kennedy would stay with singer Bing Crosby—a Republican!

During the Kennedy years, Sinatra was never invited to fly on Air Force One or attend any of the state dinners (as guest or entertainer) or pay a visit to Camp David. Although, early on, he copped an invite to a luncheon, but that was it.[4]

Sinatra's disillusioning experience with JFK did not prompt him to retreat from Democratic affairs, but (like many others) he took a hiatus from national politics after the Kennedy assassination. He did not campaign for Lyndon B. Johnson in 1964, although once LBJ was elected, the White House requested an FBI check on Sinatra (and other entertainers).[5] No invitation to perform was tendered, however. Sinatra famously received a fifteen-minute audience with LBJ while the latter lie prone on the massage table, but that was it.

Sinatra remained active in California politics campaigning on behalf of Democratic Governor Pat Brown's reelection bid in 1966 against Ronald Reagan. To one of his signature songs, Rodgers and Hart's "The Lady Is a Tramp," Frank again adjusted the lyrics:

Hates California
It's Reagan and damp[6]

Distaste for Bobby Kennedy and his candidacy for the Democratic presidential nomination in 1968 helped motivate Sinatra to return to the national political arena on the side of Kennedy opponent Vice President

Hubert Humphrey, for whom he organized ten fund-raising concerts. But after Humphrey's nomination at the 1968 Democratic Convention, his aides advised Humphrey to give Sinatra his walking papers, citing the singer's alleged mob ties that newspapers were then recycling. Sinatra caught the drift, and it was he who walked right into the arms of Richard Nixon and the Republican Party.

His conversion to Republicanism was not sudden (nor, in fact, ever complete).[7] In 1970 he endorsed Reagan's candidacy for reelection as governor of California (as cochair of Democrats for Reagan) and raised $500,000 in benefit concerts for the incumbent's campaign fund. Sinatra similarly befriended Vice President Spiro T. Agnew when they met in 1970, although he did not necessarily embrace the man at the top of the ticket, Richard Nixon.

The Sinatra-Agnew connection prompted Nixon advisor Chick Colson to urge the president to woo Sinatra into the administration's political camp in early 1971. "Sinatra is the most important person in the Hollywood entertainment community . . . he has the muscle to bring along a lot of the younger lights." But as far as the social secretary's office was concerned in May 1971, Sinatra was still considered "inappropriate" for White House entertainment. Yet later that year, Frank's name finally appears on a potential entertainers list prepared by the social secretary's office, along with the following remarks:

1. President and Mrs. Nixon invited him to Mexican State Dinner in San Diego.
2. He has played golf with V.P. Agnew.
3. He is the winner of the Gene Hirschould [sic] Award from Motion Picture Academy of A&S.
4. If we have him, I bet he'd package a huge show.
5. *What about his underworld friends?*[8]

All this plan dancing was rendered moot when Sinatra famously "retired" from show business in June 1971.

By 1972, however, Sinatra was firmly in the Republican camp. His reservations about Nixon were removed when the president decided to keep Agnew on the ticket. Sinatra actually financed a pro-Agnew write-in campaign in the early primaries to rouse support for the vice president. He went on to contribute $53,000 to Nixon's reelection effort, campaigned with Agnew, and briefly abandoned his "retirement" to sing at the Republican Convention in Chicago. The substitute lyrics for "The Lady Is a Tramp" had changed:

> They're both unique, the Quaker and the Greek
> They make this Italian want to whistle and stamp
> Because each gentleman is a champ[9]

Several weeks earlier, Sinatra appeared before the Select Committee on Crime of the U.S. House of Representatives to answer questions about a racetrack investment. Not only did Agnew publicly stand by his man, but Nixon also telephoned Sinatra to congratulate him on his testimony.

After the Nixon-Agnew ticket was reelected, Sinatra was sighted on December 7, 1972, among Washington officials and politicos in the stands at the night launching of Apollo 17 at the Kennedy Space Center in Florida. He sat next to Republican supporters actor Hugh O'Brien and comedian Jonathan Winters. More telling: high-ranking Genovese crime family member Angelo DeCarlo was released from federal prison in December, allegedly because Sinatra persuaded the White House to issue a presidential commutation of sentence.

Republicans, it had to seem to Sinatra, understood loyalty in the same way that he did and that Democrats did not. Could an East Room musicale starring Frank Sinatra be far behind? Yes but, Frank, in his inimitable style, almost blew it.

Booked to host an inauguration-eve event at the Kennedy Center in 1973 (with the Nixons and Agnews attending), Sinatra went ballistic and withdrew as emcee when the Secret Service denied his last-minute request to put comedian Pat Henry on the bill. But that wasn't the worst of it. Later that night at a party, Sinatra exploded at *Washington Post* society columnist Maxine Cheshire. "Get away from me, you scum," he shouted. "Go home and take a bath." And it didn't stop there: "You're nothing but a two-dollar broad. You know what that means, don't you? You've been laying down for two dollars all your life." Before stalking off, Sinatra stuffed two one-dollar bills into Cheshire's glass.[10]

Official Washington was shocked of course and Nixon was said to be enraged, but despite aides' advice to cancel his upcoming appearance at the White House, he held firm. Sinatra's long journey from Democrat to Republican, from outcast to respectability, was finally over. He would appear at the state function for the prime minister of Italy on April 17, 1973.

To his everlasting credit, Frank Sinatra brought orchestrator Nelson Riddle with him, the one man who was most responsible for Frank Sinatra becoming FRANK SINATRA. It is hard to imagine at this remove that Frank Sinatra—the bobby-soxers' delight, the swinger extraordinaire, the top, the king of the hill—was once almost washed up:

> By the early 1950s, the luster had gone from Frank Sinatra's career: Columbia Records had released him when his record sales dwindled; CBS had canceled his weekly television variety show after two dismal seasons; MGM had dropped him after a succession of box office failures; and MCA, the talent agency that represented him, had given him his release because he became difficult to sell and he was often a problem; if that wasn't enough, he owed the government over $100,000 in back taxes.[11]

But then in early 1953, Sinatra famously landed the role of Maggio in *From Here to Eternity* and signed a contract with Alan Livingston of the newly formed Capitol Records. Livingston felt strongly that Riddle could do for Sinatra what he had done for Nat King Cole: "Unforgettable," "Mona Lisa," "Pretend." Nelson Riddle's orchestral arrangements would fuel the engine that powered Sinatra's musical comeback.

He had his first recording session with Riddle on April 30, 1953, and of the four tunes recorded, two became hit singles: "I've Got the World on a String" (which Frank often used as a concert opener, although he used it to close the White House set) and "Don't Worry 'Bout Me." Capitol Records producer Alan Dell recalled that after the final take on "World on a String," Sinatra asked him, "Who wrote that arrangement?"

Dell replied, "This guy—Nelson Riddle."

Frank said, "Beautiful."

Session photographer Sid Avery also recalled, "When Frank listened to the playback of the recording, he was really excited about it and said, "Jesus Christ, I'm back. I'm back, baby, I'm back."[12]

The first album Sinatra recorded with Riddle was *Songs for Young Lovers*. Nelson conducted but only contributed one chart, the rest were songs Sinatra had been featuring in his nightclub act charted by George Siravo. Nelson then provided Sinatra with a lush string background on the single "Young at Heart." The song became a number one hit in early 1954, his first in six years, and perhaps even more important, it marked the first million-selling record of his career.

That same year, the jazz element that had always been part of Sinatra's musical legacy was brought to the forefront in the concept album *Swing Easy*. Arranged by Nelson for Sinatra and ten musicians, the tunes were all swingers, featuring solos by prominent studio jazz musicians. The album cover of *Swing Easy*, and especially the music, were important in introducing the new image Sinatra had created: the confident, carefree, big-city hipster gliding atop a swinging jazz beat, his Windsor-knotted tie pulled away from his collar, and the proper lid on his head—a Stetson felt hat.[13]

But then Frank and Nelson moved on to something different, an album of torch songs, ballads of desperation that would be released in 1955 as *In the Wee Small Hours of the Morning*. This concept album, with its sustained mood of wistful melancholy, received astounding critical praise and served to separate Frank Sinatra from his male contemporaries for all time. He had finally won over the leading musical critics and was finally accepted as a truly formidable musical artist. While Frank had always been a fan favorite among readers of *DownBeat*, the leading jazz magazine of that time, winning male singer of the year for five straight years at the start (1941–1947) and nine straight years after his comeback (1954–1962), he won the critics poll for the first time in 1955 on the strength of *Wee Small Hours*. He earned the accolades of *DownBeat* critics again in 1957 for his three subsequent concept albums: *Songs for Swingin' Lovers, Close to You,* and *A Swingin' Affair,* all orchestrated by Riddle.[14]

The stream of thematic concept albums on Capitol that began with *Young Lovers* and *Swing Easy* in 1954 reached its *Point of No Return* in 1962, when Sinatra launched his own Reprise label. But in the mind of many, it is Sinatra's Capitol albums that represent near perfection in the context of popular recordings of the era.

All told, Capitol released sixteen albums, nine arranged by Nelson Riddle, the others orchestrated by George Siravo (one), Billy May (three), Gordon Jenkins (two), and Axel Stordahl (one).[15] But as Sinatra's biographer Will Friedwald has said,

> It remained for Riddle to develop both the ballad side and the swinging side of Sinatra, or rather to extend the legacies of Axel Stordahl and George Siravo . . . And the Sinatra-Riddle sound has since become what we think of when we think of Sinatra; the pre-Riddle period can be reduced to a prelude, the post-Riddle period era to an afterthought.[16]

That does not mean that the Sinatra-Reprise era, noted perhaps for its versatility more than its quality, was an "afterthought," as a horde of Ol' Blue Eyes' latter-day fans would be quick to point out. In fact, Riddle orchestrated four of the twenty-six Reprise albums over its twenty-year run, notably *The Concert Sinatra* (1963), which holds its own in comparison with any Capitol album.[17]

But what is it about Riddle's arrangements that made them so special? As Nelson himself characterized it,

> Perhaps unconsciously, my ear recalled some of the fine arrangements Sy Oliver had done for Tommy Dorsey [in whose band Nelson played trombone] using sustained strings but also employing rhythmic fills by brass and saxes to generate excitement. The strings, by observing crescendos in the right places, add to the pace and the tension of such writing without getting in the way. It was further embroidery in this basic idea to add the bass trombone of George Roberts plus the unmistakably insinuating fills of Harry "Sweets" Edison on Harmon-muted trumpet.

There was more, as flautist Paul Horn put it: "The flute has always been used in film scoring with a symphony orchestra. But for pop arrangements to use woodwinds like he used was unique, and the flutes played a major part in it . . . he was really a painter of sound."[18]

Riddle's string writing, heavily influenced by the impressionists Debussy and Ravel, perfectly melded with his jazz sensibilities for scoring reeds and brass. To this unique blend, he would add the "embroidery" using all manner of accent instruments (celeste, guitar, violin, flute, alto saxophone, French horn) in solo or in tandem without taking away from Sinatra's vocal line and, in fact, enhancing it.

THE SHOW

On the evening of April 17, 1973, at the White House, after the president introduced him as "the Washington Monument, the top," Francis Albert Sinatra for the first time in his career strode across the East Room stage to thunderous applause. Following his customary bows, he signaled to Nelson Riddle, who fronted the Marine Corps Orchestra augmented by two guest musicians, and began his ten-song set for President Nixon, Italian Prime Minister Andreotti, their wives, Vice President Agnew, members of diplomatic Washington, cabinet members, union leaders, businessmen, and members of Congress, many of them Italian Americans.

"You Make Me Feel So Young"
Arranger Nelson Riddle | *Songs for Swingin' Lovers* | Capitol (1956)

Frank opened with a zesty "You Make Me Feel So Young," the Myron/Gordon song that was his standard concert opener in the 1950s.[19] In fact, it opened the *Songs for Swingin' Lovers* album, in many critics estimation an all-but-perfect album. John Rockwell, for example:

> Sinatra's singing on this album has a verve and conviction that makes his records from the Forties sound bland. He has learned to tease and twist a vocal line without violating its integrity. By now he knows how to kick forward a song's rhythmic impetus by the percussive articulation of key one-syllable words . . . The album as a whole breathes with a delightful blend of Riddle's naughty sweetness and Sinatra's witty bravado.[20]

The "naughty sweetness" was not accidental. For this recording, Nelson put together a thirty-five-piece orchestra, consisting of a big band with a full string section. Most of the songs on the album are in "heartbeat" tempo ("the rhythm of sex," in Riddle's words), and "You Make Me Feel So Young" is no different. All the elements are there: the sustained strings (nearly imperceptible until the close) and the brass and sax sections swinging back and forth with a lonely flute seemingly weaving at will in between the lines of the orchestra and vocalist. And Frank kicking the music forward with his adroit use of the song's key word—"you." Sometimes it's "YOU!" Other times "you-ooo." Still other times "yooooooooo." Lastly and softly: "Ooo-oooh, yooooo make me feel so young."[21]

In the East Room, "Young" proved to be a solid opener for the Voice and his backup thirty-three-piece Marine Orchestra: eleven strings, ten woodwinds, nine brass, and three rhythm (see the end of the chapter for the complete roster). Riddle's charts—rehearsed the day before without Frank and then with him that afternoon—fell in the orchestra's wheel-house. A film of the event reveals surprisingly full-sounding saxes and brass; no one familiar with the classic recording would have slighted what they heard. The strings sound thinner than they do on the classic recording; there were two fewer and might have been under-recorded. Also, Frank's use of "you" to kick and punch the song along is not as effective, though that's a minor quibble. Audience reaction is less than enthusiastic but respectful; nonetheless, a great beginning.[22]

"Moonlight in Vermont"
Arranger Billy May | *Come Fly with Me* | Capitol (1958)

"Moonlight in Vermont," off the jaunty *Come Fly with Me* album that followed the *Swingin' Lovers* and *Swingin' Affair* albums, is a perfect example of why some consider the Sinatra of this period a jazz singer. In Nelson Riddle's words from a 1955 *Time* interview,

> His voice is more interesting now: he has separated his voice into different colors, in different registers. Years ago, his voice was more even, and now it is divided into at least three interesting ranges: low, middle, and high. [He's] probing more deeply into his songs than he used to. That may be due to the ten years he's put on, and the things he's gone through.[23]

By then Sinatra had perfected his fluid, legato-style phrasing, elon-gating the ends of phrases and reconfiguring the tempo of his vocal line within the confines of each measure. This he learned with the Tommy Dorsey Orchestra in the 1940s:

It was my idea to make my voice work in the same way as [Dorsey's] trombone or [Jascha Heifitz's] violin: not sounding like them—but "playing" the voice like those instruments. The first thing I needed was extraordinary breath control, which I didn't have. I began swimming every chance I got in public pools—taking laps underwater and thinking song lyrics to myself as I swam, holding my breath. I worked out on the track . . . running one lap, trotting the next. Pretty soon I had good breath control, but that still wasn't the whole answer. I still had to learn to sneak a breath without being too obvious.

It was easy for Dorsey to do it through his "pinhole" while he played trombone . . . Instead of singing only two bars or four bars of music at a time—like most of the other guys around—I was able to sing six bars, and in some songs eight bars, without taking a visible or audible breath. This gave the melody a flowing, unbroken quality, and *that*—if anything—was what me sound different.[24]

But rhythm was another critical aspect of the Sinatra style. His faultless sense of timing allowed him to toy with the rhythm of a melody, bringing syncopation and excitement to his lyric reading. Billie Holiday was a master of this technique. Sinatra once wrote in *Ebony* magazine:

With few exceptions, every major pop singer in the United States during her generation has been touched in some way by her genius. It is Billie Holiday, whom I first heard in 52nd Street clubs in the early 1930s, who was, and still remains, the greatest single musical influence on me.[25]

While roundly recognized as one of the greatest male popular interpretive singers of the twentieth century, one of its most recognizable singing voices, and the definitive male essayist of the American Songbook, Sinatra is not universally acclaimed as a jazz singer per se.[26] True, Frank's singing was not steeped in the blues or later jazz styles (bebop, for example); it belonged mostly to the Swing Era. But Sinatra, at his peak—the decade 1953–1963—was a jazz singer, subtly so perhaps, particularly in the way he handled lyrics.

Yet, in the notes to the *Sinatra Reprise Collection*, we find David McClintick asking this:

> Why has Sinatra, who is not, strictly speaking, a jazz singer, always been a universal favorite of jazz musicians? Why is he the all-time favorite singer—by far, no contest—of Miles Davis, Duke Ellington, Stan Getz, Benny Goodman, Gerry Mulligan, Oscar Peterson, Andre Previn, Lester Young, and many others?[27]

McClintick does not venture an answer. But it's simple, really: in that decade, Frank was a jazz singer. Sure he sang pop—they all do. So, okay, a pop jazz singer.

On "Moonlight," we hear it all: the different registers, especially low to middle, the gradations of color and tone, attention to the lyrics, and Sinatra's liquid style. Many commentators have highlighted the way Sinatra imparts a half-step key change as he glides out of the bridge with the word "lovely" to the word "evening" in the second chorus: "By the loveleeeeee eeeeeeevening summer breeze."

The transition is silky smooth, a simple maneuver to heighten the listener's anticipation at a critical point in the song (Tommy Dorsey would have been proud!). Frank adds his singerly touch throughout:

Falling leeeeeaaves
Ski traaaaaaaiilllls
Telegraph cables sinnnnnnnnngg

Sinatra's jazz style, so evident on "Moonlight," centers on the lyrics—how best to tell the story. He adds words (second time through, he adds "how" and "they"to bounce the line, hurry it up, and substitutes "as" for "and"), takes words out, emphasizes words by changing tone (a lower "sing," a higher "bend"), shortens words, elongates them (within or across the bar), and bends them. It's always the words with Frank.

The East Room lights dimmed as he introduced the romantic ballad as "one of the prettiest songs about one of the prettiest states in our great country." Unfortunately, for aficionados at least, the version heard by those gathered in the East Room did not quite measure up to the classic ones heard on the *Come Fly with Me* or *Frank Sinatra: Live in Australia 1959* (Blue Note) albums. Emphasis is on the words all right, but the singer's delivery of the key phrases is forced, and the "lovely evening" transition is botched the first time around—instead of "eeeee eeeee," he sings "eeee ah eeee." Only diehard fans would have noticed; the East Room crowd doled out generous applause for the performance, perhaps responding more to Sinatra's dramatic gesturing of ski trails (a dropping V-sign), cables (a horizontal wipe), and icy finger waves (fluttering fingers). Ol' Blue Eyes acknowledged the crowd by saying, "Isn't that a pretty song? What a great song that is."

"One for My Baby"
Arranger Nelson Riddle | *Only the Lonely* | Capitol (1958)

In the June 2004 issue of *DownBeat* magazine, a diverse group of seventy-three jazz singers (twenty-one male, fifty-two female) were asked to name their top all-time favorite jazz vocal albums. The top thirty were listed; *Only the Lonely* placed sixth. If there were a twentieth-century time capsule and if only one Sinatra album were allowed, this would surely be it.[28]

Originally to be titled *Songs for Losers*, until Sinatra's favorite songwriting team Sammy Cahn and James Van Heusen came up with the title song, the album is a sustained evocation of loneliness and despair. The 1975 popular song "On and On" by Stephen Bishop has the lyric "Puts on Sinatra and starts to cry." *Only the Lonely* is the implied record of course with its definitive readings of "What's New," "Angel Eyes," "Willow Weep for Me," and "Guess I'll Hang My Tears Out to Dry."

Many commentators have referred to *Lonely* as Frank's confessional album—publicly airing his heartache over the loss of actress and former wife, Ava Gardner. But that took place five years before, and as Columbia's Mitch Miller has astutely observed,

> I always tell this to singers: emotion is not something *you* feel—it is something you make the *listener* feel. You have to be very cool, and know what you're doing. You get a little tear in your voice, you put it there if the lyric calls for it. So it's craftsmanship . . . and Sinatra had craftsmanship. It's bulls—t to say that he draws on emotion from his personal life, because what he's drawing is the emotion from *your* personal life, and he's saying it to you.[29]

On the other hand, Nelson Riddle, in the months prior to the sessions, had lost both his mother and his baby daughter, and perhaps that contributed to the overall somber mood of the album.

Unlike previous collaborations, *Lonely* had almost unlimited musical resources for Riddle to tap, not the least of which were sixty or seventy players (not all used on each number of course) and a complete symphonic woodwind section, which Nelson used as though he were writing for strings. It also allowed him to double up on his accent instruments at the same time: two trombones, for example, one playing melody, the other playing jazz figures underneath.

No doubt, another contributing factor to the mood of the album was concertmaster and violinist Leonard Slatkin's role as the conductor for most of the songs. "The best of both worlds," Frank later remarked about Riddle as arranger and Slatkin as conductor. What is perhaps anomalous is that the last song recorded for the album would be the Harold Arlen/Johnny Mercer classic "One for My Baby (And One More for the Road)," the ultimate Sinatra saloon song. Anomalous because its arrangement is (rightfully) spare, a loping tinkling background piano by Sinatra's longtime pianist, musical director/confidant, and occasional conductor, Bill Miller. And again, to his everlasting credit, Frank brought Miller to the White House to accompany him on the one song that will forever be Frank's . . . and Bill's.

Sinatra had first recorded this tune in 1947 (Columbia) and had been featuring it in his nightclub act off and on for some time, which no doubt influenced how the song was recorded. In Frank's words:

> I'd always sung that song before in clubs with just my pianist Bill Miller backing me, a single spotlight on my face and cigarette, and the rest of the room in complete darkness. At this session, the word had somehow got around, and there were about sixty or seventy people there: Capitol employees and their friends, people off the street . . . anyone. Dave Cavanaugh was the A&R man, and he knew how I sang it in clubs, and he switched out all the lights—bar the spot on me. The atmosphere in that studio was exactly like a club. Dave said, "Roll 'em," there was one take, and that was that. The only time I've known it to happen like that.[30]

And that's exactly what they did at the White House—they turned the East Room into a club: audience in total darkness, spot on Frank's face and cigarette, with Bill Miller's barroom piano tinkling away in the background. Frank even introduced the song the way he had been doing for the past twenty or so years:

> I would imagine that through the years, in this room, there has been a preponderance of entertainment . . . I assume, since its inception, but I would also have to make a bet that nobody ever sang a saloon song in this room. Or maybe they did, maybe Louis Armstrong did when he was around [Sorry, Frank, Pops didn't make it to the White House]. This particular song happens to be, I think, the daddy of all the torch songs . . . or songs that people cry in their beer with, written by Johnny Mercer and Harold Arlen, two of our nation's best writers . . . It depicts the problems of a man who has problems with his lady.
>
> Consequently, in order to become a winner, he decides to get bombed. It's his only way out, he can't figure it out sensibly. And after three or four days of much imbibing he decides that he better go out among us again, to see if he is still fairly

normal . . . he falls into a small bistro about two o'clock in the morning, and his victim is the bartender.

Sinatra gave as dramatic a reading of his signature saloon song as he'd ever given. He benefited by stellar accompaniment from Bill Miller and orchestra members who provided the occasional filigree: a lonely flute, soft cushiony strings, and a muted trumpet à la Harry "Sweets" Edison. A third of the way through "Baby," Frank finally lit the cigarette he'd been holding, interspersing puffs between the lyrics before he turned away from the spot toward that long road away from his baby, mumbling, "The long, it's mighty long, too long" to an inaudible whisper. The spot dimmed. Total darkness. Lights up. Applause. Still in character, the melancholy loser thanked the audience, "I hope the surgeon general is not in the room. Smoking is enough, but singing and smoking at the same time?!

"I've Got You Under My Skin"
Arranger Nelson Riddle | *Songs for Swingin' Lovers* | Capitol (1956)

The pièce de résistance from the *Songs for Swingin' Lovers* album of 1956 is Cole Porter's "I've Got You Under My Skin." Along with a tote bag full of other Sinatra songs, this quintessential gem belongs to the twentieth-century time capsule, as much for Riddle's arrangement as for Frank's vocalizing. Ironically, it almost never came to pass.

Early on January 11, the day after the second session for the album was completed, Sinatra called Riddle at home to inform him that he had to arrange three more songs posthaste. Capitol brass wanted them to flush out the new twelve-inch disc format, and they had to be recorded the next night. Sinatra gave Riddle three tunes: "It Happened in Monterey," "Swinging Down the Lane," and "I've Got You Under My Skin." Whether they had previously discussed them or Sinatra pulled them out of his Stetson is not known.

Nelson got busy. By seven o'clock the next morning, he got the first two to the copyist (who then wrote the charts for each instrument). Nelson had a few hours of sleep and started writing again about one o'clock in the afternoon. He had put this one off for last because Frank had given him special instructions, as bass trombonist George Roberts remembered,

> Nelson called me up, and said, "Frank wants a long crescendo for the middle of "Skin." Do you know any Afro-Cuban rhythmical patterns?" And I said, "Well, why don't you steal the rhythmic pattern out of [bandleader] Stan Kenton's "23 Degree's North, 82 Degree's West?" He said," How does it go?" And I gave him the beginning trombone lines, the Afro-Cuban-sounding thing, which he developed into the bop-bop/bom-bom-bom/bom-bom-ba-bop crescendo that led up to [Milt Bernhart's] trombone solo.[31]

Nelson chiseled away at the arrangement for the remainder of the afternoon, and then with his wife, Doreen, at the wheel of their station wagon, the two motored their way from home to the Capitol Records studio in Los Angeles. Nelson sat in the backseat finishing the arrangement by flashlight. When the pair arrived at the studio, the copyist had ten of his assistants there. While they copied the arrangements, Sinatra recorded the first two tunes with Nelson and the orchestra.

Then it was time for "Skin." After the first run-through, the band stood and applauded. Bill Miller thought it was because everyone knew Nelson had done the arrangement in a hurry; no, Bill, it was just that good.[32]

Like many of the songs on the album, "Skin" begins in an unhurried fashion, swinging away in 2/4 time as a lone accent instrument—the percussionist's chimes punctuating a low repeating figure—awaits a relaxed Sinatra to enter in his smoky register voice:

chime chime chime
chime chime chime

chime chime chime
I've got you . . . chime chime
Under my skin . . . chime chime chime

The song's temperature steadily rises as the rest of the instruments enter the fray, the strings softly underneath as Frank limns the familiar Porter lyrics through the chorus and across the bridge. A sudden switch to 4/4 time—watch out, here comes Frank's crescendo with George Roberts's burping bass trombone leading the charge, volume steadily rising, the strings following suit as if channeling Hitchcock's orchestrator Bernard Herrmann and then wham! Rising above this organized cacophony comes a blistering trombone solo by Milt Bernhart, only eight bars long, but one for the ages.[33] Riddle, averse as always to over-the-top endings, switches back to 2/4 time as Frank reenters for the postcoital cooldown: chime chime chime.

Joining Roberts and Bernhart that night in the trombone section was big-band veteran Jimmy Priddy, along with Nelson himself (to give the section more weight) and a ringer, Juan Tizol, who performed in Duke Ellington's famous orchestra for many years and composed "Caravan" for Duke.

Milt's short epic solo is a *montuno*, a musical figure that Afro-Cuban bands like Machito, Perez Prado, and Dizzy Gillespie popularized. Dizzy's record of "Manteca" is a perfect example. As they say, success has many fathers. According to Milt, he even got an assist from Sinatra.

Frank kept saying, "Let's do another." This was unusual for Sinatra! I was about ready to collapse—I was running out of gas! Then, toward the tenth take or so [there would be twenty-two overall], someone in the booth said, "We didn't get enough bass—could we get the trombone nearer to a microphone?" I mean, what had they been doing? There was a mike there for the brass, up on a very high riser. "Can you get up to that one?" they asked. And I said, "Well, no—I'm not that tall." So they went looking for a box, and I don't know where he found one, but none other than Frank Sinatra went out and got a box, and brought it over for me to stand on!

Everyone in the studio—especially Frank—knew immediately what had been accomplished. Milt Bernhart further recalled:

I was packing up [and he] stuck his head out of the booth and said, "Why don't you come in the booth and listen to it." So I did—and there was this chick in there, a pretty blond, and she was positively beaming. He said to me, "Listen!" That was special! You know, it never really went past that. He never has been much for slathering around empty praise.[34]

The following week, Frank invited Nelson and his wife over to his house and he played the acetate of "Skin" over and over the entire weekend. Frank wasn't the only one who went bonkers. Jazz pianist Lou Levy (who spent several years with singer Peggy Lee) rhapsodized: "You can tell Frank is into it. They tore the world apart. It's one of the outstanding vocal arrangements—'My Way' and 'New York, New York,' if that's your bag, fine. But forget it, this one wipes 'em all out."[35]

Time magazine agreed. It was the only musical arrangement cited in its 1998 study of the most important entertainers of the twentieth century. By the way, Frank was picked top pop singer, albeit noted as jazz-inspired.[36]

Switching the mood again in the East Room, Ol' Blue Eyes loosened his tie, donned a Stetson, snapped his fingers (figuratively, of course) and said to his conductor, "Are you ready, Nelson? Go." To the audience, he said, "One of the best of Cole Porter and one of the best of Nelson Riddle's arrangements." Pianist Bill Miller chorded the familiar chime-chime-chime opening that elicited no peep of recognition from the crowd, which would not have been the case at any other concert almost anywhere else in the world. Undeterred, Frank voiced the familiar lyrics in his best smoky register baritone. The scarlet-uniformed orchestra provided swinging support, interpreting Riddle's chart to a tee. Marine bassist Dave Wundrow brought the toe-tapper to a close with a solidly plucked eight-note figure.

The White House version of "Skin" did not include the well-known bop-bop/bom-bom crescendo and thereby denied a once-in-a-lifetime opportunity for a young marine to recreate the searing Milt Bernhart trombone solo. Limited rehearsal time the day before and that afternoon necessitated focus on the beginnings and endings of several tunes.

"I Have Dreamed"
Arranger Nelson Riddle | *The Concert Sinatra* | Reprise (1963)

In the entire recording oeuvre of Francis Albert Sinatra, there is nothing else like *The Concert Sinatra*, an album of extended performances by Frank and a seventy-three-piece symphony orchestra. One of the best of the Sinatra-Riddle ballad albums, the recording features eight tunes (lyrics by Oscar Hammerstein on all but one), including "Bewitched," "Soliloquy," "You'll Never Walk Alone," "My Heart Stood Still," and "This Nearly Was Mine."

These are not the vocal offerings of the finger-snapping swingin' bachelor or the down-and-out sad sack propped against the lamppost. No, this is a full-voiced light classicist in the manner of contemporaries Todd Duncan, Howard Keel, Gordon McRae, or (almost) Paul Robeson. In other words, Frank gets as close as a pop jazz singer can to the bel canto style. On no other album does Sinatra reveal such strength in his low register and overall dynamic range.[37]

The arrangements throughout are symphonic, rarely to be found on pop recordings of the period, as on Rodgers and Hammerstein's "I Have Dreamed" from *The King and I*. Did Sinatra know that Richard Rodgers was Nixon's favorite composer? Did he know that next to *South Pacific*, the president's favorite musical was *The King and I*? Nixon would definitely know the song; he saw the theatrical version several times in New York City and, only six months before, had screened the movie at Camp David.

Respectful of Richard Rodgers's beautiful melody, the song opens in restrained fashion: flute arabesques, underpinned by a plucked-harp-and-bass-violin figure, introduce Sinatra's low register baritone, and woodwinds join the flutes atop a soft string pillow. Given the song's origin, Nelson's harmonies suggest the Orient. The strings commence to sweep and swirl as Frank modulates to his medium register voice, and then comes the dramatic first line of the bridge: "In these dreams, I have loved you so."

Tension builds, strings and French horns roil, the end is near, but, no, a return to that memorable first bridge line. Frank now in his best, dare say, operatic voice builds to the climatic symphonic ending—symbols clash, trumpets blare, high-pitched strings sing, and the Warner Brothers picture comes to "The End." Whew!

Nelson here, as he did on most of the album's songs, broke his own rule of not reaching orchestral climax at the end of the piece. No doubt, he had in mind the Broadway theatrical stage and the high-drama Hollywood soundstage (where the album was recorded).

Perhaps feeling a mite claustrophobic in the filled-to-capacity East Room, Sinatra remarked, "I feel like I'm blocking a parade or something up here," referring more to the Marine Orchestra that surrounded him than the dignitaries and guests assembled in front of him. The remark drew the expected laughter. Back to the show: "Ah, yes, here's Rodgers and Hammerstein and Nelson Riddle."

With that, Frank sang the supremely gorgeous "I Have Dreamed." The undersized Marine unit (compared to the seventy-three-piece Hollywood soundstage behemoth on the album) performed admirably. The string section executed Riddle's oriental-sounding countermelody to perfection, as did the entire orchestra on Nelson's exciting over-the-top Tinseltown ending.

As for Frank, his performance is a notch below that on the album. Perhaps, he was fearful of striving too hard to reach the previously recorded vocal summit and not making it. Three quarters up the mountain is good enough. Quibbles aside, this would still be considered a quality outing for those familiar with the album.

Audience reaction: nothing out of the ordinary—about the same as before. Respectful.

"Fly Me to the Moon"
Arranger Quincy Jones | *It Might as Well Be Swing* | Reprise (1964)

Next up, Bart Howard's "Fly Me to the Moon," from the second Sinatra-Basie album, *It Might as Well Be Swing*, arrangements by Quincy Jones. The first album between Frank and "Splank," arranged by Neal Hefti, retained much of the legendary Basie sound, but this one scored by "Q" had a different feel—tighter and jazzier—and included more contemporary tunes.

Most frequently identified with Sinatra nowadays, this pop standard was introduced by Felicia Sanders on the cabaret circuit in 1954, where it was originally known as "In Other Words." The song was first recorded by Kaye Ballard in 1954 and then by Johnny Mathis in 1956 under the new title "Fly Me to the Moon," the song's first line. Bossa nova versions were heard in the early 1960s before Sinatra claimed it for all time in late 1963.[38]

The song was an obvious choice for Sinatra's East Room inaugural. After all, it was under Nixon's first term that humans first set foot on the moon. U.S. astronauts in space were awakened more than once by Sinatra's recording.

Clearly in touch with the sound of the Count's Second Testament Band—its ensemble power, precision, and, most of all, dynamic range (whisper to shout in three seconds)—Quincy shot the "Moon" in his now-classic arrangement. The song is kicked off by a simple skippin' down the sidewalk ta-tata/ta-tata beat from drummer Sonny Payne, which is carried throughout (later by the brass and reed sections). Bassist George Catlett and solid rhythm guitarist Freddy Green are summoned by a Basie keyboard tinkle as Frank voices the familiar lines "Fly me to the moon / Let me play among the stars."

With the 4/4 rhythm firmly established, the whistling flute of Frank

Wess playfully darts between Sinatra's lines. Then the world-famous sax section joins in as Sonny adds a rim-shot backbeat to emphasize the tempo. And then surprise, it's "Sweets" Edison on muted trumpet adding some pepper to the mix. The brass is marshaled by a patented Sonny Payne drum break—a rapid fire, increasing-volume bam-bam-bam—a blast by the full band, and then quiet.

Through all these goings-on, Frank as always sings true to the lyrics. Verse and chorus complete, he takes a break as the band plays its version close to the melody. A Sonny drum break and Frank is reintroduced for the second run-through. This time the saxes swing, and the brass punch repetitively to recreate the skipping ta-tata/ta-tata rhythm Sonny had established at the start. Another escalating bam-bam-bam drum break by Sonny and the full ensemble roars as Sinatra shouts out the famed closing:

In other words
Ba-da da-dada da [band roaring]
In other words
[silence]
I loooove
splank splank splank [who else but Basie]
YOU!

Quincy's experience arranging the *It Might as Well Be Swing* album was markedly different from that of Nelson Riddle. Sinatra was not as involved. In Q's words:

We started to talk about the tunes. And it's very funny the way songs come up. I'd suggest one, and he'd suggest a couple, and you keep thinking them up and you just come up with a real nice mix. . . .

[Jones arranged most of the songs in Hollywood.] I moved in at Warner Bros. in Dean Martin's dressing room while Frank was next door, shooting the picture [*None but the Brave*] . . . I locked myself there for a week and kept writing. I fell asleep late Sunday night and then on Monday morning I looked up and there's Frank in a military uniform [costume from the film], asking me how I wanted my eggs. He was cooking breakfast![39]

Taking a break before flying to the moon, Sinatra engaged the East Room audience in some stage patter accompanied by a snappy little tune by the piano trio—Bill Miller (piano), Dave Wundrow (bass), and Mark Sunkett (drums).

This next song I've been singing for quite a few years. And . . . during the time of one of our space shots, like all of us in the country, I was watching the television report on it, and lo and behold in the middle of the reporting and the pictures that were coming through, I heard myself singing this song from up there [points overhead].

And I want to tell you it was quite a thrill. It really was. I've been to some altitudes before but never that high, never that high. [Laughter.] It was a great honor, too, to have them choose this song.

Soliloquy over, the bouncy tune morphed into "Moon" as Frank sang the opening lines nearly everybody on planet Earth knew by heart. Working off Quincy Jones's charts, the Marine Orchestra did its best to mimic the Basie aggregation. The flautist darted in and out like Frank Wess; the drummer executed a Sonny Payne drum break; and the strings, an afterthought on the original recording, are in the mix, live, as Q would have wanted them. The sax and trumpet sections traded punches to recreate that skippin' feel before they joined forces at the close to shout encouragement to their star vocalist, who at the end, hummed Count's signature triple splank with a "hmm uh uh hmmm hmmm . . . You!" Audience reaction to this swinger was as before—generous but polite.

"Try a Little Tenderness"
Arranger Nelson Riddle | *Nice and Easy* | Capitol (1960)

In addition to key collaborators Nelson Riddle and pianist Bill Miller, Frank also brought to the nation's capital his favorite guitarist, Al Viola. The two first met when Al, as a member of the Page Cavanaugh Trio, backed Sinatra on two singles for Columbia in 1946. Al later hooked up with Sinatra in the mid-1950s and stayed with him throughout his career, working on most of his Las Vegas and concert appearances and on his TV specials and album recordings (five for Capitol and all but two for Reprise). Most would know his movie soundtrack work (*West Side Story*, *Dr. Zhivago*, and *The Godfather*), if not his name.[40]

At the White House, Frank gave a lengthy introduction to the next number:

> I would like to relate to you, Mr. President, a wonderful thing that happened to me right after rehearsal [this afternoon]. I was sitting in the greenroom and one of the young men came in and said, "Mr. Sinatra, my father is a great fan of yours." And that was thrilling to begin with! [Laughter.] But, really, seriously, he was really sweet. He said he had a stack of records that high [extends arm, knee high off the floor], and I said, "That's wonderful! It's very nice—except for that I made a stack of records *that* high [raises his arm above his head] [More laughter.] It's true. It happened this afternoon!
>
> We'd like to do something for all the ladies in the room, or all the ladies all over the world. A very pretty song, I guess some forty years old . . . We brought along with us from California one of the finest guitar players in [Nixon's birthplace] Whittier. [Laughter.] Mr. Viola is his name—Mr. Vi-o-la [said in a familiar, swaggering sort of way]. Another Italian gentleman. [Al strummed a chorded introduction on his lap-held acoustic guitar.] When you finish fooling around, I'm ready to go, you know. I don't dig those Wagnerian introductions [said in jest].

Accompanied only by Al's guitar, Sinatra sang a rather touching "Try a Little Tenderness," a song he had recorded first on his initial concept album, *The Voice of Frank Sinatra* in 1946, and then again in 1960 on the *Nice 'n' Easy* album, backed by Riddle's strings and flutes. This version is laid back, at times almost spoken instead of sung, sort of like a rehearsal run-through for the benefit of his guitarist. Very unlike Sinatra, but then again, maybe not. Ever the dramatist, Frank could have felt the song deserved a low-key delivery aimed, as he said, at all the women in the room and their common need for a little salve from their men every once in a while to soothe their concerns and unmet wants.

At the conclusion, the White House crowd gave the duo more than its due, spurred on by the singer's clapping and call for Mr. Viola to take a bow. The "Tenderness" vocal/guitar duet was a rare treat for those in the East Room that night—although most would not have realized it. While the two had played the song together in duet many times before in concert, it had never (and has never) been captured on record. Al and Frank performed it again in a benefit concert on September 27, 1979, in a most majestic setting beneath the dramatically lit Pyramids and Sphinx. Frank dedicated the song to Mrs. Sadat, wife of Egyptian President Anwar Sadat, who had only recently signed a peace deal with Israel.[41]

"Ol' Man River"
Arranger Nelson Riddle | *The Concert Sinatra* | Reprise (1963)

Surely, when one thinks of "Ol' Man River," that venerable Hammerstein and Kern song from *Showboat* (1927), someone other than Ol' Blue Eyes comes to mind—perhaps a large, broad shouldered, and barrelchested man, with a voice as deep and resonant as Carlsbad Caverns. But Frank Sinatra? His *Concert Sinatra* version is a belief changer.

In his *Sessions with Sinatra*, Charles Granata has this to say:

Sinatra demonstrated an impressive range . . . on "Ol' Man

River," which he sings wide open. But after the verse, which is sung with a fairly bright vocal inflection, Sinatra darkens the hue, instantly highlighting the seriousness of the song. Inspired by the powerful lyrics and Riddle's opulent textural setting, Sinatra ponders each syllable, searching to extract every gradation of color possible. Here his acting skills serve him well. Near the finale he reaches the line:

You get a little drunk and you lands in jaiiiiiiiiillllllllllllllllll

And without pause, slides into the next phrase:

I . . . gets . . . weary . . .

then plummets way down, lower than you've ever heard him go, and then half an octave lower than *that*. Finally, without the slightest trace of vibrato, he smoothes it out, seamlessly flowing into the finale:

and sick of tryin' . . . I'm tired of livin', but I'm scared of dyin' . . . and old man river, he just keeps rollin' along.

As Sinatra blazes across the final notes, the strings soar, the brass screams, and the percussion pounds, bringing the vocal and the instrumental crescendos to a dramatic close. This ending powerfully captures the breadth of Sinatra's vocal range and the strength of his voice . . . With the line "Oh, I gets weary" comes, in my opinion, the most riveting moment of his entire recording career.[42]

Sinatra recorded numerous songs that have become forever associated with him, and him alone. His version of "River" does not rise to that level but comes awfully close, although Sinatra's longtime percussionist Emil Richards might disagree:

Frank used to do one thing that really freaked me out . . . He would hold his hands behind his back as if he were handcuffed, pull his shoulders forward, or his chest forward and his shoulders back to get more air. [Then he'd sing the last line without pausing for a breath.] I tried doing that along with him a couple of times, and it was almost impossible. But he did it with one breath, and it was so effective, it gave me chills or made me cry every time.[43]

Some might consider this selection a bit risky for a White House debut after a spell of semi-retirement, but Frank obviously did not. In preparation for his big night, he left nothing to chance. To get his voice back in shape, the fifty-six-year-old legend subjected himself to a rigorous program of breathing exercises and vocal scales. (No word on running track or taking laps in pools.) Sinatra introduced the song quietly to set the mood:

From the finer music in the American repertoire, I'd like to do something by the late Oscar Hammerstein and Jerome Kern— one of the traditional songs that has come through the years unscathed and becomes more mellow as the years go on.

He didn't name the song, and it can be assumed many in the audience didn't know what it was even after several lines of the verse had been sung, given Frank's placid delivery and the spare solo piano accompaniment by Bill Miller. The emotional content would inexorably grow as the words became more familiar. Building, building to the point where the singer would attempt to defy gravity and leap the wide gorge, exhibiting superhuman breath control as he slid out of "jaiiiiiiiiillllllllllllllllll" to "I gets weary" without a fault. The strings entered at this critical juncture to highlight the tension, and the rest of the orchestra soon followed as Riddle, the Marine Orchestra, and Sinatra in full operatic mode did their damnedest to match the Hollywood soundstage-orchestra ending achieved on *The Concert Sinatra* album.

They succeeded. The two-hundred-plus guests, finally awakened, began clapping even before the long last note had concluded. They rose en masse to give a standing ovation, the longest of the evening. President Nixon was the first on his feet. Frank's preparation reaped dividends.

The singer tried to tamp down the enthusiastic response: "You're very kind," and "Oh, come on," in addition to his usual thank-yous. Italians and Italian Americans in the audience had to be pleased. A favorite son had made them proud.

"I've Got the World on a String"
Arranger Nelson Riddle | Single Release | Capitol (1953)

After the emotional outpouring died down and the East Room crowd settled back in their seats, Frank thanked them again and said, "We'll change the mood a little bit now."

For his mood changer, Frank picked the song that started it all for both him and Nelson some twenty years before, Harold Arlen's "I've Got the World on a String." More than any other song, Sinatra would open club dates and concerts with this number for the rest of his life. A sentimental, nostalgic pick perhaps, but oh so appropriate. It was the song that led Frank, upon first hearing it on playback, to exclaim: "Jesus Christ, I'm back. I'm back, baby, I'm back."

The singer in good voice from his "Ol' Man River" workout and his backup band in total synchronization, the medium-up tempo "String" proved to be an unabashed finger-snapping swinger. This rendition would make a good selection for a blindfold test. It's hard to imagine many jazz critics or aficionados nailing this one. Most would place the recording in the 1950s, backed by a Nelson Riddle studio orchestra or even Count Basie, and nary a one would guess it was the Marine Orchestra backing Ol' Blue Eyes at the White House in 1973. It's that good.

When Sinatra concluded, the crowd applauded wildly again but remained in their seats.

"That's America to Me"
Arranger Nelson Riddle | Single Release (1945)

Before the final number, Frank spent a few minutes expressing his gratitude:

> I begin by telling you that, when I was a small boy from New Jersey, I thought it would be a great boot if I could get a long-distance glimpse of my mayor in a parade . . . so that, you know, after all of these many years, to be here in this great house and entertaining my president and my vice president and their guests, is quite a boot to me! I . . . hmm, it's difficult to put into words, except that I am honored, and I am privileged to be here.
>
> Today during the rehearsal I was looking at the two magnificent paintings of President Washington and Mrs. Washington [on the East Room wall], and thought about what a marvelous dignity has come from this one particular man up through the years, all the way down now to this moment with our own president, the dignity that has been given to the office . . . and it makes me very proud of my country. I love my country, as we all do . . . and that's just it, I thank you, Mr. President, for inviting me here and to perform for you. [Extensive applause.] And, of course, I can't omit the fact that I am also performing for the wonderful prime minister of my father's country. [Applause.]

Sinatra then launched into "That's America to Me," a patriotic anthem originally titled "The House I Live In," which he sang in an award-winning short film of the same name back in 1945. The "House" is a metaphor for the country, and the lyrics, written in 1943 by Abel Meeropol, are a plea for racial and ethnic tolerance. Meeropol also wrote "Strange Fruit," which sketched the horrors of lynching and became Billie Holiday's signature song. While "America" has been and continues to be sung by many famous artists, it is most often associated with Sinatra, another of his signature songs. Deservedly so. No matter his

Frank Sinatra (*center*) following his first performance at the White House, with Prime Minister and Mrs. Andreotti (*left*) and President and Mrs. Nixon (*right*).

national politics, Frank was a steadfast liberal on the matter of civil rights. In practice, he lectured for tolerance and bent over backwards to hire black musicians for all his record dates.[44]

His White House performance of "America" stands as one of his best. He benefited immensely from the solid accompaniment provided by the Marine Orchestra, to be expected given the numerous numbers with patriotic themes in their book.

As the audience embraced the singer with another round of tumultuous applause, the Nixons and the Andreottis went up to Sinatra and stood beside him for photographs. A few seconds later, they were joined by the Agnews. The president then went to the microphone to praise Sinatra:

> Mr. Prime Minister and our distinguished guests [Nixon points in the direction of Frank] I want you to hear this, Frank, don't leave. Those of us who have had the privilege of being in this room have heard many great performers, and we are always very privileged to hear them, particularly in this room. But once in a while, not always, once in a while, there is a moment when there

is magic in the room, and a great performer, a great singer, entertainer, is able to capture and move us all. And Frank Sinatra tonight has done that. We thank him.

At that point, according to *Washington Post* reporter Donnie Radcliffe,

Sinatra slipped around to the side of the bandstand and stood quietly with tears welled in his eyes as the Nixons and their guests passed by.

"Lovely words, sir," Sinatra told the President. "See you very soon."

"July," said the President. "I've got to practice. I haven't played (golf) for a year."

While the Nixons escorted their guests to the North Portico, Sinatra slipped through the Green Room in what appeared to be an effort to avoid reporters in his way. When one asked him why he had chosen those songs, the spell of the evening's "magic" was broken.

"How else could I put a program together," snapped Sinatra, moving quickly away. Nearby, on what appeared to be a rescue mission, stood White House Press Secretary Ron Zeigler who whisked him through the Blue and Red Rooms into the Great Hall and an adjoining anteroom, where an elevator was to take him to the Nixon family quarters.

Zeigler explained later that the President had invited Sinatra upstairs for a chat.[45]

What a shame Sinatra chose to dismiss the reporter's question. It would have been nice to hear why he performed the songs he did. Nelson's charts were used on seven of the ten songs, and Frank didn't include anything recorded after 1964 from his last eleven albums—no "That's Life," "My Way," "Summer Wind," or "Strangers in the Night." It would have been nice to hear Frank's comments about Nelson, Bill

Miller, and Al Viola, beyond the onstage acknowledgments. Indeed, to also hear about the Marine Orchestra that accompanied him. After all, the program was as much about them as it was about him.

Two years before, Frank had privately acknowledged Nelson's contributions when he sent him a copy of the Francis Albert Sinatra Tribute in the Congressional Record of 1971 with a note signed on his stationery: "Dear Nelson: You are as much a part of what was said about me by these great men in the Senate . . . I wanted you to have a copy."[46]

With his first White House gig under his belt and his "comeback" fully under way, Frank got busy. That September, he released the appropriately titled *Ol' Blue Eyes Is Back*, and the following March he appeared at Madison Square Garden in a huge affair billed as the Main Event, where he sang "I've Got You Under My Skin" and "That's America to Me." Four years after that, at his Radio City Music Hall opening, he sang for the first time his ultimate signature closer "New York, New York" and thereafter at concert after concert into the 1990s.

Nelson never recorded with Frank again, although they did an occasional TV special and concert together. In 1985, they had both agreed to return to the studio to record some songs that Frank had missed along the way. Sadly, the fates intervened. Riddle died that October.[47]

As previously mentioned, five members of the Bob Crosby Bob Cats stepped upon the East Room stage during the Nixon administration (Butterfield, Conniff, Haggart, Lawson, and Miller). Make it six: Nelson Riddle arranged for the Bob Cats band during 1946–47.[48]

Three days after Frank's starring role at the White House, the president, obviously smitten with his new golfing buddy, viewed *Some Come Running*, the first of six Sinatra movies he would screen before leaving office sixteen months later. The last film he would see in office was his all-time favorite *Around the World in 80 Days*, in which Frank had a bit part as a saloon singer.[49]

Twenty-three days after the White House event, pal Richard Nixon addressed a letter to Frank:

Once in a great while, a performer manages to hold everyone in the audience spellbound. You did just that during your appearance at the April 17 dinner for Prime Minister Andreotti. The selections which were included in your program were those which many of us have associated with you over the years, and that evening you made them sound even better than ever! Incidentally, your graciousness in rehearsing before the members of the White House staff really made their day—and some of the young ladies present were nearly walking on air when they returned to their desks.

Sincerely, Richard Nixon[50]

Spiro T. Agnew resigned from the vice presidency six months later after pleading no contest to criminal charges of tax evasion and money laundering while governor of Maryland. He was fined $100,000 and given a three-year probation. Through it all, Frank maintained his loyalty, supporting Agnew both publicly and privately.

His political conversion complete, Frank remained a red-blooded Republican for the remainder of his life, notably supporting his Hollywood buddy Ronald Reagan for president. He raised funds and organized inaugural galas for Reagan in 1981 and 1985 (hiring Nelson Riddle to arrange and conduct the orchestra as he did twenty years prior for JFK) and was a frequent visitor at the White House in both terms, as an entertainer (three times) as well as a guest. He even served as White House impresario for a spell, à la Paul Keyes! Finally, in 1985, President Reagan awarded Sinatra the Medal of Freedom—knighthood, at long last.

It should come as no surprise when George Herbert Walker Bush was elected president in November 1988 that Frank Sinatra would be at the inaugural festivities the following January—as a performer only, however.[51]

Mt. Rushmore doesn't have the room to display all of Sinatra's signature songs and classic albums. In its stead, thankfully, we have the Grammy Hall of Fame, which holds these Ol' Blue Eyes songs: "I've

Got You Under My Skin" (1998), "The House I Live In" (1998), "I've Got the World on a String," (2004), and "One for My Baby" (2005), and his albums *In the Wee Small Hours* (1984), *Only the Lonely* (1998), *Songs for Swingin' Lovers* (2000), and *Come Fly with Me* (2004).

Marine Orchestra Roster
April 17, 1973 | Italian Prime Minister Andreotti Musicale

Flute: Leslie Hunt
Oboe: John Renzi
Bassoon: Robert Kalman
Clarinet: Timothy Foley (retired director of the Marine Band), Vincent Ognibene (possibly bass clarinet), Craig Nordstrom (also sax), Dennis Burian (retired asst. director of the Marine Band)
Sax: Errol Schlabach. Ronald Hockett, Walter Blauvelt
Trumpet: Kenneth Emenheiser, John Wright, James Redfield, J. Carlton Rowe
Horn: James Basta
Trombone: Dale Weaver, Mitchell Rausch, James Crowe, Thomas Wilson
Percussion: Mark Sunkett
Violin: Peter Tramontana (concertmaster), Joseph Gatwood, Robert Zelnick, Geoffrey Maingart, Benjamin Sanger, Bryan Johnson
Viola: George Woshakiwsky, Jerome Guilbeau
Cello: Paul DeBourg, James McWhorter
Bass: Dave Wundrow
Piano: Tony Matarrese
Harp: James Pinkerton

Personnel listed in seating order (i.e., 1st trumpet, 2nd trumpet, etc.)

Information courtesy of Gunnery Sergeant, USMC, Kira Wharton, Assistant Chief Librarian/Historian, U.S. Marine Band, Washington, DC.

Billy Taylor Trio

*Nixon was extremely supportive of jazz and made me
feel most comfortable—and I'm a registered Democrat!*
—Billy Taylor

October 9, 1973 | Ivory Coast President Houphouët-Boigny Dinner

BILLY "BT" TAYLOR HAD APPEARED twice at the White House—first
as a guest pianist at the Ellington all-star seventieth-birthday bash
in April 1969, and then as a performer and musical conductor for the
David Frost Christmas show in December 1970. So Taylor was a known
quantity and a safe choice for providing the after-dinner entertainment
for the state visit of President Houphouët-Boigny of Ivory Coast.

Taylor's third appearance on the East Room riser resulted from his
talent, of course, but also from a shift in internal entertainment-booking
policy: from the West Wing to the East Wing, from the president to
the First Lady. Pressures had been mounting, both within and outside
the White House, over the questionable entertainment choices made by
the president's designated impresario, his longtime friend Paul Keyes,
the TV executive.

Once Keyes took over the White House talent-booking function in
early 1973, according to a *Washington Post* article by Donnie Radcliffe:

"He just kind of took over," recalled a White House staffer. From then on Keyes became the point man on decisions about who would and would not entertain at the White House. He lined up performers for seven White House events from his Los Angeles office and at times his choices were not known by even the White House staff members until a few days before the event.

Working through the West Wing of the White House, the President's side, rather than Mrs. Nixon's East Wing [where the social secretary's office was housed], Keyes bypassed efforts to match entertainers with the honored guests' preferences. Unlike in the past, both under President Johnson and in the first term of President Nixon, no embassies were consulted. Keyes simply matched up visitors with a Hollywood star who was available at the moment, according to a White House aide.[1]

Keyes first matched Frank Sinatra with Italian President Andreotti (assist to Nixon and Vice President Agnew), then paired the pop-duo Carpenters with German Chancellor Brandt; Bob Hope and company with the Vietnam POWs; balladeer Johnny Mathis with Liberian President Tolbert; Johnny Mann Singers with Soviet Premier Breshnev; and singer Tony Martin with the Shah of Iran. During the Shah's first visit to the Nixon White House in 1969, he fared a lot better, drawing the Modern Jazz Quartet.

Starting with the dinner Nixon gave for the Vietnam POW families that featured a Who's Who of mostly Hollywood Republican supporters (Roy Acuff, Edgar Bergen, Vic Damone, Sammy Davis Jr., Connie Francis, Phyllis Diller, Joey Heatherton, Bob Hope, Ricardo Montalban, Jimmy Stewart, and John Wayne), Keyes described his talent-scouting efforts thus:

"I blindly took the Pentagon's list of entertainers who had been in Vietnam and from it built the best variety show I'd ever done. Believe me, I had stars begging to get in. It was . . . the highlight of my life."

Keyes's producing formula for the POWs was patriotism and

variety. For the [other] dinners it was simple: either patriotism and soft rock (Carpenters and the Johnny Mann Singers) or patriotism and plaintive (Frank Sinatra) or maybe just romantic and bouncy (Johnny Mathis and Tony Martin).[2]

And what did *Washington Star* society reporter Betty Beale think of all this? Her headline five days after the Martin event tells all:

LOWBROW ENTERTAINMENT AT THE WHITE HOUSE
With the deglamorization of the Nixon White House by the Watergate scandal [at this point Nixon aides Dean, Haldeman, and Ehrlichman had resigned, Dean had testified before Congress, and the Oval Office tapes had just been revealed], the President and First Lady hardly need the reputation this administration has been getting for lowbrow state entertainment.

To go from the Metropolitan's Dorothy Kirsten, Birgit Nillson and Roberta Peters or [classical pianist] Van Cliburn to Las Vegas performer Tony Martin in one administration is not unlike the contrast between the President's standing after rapprochement with Red China compared to his position today.

It seems unlikely that Their Imperial Majesties, the Shahanshah and Empress of Iran, people who have the lifetime privilege of witnessing or summoning the finest artists in the world—could have been charmed, even for one minute, with such an unsophisticated performer as [Tony] Martin.[3]

Hollywood fatigue had enveloped the East Wing as well. Two days after Martin cracked, "Cole Porter was a musician as a result of not becoming a lawyer—and that's good these days," the First Lady decided enough already with the showbiz, and the press was duly informed:

From now on, an advisory committee, including National Endowment for the Arts [NEA] Chairman Nancy Hanks, will suggest "more balanced" entertainment for state functions in an effort to make the White House a showcase of what's best today among American classical and popular artists, including musical as well as theatrical arts.

Final authority will be with the First Lady Pat Nixon, who, with her daughter Julie Eisenhower, imposed the new policy in reaction to Tuesday night's entertainment by singer Tony Martin for the Shah of Iran.[4]

The social secretary's office was back in business as the procurer of talent (as far as the public would know), with NEA chair Hanks in the advisor's seat. A major beneficiary of this new policy would be jazz pianist Billy Taylor.

Ms. Hanks first booked duo pianists Richard and Francis Hadden for Prime Minister Bhutto of Pakistan on September 18—an easy sell if there ever was one. The husband-and-wife team had been the first Westerners to perform in China in modern times as a result of Nixon's recognition of the isolated nation the previous year. Next up, another easy sell: Billy Taylor, who not only had appeared twice for Nixon, but had also been appointed by the president the previous September to a six-year membership on the National Council on the Arts. Only four other jazz luminaries have been so appointed in its fifty-year history—Duke Ellington by President Johnson in 1968; conductor Gunther Schuller by Nixon in 1974; bandleader/educator David Baker by Ronald Reagan in 1987; and drummer Chico Hamilton by George W. Bush in 2006.

Hanks opened the bidding on August 9 in a letter to Social Secretary Nancy Winchester:

The attached article ["Okay, Billy"] in [the August 6, 1973, issue of] Time made me think of you and Helen [Smith] and the White House entertainment. [Assistant Michael Straight] and I would put Billy Taylor very high on your list of possibilities.[5]

Lucy responded in a letter dated August 13:

Billy Taylor is a magnificent suggestion for White House entertainment. He was a part of the Duke Ellington birthday party
and would be excellent to perform again on his own. Many
thanks for your recommendation.

Any day now the Nixons will go to California—we hope—
and we will scatter to the winds [for summer holiday]. Helen and
I would like very much to meet with you and Michael when we
all return to Washington, probably after Labor Day.[6]

According to Billy,

Nixon really perceived the arts as non-political. He saw the arts
as something that should be encouraged and nurtured and in
which the government should be the junior partner. He was
extremely supportive of jazz and made me feel most comfortable—and I'm a registered Democrat![7]

True, as the record indicates, Nixon was supportive of jazz, but like
everything else, he used the arts as a political tool to reward and culti-
vate supporters, and Billy was a well-known jazzman (his national TV
exposure on the *The David Frost Show* was second to no other jazz personality at the time), well respected, and influential. Billy was a shoo-in
"to perform again on his own." It was just a matter of when.

Sometime in September, most likely the second week, Billy was invited to provide the after-dinner entertainment for President Houphouët-
Boigny of La Côte d'Ivoire (Ivory Coast); it was the African monarch's
third visit to the United States. In 1962 JFK hosted a State Dinner for
the Ivory Coast leader with the entertainment provided by the American Ballet Theatre, and in 1967 LBJ feted him with a luncheon.[8]

Billy quickly notified his trio mates (Bobby Thomas and Buster
Williams), decided on a program (which would include a fresh composition in honor of the visiting dignitary from western Africa), and

rushed the song list to the social secretary's office, where it would be calligraphically rendered for the tasseled program booklet—the guest's memento of the evening.

A virtual Who's Who of jazz percussionists have flowed through BT's trio over the years—Grady Tate, Ed Thigpen, Winard Harper all come to mind—but none had a longer association than Robert "Bobby" Thomas, who was with him on and off in the early '70s to the mid-'90s. A solid and versatile drummer, who put real swing into contemporary rhythms, Bobby accompanied Billy at his next White House gig that took place a year and a half later under President Ford. Much appreciated by pianists as well as his drummer students, inexplicably, Thomas was another one of those below-the-radar timekeepers.[9]

BT attracted many top-flight bassists as well: Doug Watkins, Bob Cranshaw, Ben Tucker, Victor Gaskin, to name a few, and for a short time, Charles A. Williams Jr., better known as Buster Williams.[10] In the fall of 1973, Buster was on the verge of becoming known to the wider jazz audience. He had paid his dues. As a teenager, he had accompanied saxophonist legends Gene Ammons and Sonny Stitt, and in his mid-twenties, he backed a string of outstanding female jazz vocalists—Dakota Staton, Betty Carter, Sarah Vaughan, and Nancy Wilson—before joining the Herbie Hancock Sextet during their critically acclaimed 1969–1972 period. It's doubtful that anyone in the East Room audience that night elbowed their neighbor and said, "Hey look, Billy's got Buster on bass tonight." Several decades later, such a comment would have been more likely; Buster had arrived by then, on nearly every jazz fan's list of premier jazz bassists.

Four and a half years prior, at the White House all-star gathering for Duke Ellington, Billy paid tribute to the maestro by playing three of Duke's compositions. For his own star turn on the East Room riser, Billy chose to honor jazz pianist/composers as well: himself appropriately (on five of the eight numbers), George Gershwin, Oscar Peterson, and Fats Waller.[11] Billy would again revisit this theme sixteen years later, in the repertoire selected for his duo piano concert tour with jazz pianist Ramsey Lewis and on their 1990 album *We Meet Again* (Columbia).

Once seated at the White House grand piano on the riser in front of the seated dignitaries and invited guests after the state dinner, BT opened with George Gershwin's "They Can't Take That Away from Me," from the Fred Astaire/Ginger Rodgers film *Shall We Dance?* Here, we can give an assist to lyricist brother Ira for the melody. George had "started out with a brief, four-note phrase, but Ira pleaded, 'George, can you just give me two more notes?' George did and gave Ira the chance to craft a catalog of understated, even back-handed compliments: 'The way you wear *your hat* . . . The way you sing *off key.*'"[12]

No one would dare take these wry sentiments away from Fred after he sang them to Ginger but . . . although the song was nominated for an Oscar, it lost. Billy's upbeat, bouncy treatment of the familiar Gershwin tune was quite appropriate for an opening number. Over the years, BT committed eight different Gershwin songs to record.[13]

Billy followed the Gershwin tune with his own composition: "Paraphrase," a medium up-tempo finger-snapper. His solo consisted of churlish single note runs interspersed with rollicking block-chord intervals. As for the tune's melody, it's a paraphrase all right, probably something BT had heard at church, a gospel lick he took to the nearest basement jazz club, and then worked it over, secularized it, and gave it a nice bluesy feel, as can be heard on the *It's a Matter of Pride* (GRP Records, 2012).

For his second tribute, Billy chose a piece from the *Canadiana Suite* by jazz piano great Oscar Peterson, the closest exponent of Art Tatum in modern jazz, who along with Fats Waller, had the most influence on Taylor's early playing style. BT had this to say about him:

[Oscar Peterson] is not only a virtuoso pianist, he's a remarkable musician. The thing I admire about him is that he is always growing. His phenomenal facility sometimes gets in the way of people's listening, but he has a big heart and he plays beautiful things.[14]

First recorded in 1964, the eight-part *Suite* represented Oscar's first substantial venture as a composer, its pieces figuratively tracing a journey from the Atlantic coast westward to British Columbia, where the Rocky Mountains plunge into the Pacific. It was a description of the second stop on the journey, the "Laurentides Waltz," that the 174 guests heard in the East Room that night. Peterson's biographer Gene Lees characterized the piece in this way:

> [This piece] projects Oscar's impressions of the Laurentians, the pine-covered rolling mountain range of Quebec, which begins thirty miles north of [Oscar's birthplace] in Montreal. *Laurentides* is the French name for the range . . . "I've been in the Laurentians mostly in the skiing season," Oscar said, "and it's always been a happy, swinging kind of place, with a crisp effect. This is the most seasonal section of the suite—it is supposed to be a winter scene that you're facing" . . . His brilliant piano runs may evoke the weaving line of a descending skier for some; I see them in the wings of spray from the water ski.[15]

Most jazz waltzes are downright infectious, swing like hell, and whistle through your mind the whole day through. "Laurentides Waltz" is different. Billy Taylor's version, like Peterson's, is less catchy than most jazz excursions into the 3/4 (or 5/4 or 6/8) realm. Yet the piece is more sweeping and grandiose than most, majestic like its namesake mountain range. The 1-2-3 feel is there, but subtle, somewhat overwhelmed by the multinoted, weaving melodic line. Still, overall, it casts a hypnotic spell, as can be heard on the *Dr. T album* (GRP Records, 1993). BT's version is strikingly similar to OP's, down to the introductory unaccompanied piano solo—indeed, a true homage.

Billy interspersed another of his original compositions, the pretty ballad "Somewhere Soon," which can be heard on *OK Billy!* (Bell Records, 1970), accompanied by *The David Frost Show* band, and on *We Meet Again* (Columbia, 1990), in tandem with pianist Ramsey Lewis.

Next up, a tribute to another early piano influence, Thomas "Fats"

Waller. In his *Jazz Piano: A Jazz History*, Taylor rhapsodized about the importance of Waller to his life:

> My uncle Robert responded to my obvious fascination with jazz and introduced me to the records of two of the most important musical influences of my life: Fats Waller and Art Tatum. As great as Fats Waller's records are pianistically, his in person playing was even better. Once in the mid-thirties I sat at the Lincoln Theatre in Washington, D.C., for every show on a Friday, Saturday, and Sunday because Waller was making a rare appearance as a soloist. He played both the piano and the organ, and his performances were, to say the least, overwhelming. His virtuosity, his touch, his improvisation were unlike anything I have heard before. He was a master jazz artist and the most exciting stride pianist I ever heard. Even Tatum, who was a superlative stride pianist, used to say, "Fats Waller, that's where I come from."[16]

To cognoscenti, Waller is known as the preeminent stride pianist, surpassing the likes of James P. Johnson and Willy "the Lion" Smith. To the public, Fats is known as the prodigious composer of stomping hits such as "Ain't Misbehavin'," "Honeysuckle Rose," "All That Meat and No Potatoes," and "The Joint Is Jumpin'." For his tribute, Billy chose a less known but more elegant number, one he had probably committed to memory and practiced years ago, the extremely catchy "Jitterbug Waltz." Waller composed this instrumental tune late in his career, sometime in 1941, as his son Maurice tells it:

Dad arrived in New York [City] at three in the morning. Dad raced up the stairs while [band manager] Buster warmed up the organ.

"Leave the boy alone. Let him sleep," I could hear my mother say.

"No, no. He's gotta hear this. It's a killer-diller!" Dad grabbed my robe, hustled me out of bed, and brought me downstairs.

He sat at the organ and played "Jitterbug Waltz" with great gusto. A tremendous smile of self-satisfaction wrapped around his happy face.

"What do you think of that, Maurice?" he asked. But there wasn't a chance to reply before he answered himself. "Good as anything Gershwin's ever written." I thought so too, but I never had the chance to tell him. [Waller passed in late 1943].[17]

Another tale, probably apocryphal, claims that Fats composed the waltz in response to one of his son's piano exercises—an entirely believable story because its two-handed "Jack-and-Jill tumble down the hill" piano run evokes a piano duo, one desperately trying to keep up with the other.

"Jitterbug" was published and recorded by Waller in 1942, and unlike the "Laurentides Waltz" Taylor played earlier in the evening, this one—with its unforgettable, skittery chromatic fall—would have stuck in the mind of all who heard it—most likely forever. Too bad BT did not record this number; it could have taken a respected place among the many other recorded versions.

In his 2005 book, *The Fifty Greatest Jazz Pianists of All Time*, Gene Rizzo ranked Billy Taylor number seventeen on the list. Of note, Oscar Peterson got the top spot, Art Tatum polled fourth, Fats Waller thirty-first, and indirect-influence Bud Powell third. Obviously, Billy chose his idols well.[18]

Billy closed out his set with three of his own compositions, beginning with "Theodora," a beautiful, quiet ballad he wrote and named for his wife. He introduced the song at a Town Hall concert in New York City on December 17, 1954:

I actually wrote ["Theodora"] the afternoon of the concert and gave it to Earl [May, the bassist] right before the concert. Even though he had never played it before, he picked it right up. Earl has a great ear and is soft spoken, people don't realize the depth of his playing. He's one of the great ones.[19]

Reviewing the concert, critic Ira Gilter wrote, "This is a sensitive, beautiful piece that shows Billy has a heart for melody as well as a head [jazz slang for a throwaway introduction to improvise on]. Jazz pianist Marian McPartland seconded the view: "Actually I think Billy's best mood is a ballad. He plays some of the most gorgeous ballads I've ever heard."[20]

Indeed, "Theodora" is reminiscent of a late 1930s Broadway tune by Jerome Kern, or Vernon Duke or Richard Rodgers. It conjures up romantic standards like "Blame It on My Youth," "Smoke Gets in Your Eyes," or "Folks Who Live on a Hill," the sort of number pianist Keith Jarrett would record with his Standards Trio. Sure would be interesting to hear what other jazz pianists would do with this song.

It would have been more than a curious omission if Taylor hadn't included his signature song, "I Wish I Knew How It Would Feel to Be Free" in the program.[21] Composed in 1954 for daughter Kim (lyrics by Billy and Dick Dallas added later), the song became a civil rights anthem after jazz singer Nina Simone recorded it in 1967. Since then, the song has been recorded by some fifty artists, including John Denver, the Lighthouse Family, Harry Belafonte, Lena Horne, and Leontyne Price; and featured on the film soundtrack of *Ghosts of Mississippi* (1997), sung over the opening credits by Dianne Faris and by Nina Simone at the end.

"I Wish I Knew" rocketed into the global musical stratosphere when it was incorporated into a controversial Coca-Cola commercial in 2004. The ad was even translated into Spanish and Portugese. The English-language version featured a happy-faced Sharlene Hector of the UK group Basement Jaxx singing the song while walking down a busy street and passing out bottles of Coca-Cola. In the United States, the commercial appeared on *American Idol*, in movie theatres, and at Coca-Cola theme parks. Coke intended their video pitch as a twenty-first-century follow-up to the 1970s ad featuring the Hilltop Singers, who wanted to "teach the world to sing in perfect harmony." But good results don't always follow good intentions. Many deemed the spot overly exploitive of a cherished civil rights anthem.[22]

A special tribute came with the inclusion of the song's artifacts (original manuscript and 45 rpm disc recording by Nina Simone) in the *American Treasures Gallery of the Library of Congress*. "I Wish I Knew" has become—and this is its ultimate honor—the theme song of many school choruses and church choirs. A highlight for Billy, as he later recalled, was hearing "sixth graders who sang it to me when I visited their school."[23]

Clearly, the words are what have propelled "I Wish I Knew" into transcendent territory. Yet even as an instrumental, its weight can still be felt. Just knowing the title and hearing the gospel-inflected lament, with its alternatively mournful and joyous melody over the simple rhythm, as played by the Billy Taylor Trio should do it for most. How many of the president's guests in the East Room that night felt an emotional tug similar to that felt upon hearing other secular hymns from the 1960s like "We Shall Overcome" or "Give Peace a Chance"? It's not known, of course, but judge for yourself: at least five of Billy's albums include a version of the song.[24]

Taylor closed out his eight-song set with "La Côte d'Ivoire," a new composition in honor of Nixon's guest. This number would evolve over the years to become the third movement of Taylor's *Suite for Jazz Piano and Orchestra*. While the tune itself is simple, like many of BT's melodies, it has a West Indies feel, not too surprisingly, given West African emigration patterns. The improvisatory section by contrast is a showcase for Taylor's pianistic talents, which provides numerous clues to his primary influences. Taylor's right hand channels Bud Powell; his left, Art Tatum. But together, they summon the spirit of Fats Waller, the end result being an orchestral approach to jazz piano not found in many contemporary pianists, as can be heard on the *Live at IAJE New York* album (Soundpost Records, 2002).

～

The next day, the newspaper accounts of the dinner focused on the outbreak of hostilities in the Middle East and the doings of the dinner guests, especially those of newly installed Secretary of State Henry

Kissinger. Coverage of the Taylor Trio was therefore minimal (no mention of the backup musicians or numbers played, for example). Incisive as always, *Washington Star*'s Betty Beale scooped the competition with her ho-hum, pithy observations:

> The President's toes were beating time to Billy's trio and the President's face lit up when the drums knocked out a hot beat . . . It was jazz at its best—the kind that made even those devotees of highbrow music, Italian Ambassador and Mrs. Ortona, rave. They were there because starting last summer, three ambassadors of other countries [and their spouses] were being invited to every State Dinner. [The ambassadors of Korea and Romania also attended—not a bad gesture, really. International comity was being served and the East Room chairs were being filled, tasks made more difficult by the Watergate scandal.][25]

Billy Taylor's mother had been in the audience that night (a nice touch), as was Republican supporter and jazz great Lionel Hampton.

Billy Taylor at his third appearance in the East Room. *Left to right*: President Houphouët-Boigny, Mrs. Houphouët-Boigny, Billy Taylor's mother, Billy Taylor, President Nixon, and Mrs. Nixon.

Notably absent was Vice President Agnew, who usually attended the swinging events at the White House. He was unavoidably preoccupied, however. Sixteen hours after Billy took his final bows, Mr. Agnew submitted an official letter to the secretary of state (as required by the Succession Act of 1792) resigning the office of the vice president of the United States. Agnew had pleaded no contest—in effect a guilty plea—to a tax evasion charge in a Baltimore courtroom the day before.[26]

While the political career of Spiro Theodore Agnew had effectively ended, and that of Richard Milhous Nixon would end ten months later, the already accomplished musical career of Billy Taylor had just begun.

In 1975, Mr. Taylor became Dr. William Taylor with his acceptance of his doctoral thesis *The History of Jazz Piano* at the University of Massachusetts. And Billy didn't miss the second presidential tribute to jazz (the first being Nixon's Ellington all-star bash) held on the South Lawn by President Carter in 1978. Billy was in the audience to emcee the First White House Jazz Festival for the NPR Radio Network and was called to the stage after the formal program to accompany, who else but Pearl Bailey.

In 1982 Billy Taylor became art correspondent for the *CBS Sunday Morning* TV show and presented profiles of more than 125 artists, including jazz lights Dave Brubeck, Ella Fitzgerald, and Quincy Jones. He would perform at the White House five more times after Nixon: once for President Ford, twice for President Clinton, and twice for George W. Bush, for a total of eight times. Move over, Pearl Bailey, Billy's matched your executive mansion performance record! And, along with his trio, Billy would make three foreign tours on behalf of the State Department, matching Pearl's record in this regard as well.[27]

President George Herbert Walker Bush slipped a National Medal of Arts ribbon around Dr. Taylor's neck in 1992.[28] The following March, he was appointed jazz advisor to the Kennedy Center, where he inaugurated the Millennium Stage, the annual Mary Lou Williams Jazz Festival of Women, and a regular jazz series in the Center's Terrace Theatre. The academic world took note of the pianist educator as well, bestowing twenty honorary doctorates on Dr. Taylor over his lifetime.

His record of service on behalf of the music he loved often dominates any recitation of his accomplishments, but in the end, Taylor's legacy will be secured by his charming consolidation of the pianists who came before him, to which he added his own rollicking pulse and earthy feelings—to say nothing of his 350-plus compositions—preserved for all time on record.

Pearl Bailey Trio

When you come out here as often as I do, honey,
you just call it the *House*."
—*Pearl Bailey*

March 7, 1974 | Governors Dinner

I N 1974, THE LAST YEAR of the Nixon presidency, the White House
and the nation were mired down in the morass of Watergate. It was
no time for splashy spectacles at the mansion. It was no time to extend
invitations to reluctant entertainers who would jump at the chance to
decline an offer to perform on the nation's premier stage.[1]

Only eight events were held that year: three featured the Army Chorus and one the Naval Academy Glee Club; two films were screened
for the public; and two events brought back favorites: the Nurserymen
Association for the First Lady's birthday, and Pearl Bailey for the governors dinner, which was the highlight of the president's last year in
office (with the possible exception of his final trip to the Soviet Union).

Planning for the governors dinner at the White House to coincide
with their annual two-day March conference in Washington, DC,
began in January. Social Secretary Lucy Winchester jotted a note to
herself: "Be prepared to think about a dinner with entertainment for
the Governors and their wives. Entertainment should be non-classical.
[Possible candidates] would be Sonny and Cher, Debbie Reynolds,

or Lawrence Welk."[2] GOP supporters all, but with many Republican entertainers distancing themselves from the president over Watergate, the safest would be a proven commodity—who better than steadfast loyalist Pearl Bailey.

Along with bassist Milt Hinton and pianist Don Abney, who had accompanied Pearl four years before at the state dinner for the German chancellor, she brought her jazz drummer husband, Louis Bellson.

While not a household jazz name like era drummers Philly Joe Jones, Elvin Jones, Joe Morello, Max Roach, or Tony Williams, Louis Bellson was considered no less a drummer by musicians and critics.[3] Duke Ellington, for whom Bellson played in the early 1950s and again in the '60s, and at Duke's seventieth-birthday East Room affair in 1969, offered the highest praise: "Louis Bellson has all the requirements for perfection in his craft. He is the world's greatest drummer." Master of his drum kit—as his solo on "Caravan" at Duke's birthday party attested—and pioneer of the double-bass-drum set-up, Bellson was considered by many a worthy rival of Buddy Rich, of whom he was most like.

Louis recorded hundreds of albums as a leader, coleader, and sideman with—it would seem—nearly everybody in the business: all the major big bands (Basie, Dorsey, Ellington, Goodman, Herman, and James) and instrumentalists (Armstrong, Carter, Getz, Gillespie, Peterson, and Tatum), and singers (Fitzgerald, Torme, Vaughan, and, of course, wife Pearl, whom he married in 1952).

In terms of recorded output, Bellson was to the drums as rhythm-mate Milt Hinton was to the bass violin, and will likely join the latter in the DownBeat Hall of Fame someday. Incidentally, Milt had this to say about his drummer friend, "He's a very disciplined person. He practices constantly and works hard on his solos. There's no question he's gotten results. He's one of our strongest big band drummers and one of the nicest human beings in the world."[4]

Pearl and her trio had their work cut out for them. The opening act—President Nixon—was less than upbeat; in fact, according to the newspapers the next day, while the guests were still in the State Dining Room (prior to the evening's entertainment), Nixon delivered a serious, wide-ranging discourse on U.S. foreign policy that lasted some thirty minutes.[5] Not exactly the kind of warm-up an entertainer would want to spark a night of merriment. But as usual, Ms. Bailey would be up to the task. Once the governors and their spouses, along with the other guests, settled in their East Room chairs, the president introduced the headliner, as always, without notes:

> Well, Ladies and Gentlemen, the governors conference of course is one of those events where we want the finest entertainment the White House and this nation can provide. And when you want the finest, you usually have to go for a known quantity. One of the most outstanding performances ever given in the White House was by Pearl Bailey when she was here for Chancellor Brandt. Everybody remembers it, and they remember her. We also know that in addition to that, she has performed on the Broadway stage, in most states, and in many nations across the world.
>
> In 1972 Pearl Bailey, as you know, had an illness [heart disease], and she received the award of Heart of the Year. So we had to think of something special for her, who had virtually everything that could be awarded. So we made a special citation for her—we made her an ambassador: Pearl Bailey . . . Ambassador of Love. She is the only Ambassador of Love from any country in the world. And of course, our American ambassador to all the world. You can only understand this as you see her and hear her because she radiates the love she has in her heart to all people. And this house—in which many great stars have appeared—is honored to have again . . . Pearl Bailey, America's Ambassador of Love.[6]

Charlie Chaplin's "Smile" (words by John Turner and Geoffrey Parsons) opened the show. Drummer Louis Bellson clicked the tune

President Nixon presenting the Heart of the Year Award to Pearl Bailey in February 1972.

off at a quick tempo, faster than the familiar Nat King Cole version. Dressed in a flowing, African-styled red muumuu checkered in gold, with a jeweled, quadruple-heart tiara in her upswept hair, Pearl took center stage on the East Room riser. Microphone in hand, she struggled at first to mesh with the band. The tempo was bright and appropriate for an opening number, but her words sometimes led, sometimes shadowed the familiar melody.

Second time through, the tempo slowed and Pearl finally found her mates, or they found her—either way, she settled into a comfortable finger-snapping groove. Louis again kicked the tune intro high gear and Pearl found the pocket, driving the lyrics home in perfect synch. All is well that ends well. (Applause.)

The East Room lights dimmed. Two spots found the star. The room started to reverberate with a steady, funky gospel beat. It was time for Sister Bailey's sermon. But first, off the riser, face-to-face with the leader of the free world:

"I know you read the good book, sir. I want to ask you one question. You read your book? You read it? I want to ask you a personal question."

"About the book?" Nixon asked back.

"Yeah. I want to sit down because I want to talk to you a minute."

"Too many words," Nixon said.

"Yeah, a lot of words. I don't want you to get tired. Sit down, 'cause I got you coming in later in the program. You read the book? I mean the Bible."

Nixon was spared from having to answer as Pearl reclaimed the stage for a jumping version of the inspirational crossover hit written originally for Anne Murray by Canadian Gene Maclellan: "Put Your Hand in the Hand of the Man from Galilee." The tête-à-tête with Nixon was just Pearl's way of introducing "Galilee." It bordered on the indecorous, but her famed sassy repartee and outspokenness always harbored that danger.

Although "Galilee" had been covered by others before her (Joan Baez, Perry Como, and Elvis Presley), this was a Pearl song. Mr. Maclellan, who wrote it, must have been inspired by the gospel doings of southern black churches. It fit Pearlie Mae to a T, and it would be hard to imagine a more spirited interpretation. Pearl pranced and danced across the stage throughout, even during the switch from the gospel shuffle to a 4/4 beat, which sped up the performance, secularized the number, and made it jazzier. At the song's close, the room filled with an appreciative round of applause, but Sister Pearl had just begun:

Play that thing again, Louie. Play it again. Amen. Glory halle-lujah. You know what, everything I do in a show of any kind, my momma and poppa are right in the show. Somebody said, "Well, Pearl, where are they?" Well, poppa was a holy, sancti-fied preacher. That's why I want to repeat this song, put momma and poppa in here. They preached up at 6th and M [Street] right here [in southwest DC] at the Holy Sanctified Church. "Where's your momma?" You see my momma when you see me strutting and carrying on like that. That's momma, and she had beautiful dimples. Even when she was there, lying down there [gestured, as lain in a casket], she had them. They were about two inches deep. So you say, "Well, Pearl, where are your dimples?" I got 'em. Wait till I go home and take out my teeth, honey. I got 'em, about two inches deep.

This is poppa's part right here. See, he was a holy and sanctified preacher. People say, "What kind of preacher is that?" That is the kind of church where people sing and clap their hands. Children say they started rock and roll. I got two of them. Bless the beast and the children. And they say, we started it. And I always look at my children and say like [comedian] Flip Wilson, "No, you didn't either." Because it came from those churches with the tambourines and the beat was going. A lot of people laugh because I say they shouted up and down. The Baptists shout too. Methodists, too, but they are a little more snobbish about it. [Laughter.]

But something used to happen that made me want to repeat this song. About six or seven weeks after poppa had his sermon going—he's a good preacher too—the collection plate used to go down a little bit. So poppa was a very wise man. He used to send about a hundred miles away, and he would pick him up a young, exciting, new unmarried elder. And he would come to the church on a Sunday morning right here at 6th and M. I mean that collection plate would swell because every young sister turned up. Everybody had their own little shout. I was a little thing, about five or six years old, right in that crowd, and had a chance to watch them. I mean those sisters had their own little shout, the youngs had it! [Pearl did some fancy stepping to the percolating gospel beat; the band continued to play during her rap, raising the volume for her dance segments.]

Then you had the other sisters—they couldn't make that [young stepping], so they had their own bounce going, right in front of that young elder. I tell you, I mean that plate would swell. Hallelujah, elder! [Hand on hip, Pearl executed a rump-shaking twirl-around.]

Then you had the others, a little wider, never heard of Weight

Watchers. They couldn't shout, so they just walked it off for the young elder. [Pearl swooped to one end of the riser then back, arm held high.] Whooooooo! Chicken, elder! With gravy! There is something else they used to do. That's not the reason I did this song. They used to fall out on the floor, under the power. They got so happy they fell right out cold. I was a little thing, I used to stand back there and watch them and everything they would do. They would fall out cold. They called it under the power.

I fell out under the power too. I told you I was a clever little thing—I took after my father. And you know if I was wise at five years old, you know I'm a humdinger now. [Laughter.] When they fell out under the power . . . when the sisters used to shout up and down and little nickels and pennies used to fall out of the pocket, little Pearl used to see it, and my little feet would get to going and I got happy and I fell on top of the power, the financial power. I mean I was reading the *Wall Street Journal* when I was six years old. I mean I was fooling around with my hands; I got my hands on the power.

Pearl's churchified dish preceded a second helping of "Man from Galilee," which the East Room crowd enthusiastically and roundly greeted at its conclusion.

Needing to rest, Pearl sat down on a stool next to the piano. In a near repeat of their routine for Chancellor Brandt four years before, Nixon got up and placed a chair next to Pearl, prompting her to comment, "I didn't think you'd give me another chair 'cause I got a chair. I was looking for a piano this time. Yes, sir, you don't want this one back, do you? 'Cause it matches the other one. Isn't that wonderful."

But it was time for the next number, one known by most in the audience: "For Once in My Life." Contrary to popular belief, Stevie Wonder did not write the song; the credit goes to Motown staffers Ron Miller (lyrics) and Orlando Murden. Stevie's up-tempo, "definitive version" (October 1968) actually followed ballad renditions by Jean DuShon, the Temptations, and Tony Bennett.[7]

Pearl's interpretation was more in line with Wonder's, which gave her a chance to strut her stuff after she sang the song first time through. On the second go-around, Pearlie Mae's terpsichorean moves were more active, replete with modern-dance ticks and vaudeville steps— leg kicks and all—although her stuff was somewhat hidden under her large, flowing red-and-gold muumuu. Looking for all the world like an ancient Egyptian queen, she swept back and forth across the stage as if on roller skates.

The audience responded with oohs and aahs and scattered applause. Why, they must have wondered, was a fifty-six-year-old-woman with heart disease doing such a vigorous number? Pearl had obviously asked herself the same question, and wisely stopped and leaned over the piano top where she signaled pianist Abney to take another improvised chorus. She said to herself, "Pearl, you look tired . . . I'm going to rest on it. I'll rest on it."

Her turn came again and she sang out the number, but not with the same energy she had at the start. Nixon's well-referenced chair was handy, so she took it and sat down with the microphone. Her head just reached the height of the piano keyboard as she launched another monologue, so it was unlikely that many at the back of the room could see her, but they could hear her:

You know, the funniest thing last March, I went over to the State Department—I get around you know—and that was the beginning of our two-hundred-year celebrations as a country. We had all them ambassadors from all over the world. Oh, that was a fancy party. I was there, too, as an ambassador. I was the pièce de résistance. That's French for "I didn't get paid." [Bada boom!]

After a while, then Secretary of State Rogers took me over to a corner, the program was over, we were dancing away, and he said, "Pearl, meet our new ambassador from Iran." And I met this tall young man. Two days later, he called me up and said, "Pearl, our government would like for you to come over to Iran."

Hot dog! Dinner in Iran. Corn bread, greens—hey, don't

laugh, the Persians cook pretty good. They need a little more salt, though, but it was good. And I said, "Sir, you want me to sing?"

He said, "Nope. You did something the other night. I saw a light."

And my country needs to see that light, and recently I did the same thing for the Jordanians. I shall do it all over the world for everyone. I saw later that President Nixon, Dr. Kissinger, and the queen of Iran had a tape of this. I had done it on *The Oral Roberts Show* [on March 15, 1973; Nixon had ordered the White House Communication Agency to tape the televangelist's show].[8] I know what light he saw. And I went to Iran. But I laughed because I looked at those men [in Iran], pretty fancy, you know, all those ambassadors, all them fancy ribbons, all the countries of the world. The Russian ambassador was marvelous. He got up and danced, him and I carried on, carried on . . . and he was wonderful; and the French ambassador too.[9]

I looked all over that room, and I finally said something—because I was an outsider looking at the inside of life, I could say it. Gentlemen, you all look so marvelous, and tonight you are sitting in this room so full of peace. Tomorrow, you may not speak, but you can do nothing for me, your country, or anybody unless you learn to do something that I have found within myself, which is what . . . I walked down those stairs [to the dinner] a few moments ago with the gentleman who heads our country, with his wife, and I said to him, "There's only one way to do it, and that's to . . ."

With that, Pearl stood and sang the answer: "Let There Be Peace on Earth," the first line and title of the song she sang on *The Oral Roberts Show* that Nixon had taped. The song, written by Jill Jackson (lyrics) and Sy Miller circa 1955, has a universal message—if you want peace, dear people, let it begin with me. Pearl emphasized the line "Let it begin with me," which is repeated three times in the song.[10]

At the song's conclusion, she walked offstage accompanied by "Hello,

Dolly" from the band, but it was just a faux ending, a chance for Ms. Bailey to catch her breath and thoughts. She returned and joked, "I wasn't going, honey. I just wanted you to stand." [Another zinger from the sassy ad-lib master.] She resumed her monologue, mostly improvised, which served to introduce the next song as well as conserve her energy:

As I always say, corn bread goes well anyplace. I noticed one thing—I didn't get a chair with arms. I deliberately had the stool put there because I thought the president was going to say I knew why they put that there. She won't get another chair. Then I wondered about the two pots of geraniums they had the last time I was here. When I came in today to rehearse I said to [Social Secretary] Lucy Winchester, "You have planted all the flowers [in a planter surrounding the stage], I can't get one of them up, to get them out of here." So I was going to try the piano. Instead of that, I was downstairs . . . and I've got so much I want to do in this world . . . the president said, "Pearl, you just got to keep people happy." I can keep them happy. I can sing a few songs. I can say a few words of wisdom, and make you smile or cry—either one, I got to do all I can for America.

I was in an office downstairs changing clothes [for the show]. I thought, Whose office is this, because I intend to be in here [the White House] so much. I got so much to do for America I'm going to have to move in. So I finally found out—it was the housekeeper's office. So I said, "Whose office is this because it [would be] handy for me...to get my little messages up to the president." [Then to Nixon] You don't know this sir, but your house is called the White House, but onstage I never call it the White House. I just call it the *House*. When you go there once, you get so excited you call it the White House. "You know where I was, honey? . . . I was at the White House." But when you come out here as often as I do, honey, you just call it the *House*. [Applause.]

So I decided, so now I'll take the office. I checked around,

I kept checking around, see. I didn't want the Secret Service to know, because they'll know my purpose. I didn't even want the president to know. He's a magnificent man—I wouldn't even call him a politician—he's a magnificent man. But then I'm a pretty good showman. I found out something in my business. The time to give the punch line is always when you have got a crowd. Then you got him. So I decided to ask him, could I move in? [To someone at the back of the room] What are you doing peeping around the flag? I ain't going to do anything, honey. [Laughter.] Isn't that funny, when you're young, they stand in front of the flag, when you get older . . . they get behind the flag and peep out. Come on out, honey.

So I check around and found out it was the housekeeper's office. You know, I wrote a cookbook just recently [*Pearl's Kitchen: An Extraordinary Cookbook* (Harcourt, 1973).] I wrote a chapter on cleaning house too. I clean pretty good. I looked at this big house.

I said, "Well, this one I'm going to take."

"But we told you it's the housekeeper's office."

"Well, how—as big as this house is—if she's doing the cleaning, to keep up with it, she don't need an office to sit down."

So, sir, I can move in anytime . . . anytime.

I wanted to do something for you tonight. The president loves . . . [to Nixon] I don't want to make you feel bad in front of your friends . . . I say he loves the piano . . . I started to say he really can't play the piano but . . . [crowd gasps] . . . he plays well. He loves the piano. He loves jazz and music. So I thought, I got a red-hot one [in fact, Pearl had two songs on the program she didn't get around to singing], but I thought I would give you a moment of pleasure. But I tell you, sir, I don't know what adrenaline or truth God got into you tonight. Because you look happier and better than I have seen you in a long time, may you continue [Extended applause.]

[To Nixon again] I'm not a woman liberator [*sic*], but I got to say it because I am a woman—you got some kind of woman sitting beside you, mister. [More applause.]

So I thought, just for your pleasure, because you love music, and because I see my age group in here—everybody here is thirty-five or thirty-four—we would play just one jazz number. It's got nothing to do with me. [Louis Bellson's brushes signal a lively up-tempo number.] But a gentleman came here [to the United States] named Irving Berlin. A magnificent man. Just so you could hear a little swing. To keep your spirit up—this is for the president.

Pearl could have added a bit of interesting folklore here on "Always," the song she was about sing, but she chose not to. A shame really. "Always" originated when a young woman named Mona implored Irving Berlin to write a song for her. He obliged with the line "I'll be loving you, Mona." Later, when Berlin was working on a stage musical, he changed "Mona" to "Always." But the song didn't make it into the show. Much later, in 1925, inspired by his love for his wife-to-be, Ellen, Berlin went back to work on the uncompleted song. The lyrics took Berlin two years to complete; the memorable ending came in an inspired moment: "Not just for an hour, not just for a day, not just for a year—but always."[11]

Pearl sang the first verse and then said, "I'm going to sit down as soon as I get them swinging." At the end of the first chorus, as the band kept playing, she introduced the musicians, something she didn't do at her first appearance for Chancellor Brandt four years before:

This gentleman is Mr. Don Abney, one of the greatest jazz pianists in the country. [Applause.]

This gentleman here is Mr. Milt [the "Judge"] Hinton. He was about fifteen to thirty years with Mr. [Cab] Calloway, ten to fifteen with Duke Ellington [years of service exaggerated]. One of the great bassists. All three went to Iran. [Applause.]

I know him. [She looks toward her husband.] So very few

people know that Louis Bellson originated the idea of the double-bass drums [Pearl strolled over to the drum kit, pointed to each drum], the two-bass idea, in America. The greatest drummer in America today, Louis Bellson. [Applause.]

Pearl sang a couple of lines of "Always" and said, "With my apologies, sir," as she took a seat on her much-discussed chair at the foot of the gold-inlaid grand piano, the microphone in her hand. Pianist Abney took charge and improvised a chorus of scattered single-note runs over the peppy 4/4 rhythm provided by his section mates. The Berlin song, originally written as a waltz with an unusual (for him) A-B-C-D structure, was a straightforward, lightweight pop song but had long been a favorite of jazz musicians; it gave them room to do whatever they wanted, and Abney sure did.

Comfortable on her chair, Pearl commanded, "Just play one more time, one more time . . . one more, Don." The keyboardist plunged into his next chorus as Pearl sang out: "The man wants to learn piano. Play, Don. [To Nixon] This is going to keep you up all night. I can see you upstairs rehearsing this now. One more chorus, one more chorus."

Abney played on, intermixing block chords with right-hand runs. Though not too animated, the audience seemed to be digging it; a few heads nodded in time. "The place may not close till twelve, you all realize that, just a little bit more, Don. You don't have no place to go, Mr. President, right now. I don't come often, so I might as well enjoy myself."

After four choruses by the pianist—a good stretch-out for a White House gig [Pearl made up for the lack of solo playing time she gave the band four years ago]—it was time for the "Judge." Midway in his solo, Milt slipped in an old-fashioned slap-bass routine that drew smiles from the musicians and, finally, applause from the audience. Back to pizzicato, Milt referenced two lines of the melody to signal his battery mate, "Get ready to strut your stuff."

A lengthy drum solo followed, a worthy rival to the one he performed five years prior at the Duke Ellington seventieth-birthday bash. Louis swished-swished his brushes on the snare for a while before he switched to sticks to showcase the full sonorities of his kit—snare, tom-tom, cymbals, and of course his double-bass drums. Hinton leaned over to Bellson with an obvious congratulatory, "Yeaaah!" (Applause.)

Pearl sang out the memorable but troublesome last lines that Berlin toiled over for two years: "Not for just an hour, not just for a day, not just for a year—but always." Pearl asked the band to take their bows and the East Room crowd responded warmly. The number clocked in at seven minutes, the longest musical number without an extended Pearlie Mae rap and the highlight of the show, at least for jazz fans and perhaps for others as well. It's a shame this trio never recorded an album together and worked clubs in the United States. They would have been considered a top-notch, mainstream, straight-ahead jazz trio (would be today too). It's a double shame Ms. Bailey didn't record an album of standards with this group in the studio, just singing, no jiving. Her jazz credibility would have risen.

The band began another medium-tempo romper, with Abney tinkling away at the keyboard. Pearl, center stage, addressed the crowd: "Bye, bye, I had a good time. You know, for two years, three months, and four days, the longest running Broadway company was my company, and every night I used to say: 'Well, hello, Dolly. Well, hello, Dolly, it's so nice to have you back where you belong.'"

Pearl closed out her second appearance at the Nixon White House as she did the first: "Always leave them with something they know." The Washington bureaucrats, governors, their families, and invited guests stood and sang along. Encouraged by the star, many clapped in rhythm. She plucked a surprised Secretary of Agriculture Earl Butz out of the front row to twirl a few halting dance steps before she began her exit bows while the band played on.

Fully prepared to end the evening's festivities, the president joined Pearl onstage. He shook hands with each member of the trio and congratulated Ms. Bailey. But there was more to come. Facing the audience at the microphone, Pearl asked Nixon, "Did you have a good time?"

Nixon gave an indifferent shrug for all to see. [Take that, Pearl. Next time, don't say the president can't play piano.]

Undaunted, Pearlie Mae pressed on, but Nixon interrupted, "I get the last word."

"You can have it, but you're going to be sorry." Pearl continued, "I know, no one has ever had the privilege in America or few other countries, and I realize, with my talent and your governing authority, that you don't play as well as I sing, and I don't sing as well as you govern. [Laughter.] However, there is no place in the world that anybody ever had a head of state play the piano while they sang a song. Would you?"

Nixon acted out a schoolboy response to an unpleasant situation, burying his wagging head in his hands.

"Wouldn't it be nice to have the president play?" Pearl asked the audience.

"I don't know anything," Nixon replied.

"Anything you play, I know. Would you please? It would be history. We all know how you play . . . it doesn't matter. Would you?"

Nixon whispered to Pearl and turned toward the piano. She said to the crowd, "To show you a real ham, you know what he said when

At the final jazz event at the White House during Nixon's administration, the president and Pearl Bailey entertain the audience.

he turned his back? What do you think would be our best number?"
[Laughter.]

Nixon sat down at the piano bench and began to play "Home on
the Range." Pearl joined in, but after the familiar first lines, she broke
it off. "Mr. President. Mr. President. Wait a minute. I want to say one
thing. I want to sing a song, not ride a horse."

The accompanist continued undeterred. Pearl voiced a few more
lines, shaking her head. "I don't know if I'm finding him, or he's finding me." Fortunately, both reached the same conclusion—it wasn't
working—and stopped.

The chief executive knew what to do: "Wild Irish Rose in the key of
G," and the assembled were treated to a passable "amateur hour" duet.
Without a break, the opening chords of "God Bless America" were then
heard around the room.

"Wait, wait. Now he's singing and playing," Director Pearl said as
she waved for the inspired pianist to stop. Properly cued, the audience
stood and joined pianist Nixon to pay their vocal respects to Irving
Berlin's unofficial national anthem. At the song's end, the president
rose, approached pianist Don Abney, shook his hand (a nice touch),
and then took his place at the microphone amid prolonged applause:

I want to say to our distinguished guests, that piano will never
be the same and neither will I. [Laughter.]

Now, it was well known and reported in the press—accu-
rately I might say—to the effect that the last time Pearl Bailey
was here . . . she picked up various things. The one thing she
picked up was one of these chairs, and carried it off, and so when
she carried it off, I knew they weren't much good, because the
last time Secretary Morton sat in one, it broke. So I thought she
might as well take it. And that chair has traveled more than Air
Force One since that time [an oblique reference to Pearl's several
trips abroad on behalf of the U.S. government].

So this time, Pearl indicated that she would just pick up the
piano, and so when the social aide said, "What piano should we

put in?" I said, "You get the biggest and heaviest one you can find." And here it is [Nixon pointed to the grand piano.] But she can't take the piano.

But we did want our Ambassador of Love—and I'm going to give her another assignment in the near future. [Nixon faced Pearl] You and I will pick out the country. (Pearl replied, "I picked the office, already.") We'll pick a nice country, but make sure the combo goes too. Fair enough. [They did—to Jordan, Egypt, and Iran three months later.][12] But we thought she ought to have something special for this occasion, and as you know, many of the ladies in the audience—those who are wives of cabinet officers—have the presidential seal made into a pin. We also have made up pins just for a few special people. [For Pearl we have] the seal of the president of the United States surrounded by pearls [held high for all to see]. And so we have here tonight for our Ambassador of Love what I would call the Pearl Bailey Presidential Seal—a seal surrounded by pearls [long applause while the pendant is pinned to Pearl's frock by the president].

We all love you, but if you could leave, we just can't afford you any longer.

Following the president's off-the-cuff remarks, Pearl expressed her appreciation:

Thank you all. Thank you, Mr. President, Mrs. Nixon. We know we have some things to do. You said you would have the last word. You and I have had our last word. God always has the last word. And whatever we need he is going to supply. God bless you all.

Exit Pearl to another round of "Hello, Dolly" and sustained applause. As to be expected, the newspapers the next day focused on Pearl coaxing an obviously unrehearsed and discomfited President Nixon to play piano as she sang. The *Washington Star*: "No, he didn't know I was going to ask him to play; if he had, he'd of [*sic*] rehearsed," she told reporters later, still making jokes about the president's piano-playing talent even after he had gone upstairs.[13]

The president may have had an inkling of what was coming; after all, Pearl had visited with him at his upstairs quarters for ten minutes before dinner, and she even told him to his face at the start of the show, "Sit down, I got you coming in later in the program." No matter, it was—as it would turn out—a fitting end to evening jazz performances at the Nixon White House.

At the first jazz event in the East Room, three months into his administration, Nixon played the piano and sang "Happy Birthday" to Duke Ellington. At the last jazz event, only four months before his infamous resignation, he played the piano and sang "God Bless America" to Pearl Bailey. A good beginning, a good ending . . . as far as jazz is concerned.

Nixon would vacate 1600 Pennsylvania Avenue on August 9, 1974, for all time. Pearl, on the other hand, would return countless times over the next sixteen years as an official (she was appointed special delegate to the U.N. by presidents Ford, Reagan, and George H. W. Bush), as an award recipient (she received the Medal of Freedom from Reagan in 1988), an entertainer, and an invited guest. No entertainer, save possibly for Bob Hope and Billy Graham (if one can include the reverend in that category), spent as much time in the *House* as Pearl Bailey.

Notes

SETTING THE STAGE

1. Memo, Nixon to Rose Woods, February 17, 1969, Special Files, EX SO3, February 17, 1960–March 18, 1969, Nixon Library, National Archives, College Park, MD.

2. Memo, H. R. Haldeman to R. Woods, March 23, 1970, Special Files, SO3, July 1, 1969–July 17, 1969, Nixon Library, National Archives, College Park, MD.

DUKE ELLINGTON

1. Edward Allan Faine, *Ellington at the White House, 1969* (Takoma Park, MD: IM Press, 2013). A short clip of the first jazz band to appear in the White House—the Paul Winter Sextet on November 19, 1962—is available for viewing at http://www.paulwinter.com/videos/ under "Count Me In." The sextet was, in fact, the first entertainment of any kind filmed at the president's mansion.

2. The recording of the all-star concert is available on CD: *Duke Ellington 1969: All-Star White House Tribute*, Blue Note, 2002.

3. Terence M. Ripmaster, *Willis Conover: Broadcasting Jazz to the World* (Lincoln, NE: iUniverse, 2007), 142.

4. The seventeen-minute USIA documentary of the Ellington tribute is available on YouTube under "Duke Ellington at the White House": https://www.youtube.com/KQTE2EWH5UY.

5. Leonard Feather, *From Satchmo to Miles* (New York: Stein and Day, 1974), 57.

HENRY MANCINI

1. Jerry Beck, *Pink Panther: The Ultimate Guide to the Coolest Cat in Town!* (New York: DK Publishing, 2005), 14; Henry Mancini and Gene Lees, *Did They Mention the Music? Autobiography of Henry Mancini* (New York: Cooper Square Press, 2001), 238, 239.
2. Fred Binkley, "Mancini's Movie Manifesto," *DownBeat*, March 5, 1970, 16.
3. Sammy Mitchell, "Unbuggable Henry Mancini," *DownBeat*, March 6, 1969, 36.
4. Donald Fagen, liner notes, *Ultimate Mancini*, Concord Records, 2004, CD.
5. Mancini's performance numbers/comments transcribed by the author from "Henry Mancini," White House Communication Agency Sound Recordings, Tape J-105, June 30, 1969, Nixon Library, National Archives, College Park, MD.
6. Glen T. Eskew, *Johnny Mercer: Southern Songwriter for the World* (Athens, GA: University of Georgia Press, 2013), 294.
7. Ibid., 371.
8. Phillip Furia and Michael Lasser, *America's Songs: The Stories behind the Songs of Broadway, Hollywood, and Tin Pan Alley* (New York: Routledge, 2006), 276, 278.
9. Mancini, *Did They Mention the Music?*, 187–89.
10. Mark Feeney, *Nixon at the Movies* (Chicago: University of Chicago Press, 2004), 280, 345, 349.
11. White House memo, Deborah Sloan to William E. Minshall, November 19, 1971, White House Special Files, EX SO3, October 1, 1960–October 31, 1969, Nixon Library, National Archives, College Park, MD.
12. Mancini, *Did They Mention the Music?*, 187–89.

MODERN JAZZ QUARTET

1. Donnie Radcliff, "No House For Show Biz," *Washington Post*, July 27, 1973; Elise R. Kirk, *Musical Highlights from the White House* (Malabar, FL: Kreiger Publishing Co.,1992), 151, 183, 186; and Hollie I. West, "Jazz Elite," *Washington Post*, October 22, 1969.
2. Betty Beale, "President Lauds Shah," *Washington Star*, October 22, 1969; editors, "Jazz Soiree at the White House," *DownBeat*, December 11, 1969.

3. Ben S. Page, "Open Bags: An Interview with Milt Jackson," *DownBeat*, April 30, 1971.

4. White House Press Release, White House Special Files, EX SO3, October 1, 1960–October 31, 1969, Nixon Library, National Archives, College Park, MD.

5. Gary Giddins, *Visions of Jazz: The First Century* (Oxford: Oxford University Press, 1998), 382; Andy Davis, liner notes, *Space*, Apple Records, October 1969, CD; and Francis Davis, *In the Moment: Jazz in the 1980s* (Oxford: Oxford University Press, 1986), 228–32.

6. Rob Mariani, "Connie Kay Plays the Drums Impeccably," allaboutjazz .com, December 27, 2006, http://www.allaboutjazz.com/connie-kay-plays-the-drums-impeccably-connie-kay-by-rob-mariani.php.

7. Overheard by the author at Cleveland and Columbus, Ohio, jazz clubs, circa 1957–1962.

8. Howard Mandel, *Miles Ornett Cecil: Jazz beyond Jazz* (London: Rutledge, 2008), 238. http://www.howardmandel.com/mocinfo.html.

9. Gary Giddins, *Weather Bird: Jazz at the Dawn of Its Second Century* (Oxford: Oxford University Press, 2004), 321–22.

10. Patrick Edward Roulet, *Milt Jackson: The Creative Genius Behind "Bags' Groove,"* Doctoral Thesis, University of Washington, Graduate School, 2002.

11. Giddins, *Weather Bird*, 129.

12. Ray Drummond, "Percy Heath (4.30.23–4.28.05)," *JazzTimes*, March 2006, 37. http://jazztimes.com/articles/25474-percy-heath.

13. Bob Dawbam, liner notes, *Under the Jasmin Tree*, Apple Records, September 1968, CD; Giddins, *Visions*, 397.

14. Thierry Lalo, *John Lewis* (Valence, France: Editions du Limon, 1991).

15. David Meeker, *Jazz in the Movies: New Edition* (New York: Da Capo Press, 1981); Scott Yanow, *Jazz on Film* (New York: Backbeat Books, 2004).

16. Davis, liner notes, *Space*.

17. Allan Kozinn, "Classical Music in Review: Joaquin Rodrigo Tribute Carnegie Hall," *New York Times*, May 12, 1992.

18. Charles Suber, "Jazz Soiree at the White House," *DownBeat*, December 11, 1969, 23.

19. West, "Jazz Elite."

20. MJQ's performance numbers and crowd reaction transcribed by the author from White House Communication Agency Sound Recordings, Tape J-110, Nixon Library, National Archives, College Park, MD.

21. Giddins, *Visions*, 397.
22. West, "Jazz Elite."
23. Davis, liner notes, *Space*.
24. West, "Jazz Elite."
25. Davis, liner notes, *Space*.
26. Page, "Open Bags."
27. Chris Albertson, "Review: *Under the Jasmin Tree*," *DownBeat*, May 15, 1969, 28.
28. Suber, "Jazz Soiree."
29. President's Personal Files, White House Social Files, 1964–1974, Nixon Library, National Archives, College Park, MD.
30. John S. Wilson, "Modern Jazz Quartet Furnishes Elegance, Polish and Precision," *New York Times*, December 22, 1969; Tami Fiofori, "Modern Jazz Quartet, Lincoln Center," *DownBeat*, May 14, 1970, 35.
31. MJQ Middle East tour, Department of State Telegram: Cultural Presentation: Modern Jazz Quartet, April 25, 1970, Box 71:17, Bureau of Educational and Cultural Affairs, Special Collections, University of Arkansas, Fayetteville.

AL HIRT

1. Marie Smith, "Governors 'Rock' in East Room," *Washington Post*, December 4, 1969.
2. To be accurate, of the twenty-four prior Nixon social events in 1969, his first year in office, only seven fell in the chamber-music category, ten were popular, four miscellaneous, and three jazz. See Edward Allan Faine, *Ellington at the White House, 1969* (IM Press, 2013), 239–40. It was the seven classical chamber events (and perhaps the un-hipness of the popular events) that some people objected to; Isabelle Shelton, "High Music," *Washington Star*, December 4, 1969.
3. Colin Escott, liner notes, *Al Hirt: Greatest Hits*, RCA 07863 69398-2, 2001, CD.
4. John S. Wilson, "Big Man with a Trumpet," *New York Times*, July 4, 1965.
5. Charles Suber, "Straight Talk from Al Hirt," *DownBeat*, September 4, 1969, 14.
6. Escott, *Greatest Hits*; Suber, "Straight Talk from Al Hirt."
7. Musicians listed in White House guest program December 3, 1969

(in the author's possession); http://www.artistdirect.com/artist/credits/joseph-t-pee-wee-spitelera-jr/496159.

8. http://www.allmusic.com/artist/wayne-devillier-mn0000736624/credits.

9. http://www.ellismarsalis.com/#biography; Escott, *Greatest Hits*.

10. Hirt's performance numbers and comments transcribed by the author from "The Al Hirt Combo," White House Communication Agency Sound Recordings, Tape J-147, December 31, 1969, Nixon Library, National Archives, College Park, MD.

11. http://en.wikipedia.org/wiki/When_The_Go_MarchingIn.

12. Marilyn McCoo and Billy Davis Jr. with Mike Yorkey, *Up, Up, and Away: How We Found Love, Faith, and Lasting Marriage in the Entertainment World* (Chicago: Northfield Publishing 2004), 93.

13. Ibid., 114.

14. H. R. Haldeman, *The Haldeman Diaries: Inside the Nixon White House* (New York: G. P. Putnam & Sons, 1994), 43.

15. Yorkey, *Up, Up, and Away*, 115.

16. Shelton, "High Music."

17. Smith, "Governors 'Rock.'"

18. Yorkey, *Up, Up, and Away*, 115–16.

19. Roy Reed, "Nixon Reassures South on Schools," *New York Times*, August 15, 1970.

PEGGY LEE

1. Peter Richmond, *Fever: Life and Times of Miss Peggy Lee* (New York: Henry Holt, 2004) 87–195.

2. Ibid.,196–246. In 2004, *DownBeat* magazine polled a diverse group of seventy-five jazz singers for their top all-time favorite jazz vocal albums (male or female). The top thirty were listed, but *Black Coffee* didn't make the cut. Ten albums were by male singers, four by mixed groups. Had the poll been limited to albums by female singer, odds are—most would agree—*Coffee* would have made the list. Frank-John Hadley, "The Singers' Albums: 30 All-Time Favorite Jazz Vocal Albums," *DownBeat*, June 1, 2004, 46–51.

3. Richmond, *Fever*, 246–48.

4. Ibid., 252–56.

5. Ibid., 256–67.

6. Ibid., 288–314; Robert Strom, *Miss Peggy Lee: A Career Chronicle* (Jefferson, NC: McFarland, 2005), 281–83.

7. Richmond, *Fever*, 316.

8. Note, Constance Stewart to Lucy Winchester, January 26, 1970, White House Central Files, Staff Member Office Files, Lucy Winchester, Nixon Library, National Archives, College Park, MD.

9. Richmond, *Fever*, 316; pp. 316–18 of Richmond are expanded by the author's transcription of the event from White House Communication Agency Sound Recordings, Tape J-120, Nixon Library, National Archives, College Park, MD.

10. Ibid., 316.

11. Ibid., 317.

12. Author's transcription.

13. Richmond, *Fever*, 199.

14. Strom, 133–36, 139–42, 146–47, 175, 182, 216.

15. Richmond, *Fever*, 258.

16. Ibid., 194.

17. Marie Smith, "Sing-Along with Peggy" in "Pompidou Honored," *Washington Post*, February 25, 1970.

18. Richmond, *Fever*, 407 and 387.

19. Vera Glaser, "Peggy's Feverish Act Leaves White House Cold," *Chicago Daily News*, February 28–March 1, 1970.

20. Smith, "Sing-Along with Peggy."

21. Betty Beale, "Nixons Fete Pompidous," *Washington Star*, February 25, 1970.

22. Betty Beale, "Low Brow Entertainment at the White House," *Washington Star*, July 29, 1973.

23. Glaser, "Peggy's Feverish Act."

24. Memo, Dwight L. Chapin to Alex Butterfield, Re: Pompidou Dinner, February 25, 1970, White House Special Files, EX SO3, Nixon Library, National Archives, College Park, MD.

25. Richmond, *Fever*, 99.

26. Hollie I. West, "No, That's Not All There Is," *Washington Post*, March 22, 1970.

27. Richmond, *Fever*, 386.

BOBBY SHORT TRIO

1. Marie Smith, "White Tie Reception," *Washington Post*, April 6, 1970.

2. Ymelda Dixon, "Party Fit for a King," *Washington Star*, April 6, 1970.

3. Richard M. Nixon, *The Memoirs of Richard Nixon* (New York: Grosset & Dunlap, 1972), 535; Herbert G. Klein, *Making It Perfectly Clear* (Garden City, NY: Doubleday, 1980), 126–27.

4. Bobby Short with Robert Mackintosh, *Bobby Short: The Life and Times of a Saloon Singer* (New York: Random House, 1995), 185.

5. Marie Smith, "Windsor Entertainment Booked," *Washington Post*, March 27, 1970.

6. Mackintosh, *Bobby Short*, 243.

7. Marie Smith, "Songs for the Duke of Windsor," *Washington Post*, March 31, 1970.

8. Ibid.

9. James Gavin, *Intimate Nights: The Golden Age of New York Cabaret* (New York: Back Stage Books, 2006), 328.

10. John Pizzarelli, "Bobby Short (9.15.24–3.21.05)," *JazzTimes*, March 2006, 41. http://jazztimes.com/articles/25485-bobby-short.

11. Nesuhi Ertegun, liner notes, *50 by Bobby Short*, Atlantic 81715-1, 1986, 4 LPs.

12. Joe Klee, *DownBeat*, February 28, 1974, 22.

13. Mackintosh *Bobby Short*, 248.

14. Nina S. Hyde, "Remember That My Name Is Ford, not Kissinger," *Newsday*, April 6, 1970.

15. Smith, "White Tie Reception."

16. Mackintosh, *Bobby Short*, 244; information about the Duke of Windsor's name in Katharine Jose, "American Girl: The Wallis Simpson Story, Told Differently," CapitalNewYork.com, February 17, 2012. http://www.capitalnewyork.com/article/culture/2012/02/5288414/american-girl-wallis-simpson-story-told-differently.

17. Short's performance numbers transcribed by the author from "Bobby Short and the Young Saints," White House Communication Agency Sound Recordings, Tape J-122, April 4, 1970, Nixon Library, National Archives, College Park, MD.

18. Mackintosh, *Bobby Short*, 249.

19. Smith, "Songs for the Duke of Windsor."

20. Ertegun liner notes, *50 by Bobby Short*.

21. Mackintosh, *Bobby Short*, 116.

22. Smith, "White Tie Reception."

23. Hyde, "Remember That My Name Is Ford."

24. Mackintosh, *Bobby Short*, 244.

WORLD'S GREATEST JAZZ BAND

1. Elise K. Kirk, *Music at the White House: A History of the American Spirit* (Urbana, IL: University of Illinois Press, 1986), 320.
2. Jon C. Hopwood, "Nicol Williamson: Biography," IMBd.com, http://www.imdb.com/name/nm0932116/bio; "1966 Tony Award Winners," BroadwayWorld.com, Wisdom Digital Media, http://www2.broadwayworld.com/tonyawardsyear.cfm?year=1966.
3. Kenneth Tynan, *The Sound of Two Hands Clapping* (New York: Da Capo Press, 1987), 13; Anne Christmas, "Hamlet Set to Jazz at White House," *Washington Evening Star*, March 20, 1970.
4. Tynan, *Two Hands Clapping*, 13.
5. Memo H. R. Haldeman to Rose Woods, February 21, 1970, Special Files, EX SO3, Box 57, Nixon Library, National Archives, College Park, MD.
6. Tynan, *Two Hands Clapping*, 35.
7. Christmas, "Hamlet Set to Jazz at White House"; John Chilton, *Stomp Off, Let's Go!: The Story of Bob Crosby's Bob Cats & Big Band* (London: Jazz Book Service) 1983, 88.
8. Bud Freeman, *You Don't Look Like a Musician* (Detroit: Balamp Publishing, 1974), 104.
9. Chilton, *Stomp Off*, 81, 107, 125, 31.
10. Ibid., 72–73, 191.
11. Chilton, *Stomp Off*, 207 (Billy) and 245 (Yank); Richard Sudhalter, *Lost Chords: White Musicians and Their Contributions to Jazz* (Oxford: Oxford University Press, 1999), 647.
12. Chilton, *Stomp Off*, 252.
13. Ibid., 198, 253.
14. Bob Wilber with Derek Webster, *Music Was Not Enough* (Oxford: Oxford University Press, 1988), 114–15.
15. Sudhalter, *Lost Chords*, 782 (Hawkins), 255 (Webster), 271 (Young).
16. Wilber, *Music Was Not Enough*, 50, 68, 70, 96, 108.
17. Freeman, *You Sure Don't*, 9.
18. Ira Gitler, "'Now Is the Renaissance': The World's Greatest Jazz Band," *DownBeat*, May 1, 1969, 16.
19. Editor, "Hottest Sounds This Side of Manhattan," *DownBeat*, December 25, 1969, 10.
20. Tynan, *Two Hands Clapping*, 19–20.
21. Ibid., 19, 22.

22. Ibid., 29.
23. Ibid., 33.
24. Ibid., 39.
25. Ibid., 42, 43.
26. Ibid., 43.
27. Ibid., 45, 48.
28. Editor, *DownBeat*, January 1969, 14.
29. Tynan, *Two Hands Clapping*, 49.
30. Christmas, "Hamlet Set to Jazz at White House"; Richard L. Coe, "'Prime' Hamlet: New Acts," *Washington Post*, March 20, 1970; and Tynan, *Two Hands Clapping*, 28, 22.
31. Description of Nicol's performance transcribed by the author from White House Communication Agency Sound Recordings, Tape J-122, Nixon Library, National Archives, College Park, MD, augmented by Tynan, *Two Hands Clapping*.
32. Chilton, *Stomp Off*, 88; Tynan, *Two Hands Clapping*, 21–22.
33. Tynan, *Two Hands Clapping*, 56.
34. James Lincoln Collier, *Louis Armstrong: An American Genius* (Oxford: Oxford University Press (1983), 66–67 and 70–71.
35. Tynan, *Two Hands Clapping*, 45.
36. Ibid., 57.
37. Ibid., 51, 35.
38. Ibid., 52.
39. Chilton, *Stomp Off*, 47, 56.
40. Coe, "'Prime' Hamlet: New Acts."
41. Christmas, "Hamlet Set to Jazz at White House."
42. Freeman, *You Sure Don't*, 44.
43. Christmas, "Hamlet Set to Jazz at White House."
44. Tynan, *Two Hands Clapping*, 54.
45. Marie Smith, "'Prime' Hamlet: New Credits," *Washington Post*, March 20, 1970.
46. Christmas, "Hamlet Set to Jazz at White House"; Tynan, *Two Hands Clapping*, 53, 54.
47. Marie Smith, "'Prime' Hamlet: New Credits."
48. Memo, Connie Stewart to Moore, January 19, 1971, White House Central Files, Staff Member Files, Lucy Winchester, Box 7, Nixon Library, National Archives, College Park, MD.
49. Tynan, *Two Hands Clapping*, 28.
50. Coe, "'Prime' Hamlet: New Acts."

51. Kirk, *Music at the White House*, 332.
52. Mark Feeney, *Nixon at the Movies* (Chicago: University of Chicago Press, 2004), 341–42.
53. Hopwood, "Nicol Williamson."

PEARL BAILEY TRIO

1. Myra MacPherson, "Pearl Breaks Them Up," *Washington Post*, April 11, 1970; Chalmers M. Roberts, "Nixon Backs Brandt Move to East," Washington Post, April 10, 1970.
2. Alan Schroeder, *Celebrity-In-Chief: How Show Business Took Over the White House* (Boulder, CO: Westview Press, 2004), 103–4.
3. Memo, Hueber, April 9, 1970, EX SO3, Box 10, Nixon Library, National Archives, College Park, MD.
4. Milt Hinton's biography page, accessed October 10, 2013, http://www.milthinton.com.
5. Ibid.
6. The Scotsman, "Don Abney 1923–2000," *The Last Post* (blog), 2000, JazzHouse, Jazz Journalists Association, http://www.jazzhouse.org.
7. Nixon's remarks and Bailey's performance numbers and comments transcribed by the author from White House Communication Agency Sound Recordings, Tape J-123, Nixon Library, National Archives, College Park, MD.
8. Bobby Short with Robert MacIntosh, *Bobby Short: The Life of a Saloon Singer* (New York: Random House, 1995), 153.
9. Phillip Furia and Michael Lasser, *America's Songs: The Stories behind the Songs of Broadway, Hollywood, and Tin Pan Alley* (New York: Routledge, 2006), 281–82.
10. Ibid., 11–12.
11. MacPherson, "Pearl Breaks Them Up."

DAVID FROST/BILLY TAYLOR

1. Memo, Lucy Winchester to file, November 13, 1970, White House Central Files, Staff Member Files, Lucy Winchester, Box 7, Nixon Library, National Archives, College Park, MD.
2. Memo, Carol Harford to Lucy Winchester, November 19, 1970, White House Central Files, Staff Member Files, Lucy Winchester, Box 6, Nixon Library, National Archives, College Park, MD.

3. White House Press Release, David Frost Christmas at the White House, December 10, 1970, White House Central Files, Staff Member Files, Lucy Winchester, Box 6, Nixon Library, National Archives, College Park, MD.

4. Dan Morgenstern, "Taylor-Made Frostings," *DownBeat*, March 4, 1971, 18.

5. BillyTaylorJazz.com, http://www.billytaylorjazz.com/bio.php; Gene Rizzo, *The Fifty Greatest Jazz Piano Players of All Time* (Milwaukee, WI: Hal Leonard, 2005), 66–69; and Len Lyons, *The Great Jazz Pianists: Speaking of Their Lives and Music* (New York: Quill, 1983), 176–83.

6. Nixon/Frost comments and Taylor/Army Chorus performance numbers transcribed by the author from White House Communications Agency Sound Recordings, Tape J-140, Nixon Library, National Archives, College Park, MD.

7. Dorothy McCardle, "Kisses for Nixon," *Washington Post*, December 19, 1970.

8. Marian McPartland, "Blindfold Test," *DownBeat*, March 4, 1971, 28.

9. Phillip Furia and Michael Lasser, *America's Songs: The Stories behind the Songs of Broadway, Hollywood, and Tin Pan Alley* (New York: Routledge, 2006), 207.

10. Memo, Dick Moore to Dwight Chapin, December 23, 1970 White House Special Files, Box 57, Nixon Library, National Archives, College Park, MD.

11. Memo Connie Stewart to Dick Moore, January 19, 1971, White House Central Files, Staff Member Files, Lucy Winchester, Box 7, Nixon Library, National Archives, College Park, MD.

12. The U.S. Army Band website: http://www.usarmyband.com/jukebox/players/christmas-with-the-chorus/white-christmas.html.

13. Billy Taylor and Teresa L. Reed, *The Jazz Life of Dr. Billy Taylor* (Bloomington, IN: Indiana University Press, 2013), 167.

14. Julie Eisenhower Nixon, *Pat Nixon: The Untold Story* (New York: Simon & Schuster, 1986), 437.

PETE FOUNTAIN

1. Memo, L. Higby to Butterfield, Bull, and Parker, White House Special Files, EX SO3, January 1972, Nixon Library, National Archives, College Park, MD.

2. Description of the medal ceremony and entertainment, including re-

marks by Dewitt Wallace, President Nixon, and Ray Conniff, transcribed by the author from *Wallace Ceremony and Ray Conniff Singers*, DVD, NPC Collection, 1211-180-72, Richard Nixon Library and
Museum, Yorba Linda, CA. The Feraci moment can also be seen in the
film *Our Nixon*, CNN Films, released in theatres in 2013 and on DVD
in 2014.

3. Conniff song list, White House Press Release, January 24, 1972, White
   House Special Files, EX SO3, 1/72, Nixon Library, National Archives,
   College Park, MD; and Donnie Radcliff, "Look What She Did to His
   Song, Ma," *Washington Star,* January 28, 1972.

4. Dorothy McCardle, "Singer's War Protest Startles Nixon Dinner,"
   Washington Post, January 28, 1972.

5. Letter, Norman Vincent Peale to President Nixon, January 31, 1972,
   White House Special Files, EX SO3, January 1972, Nixon Library, National Archives, College Park, MD.

6. Memo, Steve Bull to Donna, White House Special Files, EX SO3, January 1972, Nixon Library, National Archives, College Park, MD; and
   Bob Thompson, "Richard Nixon and the Oobie-Doobie Girl," *Washington Post Magazine*, July 27, 1997, 16, http://comcast.rayconniff.info/
   media/nixon.html.

7. Thompson, "Richard Nixon and the Oobie-Doobie Girl."

8. Carroll Kirkpatrick, "Nixon, in South, Presses Integration," *Washington
   Post*, August 15, 1970; and Gerhard Peters and John T. Woolley, "Richard Nixon: Remarks on Arrival in New Orleans, Louisiana," American
   Presidency Project, August 14, 1970, http://www.presidency.ucsb.edu/
   ws/?pid=2627.

9. Thomas Griffin, "Letter from President Cherished By Pete Fountain,"
   New Orleans States-Item, August 27, 1970.

10. "Thank-You Note from Nixon to Fountain," *New Orleans States-Item*,
    May 17, 1971.

11. "Fountain Butt of Nixon Joke," *New Orleans Times-Picayune*, June 17,
    1972.

12. Pete Fountain with Bill Neely, *A Closer Walk: The Pete Fountain Story*
    (Chicago: Henry Regnery Company, 1972) 197. Confirmed by Pete's
    manager, Benny Harrell, October 2006.

13. "Fountain," *New Orleans Times-Picayune*.

14. Henry Mitchell, "Play the Music Loud, Pack 'Em In," *Washington Post*,
    June 16, 1972; and liner notes, *Pete Fountain: The Best of Dixieland*,
    VMG CD 314 549 364-2, 2001, CD.

15. Gunther Schuller, *Early Jazz: Its Roots and Musical Development* (Oxford: Oxford University Press, 1968), 153, 181, 193, 207.

16. Ibid., 183; Frederick Ramsey Jr. and Charles Edwards Smith, *Jazzmen* (New York: Harcourt Brace and Company, 1939), 93; Marshal Stearns, *The Story of Jazz* (Oxford: Oxford University Press, 1974), 65; and Geoffrey C. Ward and Ken Burns, *Jazz: A History of America's Music* (New York: Alfred A. Knopf, 2005), 48.

17. Nick Compagno, "Interview with Pete Fountain," ExperienceNewOrleans.com, http://www.experienceneworleans.com/pete.html.

18. James Lincoln Collier, *Louis Armstrong: An American Genius* (Oxford: Oxford University Press, 1983), 67, 71, 175, 173.

19. Mitchell, "Play the Music."

20. Ymelda Dixon, "Sympatico Party for Echeverrias," *Washington Star*, June 16, 1972.

21. Angus Lind, "Fountain of Youth: At 73, Pete and His Clarinet Are Still Blowing Strong," *New Orleans Times-Picayune*, July 7, 2003.

FRANK SINATRA

1. Edward Allan Faine, *Ellington at the White House, 1969* (Takoma Park, MD: IM Press, 2013), 243; Julie Nixon Eisenhower, *Pat Nixon: The Untold Story* (New York: Simon and Schuster, 1986), 355; and Donnie Radcliffe, "No House for Show Biz," *Washington Post*, July 27, 1973; and Michael Nelson, "Ol' Red, White, and Blue Eyes: Frank Sinatra and the American Presidency," *Popular Music and Society* 24, no. 4 (2000), doi:10.1080/03007760008591786. See also Alan Schroeder, *Celebrity-In-Chief: How Show Business Took Over the White House* (Boulder, CO: Westview Press, 2004). Sinatra's efforts to get a White House gig by changing his national politics are chronicled meticulously by both Michael Nelson and Alan Schroeder in their respective texts.

2. "Bobby-Soxers Swoon Again; 'Voice' Returns to Broadway," *Pittsburgh Press*, October 12, 1944, 5. http://news.google.com/newspapers?nid=1144&dat=19441012&id=KDEbAAAAIBAJ&sjid=pkwEAAAAIBAJ&pg=2947,44879.

3. "John F. Kennedy Fast Facts: 'High Hopes' (Presidential Campaign Song)," John F. Kennedy Library and Museum. http://www.jfklibrary.org/Research/Research-Aids/Ready-Reference/JFK-Fast-Facts/High-Hopes.aspx.

4. Elise K. Kirk, *Music at the White House: A History of the American Spirit* (Urbana, IL: University of Illinois Press, 1986), 300.

5. Ibid., 308.

6. Dick Kliener, "Show Beat," *Victoria Advocate*, November 30, 1969, 47. http://news.google.com/newspapers?nid=861&dat=19691130&id= yoxeAAAAIBAJ&sjid=UosNAAAAIBAJ&pg=1108,4868654.

7. Schroeder, *Celebrity-In-Chief*, 100. Tina Sinatra maintained that her father never stopped holding liberal positions on gun control, capitol punishment, abortion, and immigration.

8. Memo, Connie Stewart to Dwight Chapin, May 13, 1971, Special Files, EXSO3, Nixon Library, National Archives, College Park, MD; memo, Social Secretary Entertainers List, late 1971, White House Central Files, Staff Member Office Files, Lucy Winchester, Nixon Library, National Archives, College Park, MD (author's italics on the fifth remark).

9. Nelson, "Ol' Red, White, and Blue Eyes."

10. Ibid.

11. Peter J. Levinson, *September in the Rain: The Life of Nelson Riddle* (Lanham, MD: Taylor Trade Publishing, 2005), 110.

12. Ibid., 112–13.

13. Ibid., 118–19.

14. "Sinatra's Poll Winnings Detailed," *DownBeat*, August, 1998, 35.

15. Charles L. Granata, *Sessions with Sinatra: Frank Sinatra and the Art of Recording* (Chicago: Chicago Review Press, 2004), 223–24.

16. David Lehman, "Frankophilia: Why Sinatra Is Our Greatest Singer, Period," *American Heritage*, November/December 2002. http://www .americanheritage.com/content/frankophilia.

17. Granata, *Sessions*, 224.

18. Levinson, *September*, 127 and 117.

19. Sinatra song list for the White House program in various next-day newspaper accounts (*New York Times, Washington Post*, and *Star*).

20. John Rockwell, *Sinatra: An American Classic* (New York: Random House, 1984).

21. The performance description is based on the author's interpretation of the classic recording, which used a different orchestra, but the same conductor and arrangement.

22. Based on the author's transcription of the film *Frank Sinatra Entertaining at the White House (with Italian Prime Minister Andreotti in Attendance)*, DVD, NPC #1211-217-73, Nixon Library and Museum, Yorba Linda, CA. Unless otherwise noted, all subsequent remarks made by

Sinatra and Nixon that evening are also based on the author's transcription of the film.

23. Granata, *Sessions*, 137.

24. Ibid., 9.

25. Frank Sinatra, "The Way I Look at Race," *Ebony*, July 1958, 42, http://www.ejazzlines.com/BILLIE-HOLIDAY-THE-GENIUS-OF-LADY-DAY-p45161.html.

26. Gary Giddins, *Rhythm-a-ning: Jazz Tradition and Innovation* (Oxford: Oxford University Press, 1985), 226.

27. David McClintick, liner notes, *Frank Sinatra: The Reprise Collection*, Reprise Records, 1990 9263-10-2, 8.

28. "Singers' All-Time Favorite Vocal Jazz Albums," *DownBeat*, June 2004, 48.

29. Granata, *Sessions*, 13–14.

30. Ibid., 143.

31. Granata, *Sessions*, 101.

32. Ibid., 101–2; Levinson, *September*, 129–30.

33. Richard Williams, "Milt Bernhart: Trombonist Who Got Under Frank Sinatra's Skin," *Guardian*, February 3. 2004. http://www.theguardian.com/news/2004/feb/04/guardianobituaries.artsobituaries.

34. Granata, *Sessions*, 101–2.

35. Levinson, *September*, 130.

36. "100 Artists and Entertainers of the Century," *Time*, June 8, 1998, 178.

37. Granata, *Sessions*, 171–74.

38. James Gavin, *Intimate Nights: The Golden Age of New York Cabaret* (New York: Back Stage Books, 2006), 90–91; Furia and Lasser, *America's Songs*, 242.

39. Will Friedwald, *Sinatra! The Song Is You: A Singer's Art* (New York: Da Capo Press, 1997), 410.

40. All About Al: Discography, http://www.alviola.com/alviola/alviola.nsf; James Isaacs, liner notes, *Frank Sinatra: Live in Paris*, Reprise Records CD 9 45487-2, 1994, CD.

41. The concert can be viewed on request at the Museum of Television and Radio in New York City. More readily available on record is Al Viola and Frank Sinatra's collaboration on "Night and Day," a live performance from 1962 on *Frank Sinatra and Sextet*: Live in Paris (Reprise).

42. Granata, *Sessions*, 171–72.

43. Friedwald, *Sinatra!*, 23.

44. "The House I Live In," Songfacts.com. http://www.songfacts.com.

http://www.songfacts.com/detail.php?id=2306; "The House I Live In (1945)," IMDb.com. http://www.imdb.com/title/tt0037792/.

45. Donnie Radcliffe, "The World on His String," *Washington Post*, April 18, 1973.

46. Levinson, *September*, 164.

47. Ibid., 293, 299.

48. Ibid., 68–69.

49. Mark Feeney, *Nixon at the Movies* (Chicago: University of Chicago Press), 350–55.

50. Letter, Richard Nixon to Frank Sinatra, May 10, 1973, Special Files, EXSO3, Nixon Library, National Archives, College Park, MD.

51. Nelson, "Ol' Red, White, and Blue Eyes"; See also Schroeder, *Celebrity-In-Chief.*

BILLY TAYLOR TRIO

1. Donnie Radcliffe, "No House for Show Biz," *Washington Post*, July 27, 1973.

2. Ibid.

3. Betty Beale, "Lowbrow Entertainment at the White House," *Washington Star*, July 29, 1973.

4. Radcliffe, "No House for Show Biz."

5. Memo, NEA Chair Nancy Hanks to Lucy Winchester, August 13, 1973, White House Central Files, Staff Member Office Files, Lucy Winchester, Box 7, Nixon Library, National Archives, College Park, MD.

6. Memo, Lucy Winchester to NEA Chair Nancy Hanks, August 13, 1973, White House Central Files, Staff Member Office Files, Lucy Winchester, Box 7, Nixon Library, National Archives, College Park, MD.

7. Elise K. Kirk, *Music at the White House: A History of the American Spirit* (Urbana, IL: University of Illinois Press, 1986) 319.

8. Dorothy McCardle, "A Call for Harmony and Peace," *Washington Post*, October 10, 1973.

9. http://www.billytaylorjazz.com under "Billy Taylor Trio"; http://www.billytaylorjazz.com under "Discography"; and personal communication with President Gerald R. Ford Library staff.

10. http://www.billytaylorjazz.com under "Billy Taylor Trio"; http://www.busterwilliams.com.

11. Billy played "Drop Me Off In Harlem," "All Too Soon," and "It Don't Mean a Thing (If It Ain't Got That Swing)," at Duke's seventieth-birthday White House tribute, Edward Allan Faine, *Ellington at the White House, 1969* (Takoma Park, MD: IM Press, 2013), 111–15; Taylor's Program for the Ivory Coast President State Dinner, Guest Memento, White House Central Files, Staff Member Office Files, Lucy Winchester, Box 7, Nixon Library, National Archives, College Park, MD.

12. Phillip Furia and Michael Lasser, *American Songs: The Stories behind the Songs of Broadway, Hollywood, and Tin Pan Alley* (New York: Routledge, 2006), 141, 244.

13. "Discography," Billy Taylor Jazz; http://www.billytaylorjazz.com. Listen to an earlier recording of "They Can't Take That Away from Me" on *Billy Taylor Trio* (Prestige, 1995) to compare with his White House performance.

14. Gene Lees, *Oscar Peterson: The Will to Swing* (New York: Cooper Square Press, 2000) 250.

15. Gene Lees, liner notes, *The Oscar Peterson Trio: Canadiana Suite*, Limelight EXPR 1027, 1964.

16. Billy Taylor, *Jazz Piano: A Jazz History* (Dubuque, IA: WCB Publishers, 1983), 70.

17. Maurice Waller with Anthony Calabrese, *Fats Waller* (NewYork: Schirmer Books, 1977), 150.

18. Gene Rizzo, *Fifty Greatest Jazz Piano Players of All Time* (Milwaukee, WI: Hal Leonard Corporation, 2005), vii. Fair to say, Billy was a protégé of Art Tatum in New York City in the early 1940s, as was Dizzy Gillespie, who tapped Billy (in lieu of Bud Powell) for the Gillespie-Pettiford band, the first bebop band to play on 52nd Street.

19. "Billy Taylor Trio with Earl May and Percy Bryce—Prestige 24285," under "Discography," "Billy Taylor Jazz," http://billytaylorjazz.com/discography.php.

20. Ira Gitler, liner notes, *Billy Taylor Trio with Earl May and Percy Brice*, Fantasy reissue PRCD-24285-2, 2003, CD; Leonard Feather, "Marian McPartland Blindfold Test," *DownBeat*, March 4, 1974.

21. http://www.billytatylorjazz.com under "CDs/Books and Compositions": Instrumental and Vocal.

22. View "I Wish I Knew" Coca-Cola ad, http://www.adweek.com/video/coca-cola-i-wish-123645.

23. View artifacts at http://www.loc.gov/exhibits/treasures/trr105.html; Dan Morgenstern, "Taylor-Made Frostings," *DownBeat*, March 4, 1971.

24. A trio rendering of "I Wish I Knew" is also available online: "Discography," Billy Taylor Jazz; http://www.billytaylorjazz.com.

25. Dorothy McCardle, "A Call for Harmony and Peace," *Washington Post*, October 10, 1973; Betty Beale, "Jazz at Dinner for Ivory Coast Head," *Washington Star*, October 10, 1973.

26. "Agnew Quits Vice Presidency and Admits Tax Evasion in '67; Nixon Consults on Successor: Judge Orders Fine, 3 years Probation," *New York Times*, October 11, 1973.

27. Personal communique with Presidential Libraries: Billy Taylor performed at the President Ford White House for Prime Minister Bhutto of Pakistan on February 5, 1975; at the President Clinton White House in a piano duo with Ramsey Lewis in 1995 and at the 4th Millennium Night with Wynton Marsalis and Marian McPartland on September 18,1998; and at the President George W. Bush White House for Black Music Month twice: on June 24, 2003 and June 22, 2004.

28. Billy Taylor was the third jazz recipient. Since the Medal of Arts inception in 1986 through to 2011, 280 artists have been so awarded, 13 to jazz. Info on National Medal of Arts honorees at arts.gov/honors/medals/medalists_year.html.

PEARL BAILEY TRIO

1. Elise K. Kirk, *Musical Highlights from the White House* (Malabar, FL: Krieger Publishing Company, 1992), 150.

2. Memo, Lucy Winchester to file, November 13, 1970, White House Central Files, Staff Member Office Files, Lucy Winchester, Box 7, Nixon Library, National Archives, College Park, MD.

3. "Louie Bellson," Drummerworld.com, http://www.drummerworld.com/drummers/Louie_Bellson.html; and Ross Russell, "The Story of Louis Bellson, Master Drummer" *DownBeat*, March 19, 1970, 14.

4. Milt Hinton, David G. Berger, and Holly Maxson, *Overtime: The Jazz Photographs of Milt Hinton* (San Francisco: Pomegranate, 1991), 24.

5. Isabelle Shelton, "An After-Dinner Menu of Gems by Pearl, Her Host on the Ivories," *Washington Star*, March 8, 1974.

6. Unless otherwise noted, Bailey's and Nixon's remarks transcribed by the author from White House Communication Agency Video/Sound Recordings, 1211-174-74, Roll 1 and 2, Nixon Library, National Archives, College Park, MD. The president had the honor to present Pearl with the Heart-of-the-Year Award, given by the American Heart

Association. Gerhard Peters and John T. Woolley, "Richard Nixon: Remarks on Presenting the Heart-of-the-Year Award to Pearl Bailey," February 2, 1972, http://www.presidency.ucsb.edu/ws/?pid=3663.

7. Lisa Dawn Miller-Hackett, "'For Once in My Life' Honors My Father, Ron Miller," *Las Vegas Sun*, July 23, 2013, http://www.lasvegassun.com/vegasdeluxe/2013/jul/23/lisa-dawn-miller-hackett-once-my-life-honors-my-f/; and Ed Hogan, "Stevie Wonder: For Once in My Life," Song Review, allmusic.com, http://www.allmusic.com/song/for-once-in-my-life-mt0019044550: "Stevie Wonder's cover of 'For Once in My Life' is one of the Motown legend's zestiest performances. The song had been a Top Ten adult contemporary hit for Tony Bennett in 1967. Produced by Henry Cosby, the lyrics of the Ron Miller/Orlando Murden song took on an immediacy and vibrancy not heard on previous recordings and gave Wonder the definitive version. Issued on October 15, 1968, 'For Once in My Life' hit number two on both the R&B and pop charts in late 1968."

8. "'Peace in Our Time' (Spring Is Special): A Pearl Bailey Segment of the *Oral Roberts Hour*," March 15, 1973, Nixon Presidential Materials Staff, NARA, MVF #060 VCR. Ms. Bailey sings "Peace on Earth" and "In the Garden." A DVD of the Pearl Bailey segment can be obtained from the Nixon Library, Yorba Linda, CA.

9. Details on Pearl's trip to Iran can be found in her final biography: Pearl Bailey, *Between You and Me: A Heartfelt Memoir on Learning, Loving, and Living* (Garden City, NY: Doubleday, 1989). Milt Hinton's short take on the trip can be found in his photo book: Milt Hinton and David G. Berger, *Bass Line: The Stories and Photographs of Milt Hinton* (Philadelphia: University of Temple Press, 1988), 286.

10. "Let There Be Peace" lyrics at http://www.theromatic.comhttp://www.metrolyrics.com/let-there-be-peace-on-earth-lyrics-christmas-song.html.

11. Phillip Furia and Michael Lasser, *America's Songs: The Stories behind the Songs of Broadway, Hollywood, and Tin Pan Alley* (New York: Routledge, 2006), 44.

12. Memo, Mark B. Lewis, Bailey Group Mid-East Tour May 28–June 15, 1974, Office of Cultural Productions, Department of State, Box 56:15, Bureau of Educational and Cultural Affairs Historical Collection, University of Arkansas Libraries, Fayetteville, AR.

13. Isabelle Shelton, "An After-Dinner Menu of Gems by Pearl, Her Host on the Ivories," *Washington Star*, March 8, 1974.

Selected Bibliography

This bibliography is not a complete record of all the work I consulted. It indicates the substance and range of sources upon which I based my writing, and I intend it to serve as a convenience for those interested in pursuing the study of jazz and the White House.

GENERAL

Ambrose, Stephan A. *Nixon: The Triumph of a Politician, 1962–1972*. New York: Simon & Schuster, 1989. A broad political overview.

Balliett, Whitney. *Collected Works: A Journal of Jazz, 1954–2001*. New York: St. Martin's Griffin, 2002. A critical jazz review.

Feeney, Mark. *Nixon at the Movies: A Book about Belief*. Chicago: University of Chicago Press, 2004. A different but related look at Nixon's taste in popular culture.

Furia, Phillip, and Michael Lasser. *America's Songs: The Stories behind the Songs of Broadway, Hollywood, and Tin Pan Alley*. New York: Routledge, 2006. Inside information on songs in the Great American Songbook.

Giddins, Gary. *Visions of Jazz: The First Century*. Oxford: Oxford University Press, 1998. A critical jazz review.

———. *Weather Bird: Jazz at the Dawn of Its Second Century*. Oxford: Oxford University Press, 2004. A critical jazz review.

Giddins, Gary, and Scott DeVeaux. *Jazz*. New York: W. W. Norton & Co., 2009. A critical jazz review.

Kirk, Elise K. *Musical Highlights from the White House*. Malabar, FL: Krieger

Publishing, 1992. A more readily available but slightly abridged version of *Music at the White House.*

Kirk, Elise K. *Music at the White House: A History of the American Spirit.* Urbana, IL: University of Illinois Press, 1986. The definitive work on White House entertainment, available through the used-book market.

Lopes, Paul. *The Rise of the Jazz Art World.* Cambridge: Cambridge University Press, 2000. A different angle on jazz history.

Lusane, Clarence. *The Black History of the White House.* San Francisco: City Lights Books, 2011. A look at the presidency and race.

Nixon, Richard M. *RN: The Memoirs of Richard Nixon.* New York: Grosset & Dunlop, 1978. A broad political overview.

O'Reilly, Kenneth. *Nixon's Piano: Presidents and Racial Politics from Washington to Clinton.* New York: Free Press, 1995. A detailed study of the presidency and race, and Nixon's Southern strategy.

Schroeder, Alan. *Celebrity-in-Chief: How Show Business Took Over the White House.* Boulder, CO: Westview Press, 2004. An insightful account of the symbiotic relationship between entertainers and presidents.

Ward, Geoffrey C., and Ken Burns. *Jazz: A History of America's Music.* New York: Alfred A. Knopf, 2005. An overview of jazz origins and evolution.

DUKE ELLINGTON

Cohen, Harvey G. *Duke Ellington's America.* Chicago: University of Chicago Press, 2010.

Ellington, Duke. *Duke Ellington: Music Is My Mistress.* Garden City, NY: Doubleday, 1973.

Faine, Edward Allan. *Ellington at the White House, 1969.* Takoma Park, MD: IM Press, 2013.

Hasse, John Edward. *Beyond Category: The Life and Genius of Duke Ellington.* New York: Simon & Schuster, 1993.

Teachout, Terry. *Duke: A Life of Duke Ellington.* New York: Gotham, 2013.

HENRY MANCINI

Beck, Jerry. *Pink Panther: The Ultimate Guide to the Coolest Cat in Town.* New York: DK Publishing, 2005.

Meeker, David. *Jazz in the Movies.* 2nd ed. New York: Da Capo Press, 1981.

Yanow, Scott. *Jazz on Film.* New York: Backbeat Books, 2004.

Selected Bibliography

MODERN JAZZ QUARTET

Short, Bobby, with Robert Mackintosh. *Bobby Short: The Life and Times of a Saloon Singer.* New York: Random House, 1995.

PEARL BAILEY

Bailey, Pearl. *Between You and Me: A Heartfelt Memoir on Learning, Loving, and Living.* Garden City, NY: Doubleday, 1989.

Hinton, Milt. *Overtime: The Jazz Photographs of Milt Hinton.* San Francisco: Promegranate Artbooks.

Hinton, Milt, and David G. Berger, *Bass Line: The Stories and Photographs of Milt Hinton.* Philadelphia: University of Temple Press.

BILLY TAYLOR

Taylor, Billy. *Jazz Piano: A Jazz History.* Dubuque, IA: WCB Publishers, 1983.

Taylor, Dr. Billy, with Teresa L. Reed. *The Jazz Life of Dr. Billy Taylor.* Indianapolis: Indiana University Press, 2013.

PETE FOUNTAIN

Collier, James Lincoln. *Louis Armstrong: An American Genius.* Oxford: Oxford University Press, 1983.

Fountain, Pete, with Bill Neely. *A Closer Walk: The Pete Fountain Story.* Chicago: Henry Regnery Company, 1972.

Schuller, Gunther. *Early Jazz: Its Roots and Musical Development.* New York: Oxford University Press, 1968).

Ramsey, Frederick, Jr., and Charles Edwards Smith. *Jazzmen.* New York: Harcourt Brace and Company, 1939.

Stearns, Marshal. *The Story of Jazz.* Oxford: Oxford University Press, 1974.

FRANK SINATRA

Granata, Charles L. *Sessions with Sinatra: Frank Sinatra and the Art of Recording.* Chicago: Chicago Review Press, 2004.

Levinson, Peter J. *September in the Rain.* Lanham, MD: Taylor Trade Publishing, 2005.

Rockwell, John. *Sinatra: An American Classic.* New York: Random House, 1984.

Suggested Recordings

This list of recordings provides a sampling of the work of the jazz artists performing at the Nixon White House.

DUKE ELLINGTON

Live at Newport, 1956 (Complete). Columbia S12918-2, 1999, CD. Originally recorded in 1956. Ellington band with famed Paul Gonsalves twenty-seven-chorus tenor solo on "Diminuendo and Crescendo in Blue."

Never No Lament: The Blanton-Webster Band, 1940–1942. Bluebird 82876-50857-2, 2003, CD. Early versions of ten of the twenty-seven songs performed at the White House 1969 tribute.

1969 All-Star White House Tribute to Duke Ellington. Blue Note 7243 35249 2 0, 2002, CD. Originally recorded in 1969. Bill Berry, Clark Terry (tp); Urbie Green, J. J. Johnson (tb); Paul Desmond (as), Gerry Mulligan (bs); Jim Hall (g); Milt Hinton (b); Louis Bellson (d); Dave Brubeck, Duke Ellington, Earl Hines, Hank Jones, Billy Taylor (p); Mary Mayo, Joe Williams (v).

HENRY MANCINI

Henry Mancini Greatest Hits. RCA CD, 2000. Composed and arranged by Henry Mancini. Compilation of film tunes from *Hatari, Days of Wine and Roses, Charade, Pink Panther, Two for the Road*, and *Romeo and Juliet*.

The Music from Peter Gunn (1958–1961 TV series). Buddha Records, 2001, CD. Composed, arranged, and conducted by Henry Mancini. Pete Candoli (tp), Dick Nash (tb), Ted Nash (ts), Plas Johnson (ts), Vic Feldman (vbs),

John Williams (p), Bob Bain (g), Al Hendrickson (g), Barney Kessel (g), Shelley Manne (d).

MODERN JAZZ QUARTET

MJQ: The Complete Modern Jazz Quartet. Prestige and Pablo Recordings 4PRCD-4438-2, 2003, CD. John Lewis (p), Milt Jackson (vb), Percy Heath (b), Connie Kay (d).

The Modern Jazz Quartet: Under the Jasmin Tree/Space. Apple Records licensed to EMI STAO-3360, 2010, CD. Originally recorded 1968/1969. John Lewis (p), Milt Jackson (vb), Percy Heath (b), Connie Kay (d).

AL HIRT

Al Hirt Greatest Hits. RCA 100 Years of Music. RCA 07863 69398-2, 2001, CD. Al Hirt (tp). Compilation CD with hits "Java," "Sugarlips," "Cotton Candy,'" and "When the Saints Go Marching In."

PEGGY LEE

Black Coffee. Original recording remastered. Verve, 2004, CD. Peggy Lee (v).
Natural Woman/Is That All There Is. EMI Int'l, 2003, CD. Peggy Lee (v).

WORLD'S GREATEST JAZZ BAND

World's Greatest Jazz Band of Yank Lawson and Bob Haggart: Live at the Roo-sevelt Grill. Wounded Bird Records, 2007, CD. Billy Butterfield, Yank Lawson (tp); Lou McGarity, Vic Dickenson (tb); Bud Freeman (ts); Bob Wibur (cl, ss); Ralph Sutton (p); Bob Haggart (b); Gus Johnson (d): the band that played the White House with Vic Dickenson on trombone vice Kai Winding.

World's Greatest Jazz Band of Yank Lawson and Bob Haggart: What's New. Wounded Bird Records, 2007, CD. Same lineup as above with Eddie Hubbel vice Lou McGarity on trombone. Good studio recording.

BOBBY SHORT

Bobby Short Celebrates Rodgers & Hart. Atlantic, 1994, CD. Original release 1975. With Beverly Peer (b) and Richard Sheridan (d).

50 from Bobby Short [Box Set]. Atlantic/Wea, 1990, 2 CDs. Original release 1986. With White House songs "And Her Mother Came Too," "Bye Bye Blackbird," and "Gimme a Pigfoot."

PEARL BAILEY

Won't You Come Home, Pearl Bailey. Compose Memories, 1993, CD. Pearl Bailey (v). Includes "Bill Bailey" and "St. Louis Blues," both sung at the White House.

PETE FOUNTAIN

Pete Fountain: Alive in New Orleans, Laserlight 17 181, 1998, CD. Original recording 1973. Pete Fountain (cl), Eddie Miller (ts), Jack Delaney (tb), Jim Duggan (tb), Mike Serpas (tp), Earl Vulovich (p), Oliver Felix (b), Clarence Lodice (d).

Pete Fountain Presents the Best of Dixieland: Pete Fountain. Verve 314 549 365-2, 2001, CD. Recorded 1950–July 1968. Pete Fountain (cl) and numerous personnel, including Eddie Miller (ts).

FRANK SINATRA

The Concert Sinatra. Capitol Records Inc. CDP 9 47244-2, 1999, CD. Recorded 1963. Frank Sinatra (v), Nelson Riddle (arranger/conductor).

Frank Sinatra with the Red Norvo Quintet, Live in Australia, 1959. Blue Note CDP 7243 8 37513 2 7, 1997, CD. Frank Sinatra (v), Red Norvo (vb), Jerry Dodgion (as, fl), Bill Miller (p), Jimmy Wyble (g), Red Wooten (b), Johnny Markham (d).

Only the Lonely. Capitol Records Inc. CDP 7 48471 2, 1987, CD. Frank Sinatra (v), Nelson Riddle (arranger/conductor).

Songs for Swingin' Lovers. Capitol Records Inc. CDP 7 46570 2, 1987, CD. Frank Sinatra (v), Nelson Riddle (arranger/conductor).

Permissions

About the Author

EDWARD ALLAN FAINE has been a jazz fan since his early teen years in Cleveland, Ohio, where he spent an inordinate amount of time in listening booths at the back of downtown record shops. After a three-year stint in the army, he attended Ohio State University and the University of Buffalo. Upon graduating with a master's in electrical engineering, he began his first career in international satellite communications.

Many years later, he discovered his true calling when he became a writer of children's books, notably *Bebop Babies*. His first titles for adults, *Ellington at the White House 1969* and *Prisoner Chaser*, were released in 2013.

CPSIA information can be obtained at www.ICGtesting.com
Printed in the USA
BVOW04s0741260115

384759BV00004B/8/P

9 780985 795245